Bristol

ethnic minorities
and the city 1000-2001

An England's Past for Everyone paperback

Institute of Historical
Research

Bristol

ethnic minorities
and the city 1000-2001

MADGE DRESSER AND PETER FLEMING

With contributions from Edson Burton, Joe Hillaby
and Forward Maisokwadzo

Phillimore

First published 2007
Reprinted 2009

A Victoria County History Publication
Published by Phillimore & Co Ltd, Chichester, West Sussex, PO20 2DD,
England in association with the Institute of Historical Research at the
University of London.

ISBN 978-1-86077-477-5

British Library Cataloguing in Publication Data. A cataloguing record for this
book is available from the British Library.

Typeset in Humanist 521 and Minion

We wish particularly to thank the following EPE and VCH staff for their efforts
during the production of this volume:

John Beckett – Director of the Victoria County History
Matthew Bristow – Historic Environment Research Manager
Catherine Cavanagh – Project Manager
Pat Diango – Research Liaison Officer/Bristol
Nafisa Gaffar - Finance and Contracts Officer
Aretha George – Education and Skills Manager
Mel Hackett – Communications Officer
Stephen Lubell – Production and Editorial Controller
Neil Penlington – Administrator
Andrew Stokes – Web Manager
Alan Thacker – Executive Editor of the Victoria County History
Kerry Whitston – Production Manager, Victoria County History
Elizabeth Williamson – Architectural Editor of the Victoria County History

Printed and bound in Malta

Front cover image: The cover is a detail from the 1999 mural 'Grosvenor Road'
by locally based artist Gloria Ojulari Sule. It features an east Bristol street
market scene with St Paul's church and the Clifton suspension bridge in the
background.
Back cover image: Fred Walcott, originally from Barbados, in RAF uniform.

Contents

This book is dedicated to Peter Fryer (1917-2006)
and Trevor Johnson (1961-2007)
for their commitment to history and humanity.

Foreword

To make England's past a past for everyone is the laudable aim of an ambitious Heritage Lottery-funded history project, of which this present book is a central part.

All too often, the urban history of England has ignored or marginalised the history of the nation's ethnic minorities. This book aims to redress this omission by charting 1001 years of ethnic relations in one English city, Bristol. It covers the city's history from very close to its beginnings until the watershed year of 2001, when the destruction of New York's World Trade Centre and the western powers' reactions ushered in a new and more complex period of ethnic relations, in Bristol as in the wider world.

This is an area particularly prone to unwarranted generalisations, groundless assumptions and uninformed prejudice and, to counter this, the emphasis here is on interpretations based on evidence. To this end the authors have explored a diverse range of sources from medieval archaeological sites and tax documents to newly released police records, oral testimony and family histories. Volunteers from a wide range of backgrounds have contributed to the project in a uniquely interactive way and the accompanying website ensures that this dialogue will continue after the book is published.

The result is a richly textured book, full of compelling human stories, many of which have not been published before. Lavishly illustrated with contemporary representations, photographs and specially commissioned maps, this book should prove a valuable resource for all those interested in not only how Bristol, but the nation as a whole, came to be what it is today.

Trevor Phillips
Chair of the Commission for Equality and Human Rights

Preface & Acknowledgements

Writing this book has been for us both a privilege and a responsibility. Ensuring neglected groups are no longer subject to what E.P. Thompson called 'the condescension of posterity' is a crucial task and one which inspired us. But we did not intend to convey an uncritical celebration of such groups. We have aimed instead to be provocative, fair-minded and informative. Our story may span 1001 years rather than 1001 nights but, like Scheherazade, we hope to intrigue our audience into wanting to know more.

This project has involved us in collaboration with many authors from widely differing backgrounds. Chapter 1 is by Joe Hillaby, an authority on medieval jewry. Chapters 2 and 3 are by Peter Fleming with contributions from Jinx Newly and Spencer Dimmock, who have made a study of Tudor apprentices. Chapters 4 to 8, 11 and 13 are by Madge Dresser. Chapters 9 and 10 are by Madge Dresser with the assistance of Peter Newley (an engineer with a doctorate in computer aided design and a keen interest in family history). Chapter 12 is by Edson Burton, a playwright and poet whose doctorate is in history. Chapter 14 is by Dresser and Forward Maisowadzo, a Zimbabwean journalist exiled in England. Fleming and Dresser provide introduction and conclusion.

We are grateful to Andy Foyle for preparing an extensive gazetteer of religious buildings which informed the later chapters and which we plan to publish separately.

We would also like to express our gratitude to the following individuals and organisations:

Rohit Barot, Shekar Bheenuck, the Bristol and Avon Family History Society, the Manchester & Lancashire Family History Society, Simon Clarke, Peter Courtier, Steve Fenton, Paul Hoggett, Alexa Jones (copyright permission courtesy of MLFHS), Andrew Kelly, Stanisław Kucharczyk, Robin Oakley, James Powell, and Lindsey St Clair for allowing their unpublished research to be used in this book; Sophie Andrews, Raingard Esser, Angela John, Anne Laurence, Moira Martin and Keith Robbins for kindly reading selected chapter drafts and their invaluable advice.

We are indebted to Anthony Fletcher for first approaching us about this project and to the Heritage Lottery Fund and the University of the West of England for their financial support. In addition, we would like to thank our volunteers for their hard work and dedication, particularly: Gill James, Sarah-Joy Maddeaux, Gary Evans, Jinx and Peter Newley, David Large, Eira Makepeace, Marilyn Davis, James Powell, Elaine Hicks, Jill Prasad, Sîan White,

Pam Sheppard, Liz Newcomb, Rebecca Hazelhurst, Caroline Barker Bennett, and Jane Stone. They have made an invaluable contribution to this book, as has Patricia Diango, our research administrator.

Our thanks are also due to all those who have given us their time and memories as interviewees, some of whom did not wish to be named in the book. Particular thanks go to Zehra Haq, Sue Njie, Ahmed Duale, Khalif Noor, Mr Mumin, Mohammed Ismail, Abdi Jumale, Mahmoud Matan, Rais, Patricia and Rehan Hyder, Alina and Celina Domagala, Krystyna Studzinska, Ireneusz Peszyński, Mukhtyar Singh and Batook Pandya. Daniel Summerbell, Effie Romain and June Ridd members of the Bristol Black Archives Partnership, Steve Mills, Esme Peach and Claire Stern helped us with securing interviews, contacts and images. Thanks too to Jayne Mills, Bob Jones, Martin Crossley Evans, Anton Bantock, Eugene Byrne, Jane Foley and Tariq Modood for their expert help, and to James Davies, Zahir Malik, Lee Davis, Ruth Tolley and Mark Simmons for their help with photographs.

We also thank the staffs of the many libraries and archives we have used for this project, particularly those of the National Archives, the Huguenot Library, the Bristol Record Office, the Bristol Museum Service and the Bristol Central Library, without whose support this project would not have been possible. Karen Garvey, Lilleith Morrison, Margaret MacGregor, John Williams, Richard Burley, David Emeney, Sarwat Siddiqui, Rachael Vincent, Sue Giles, Julia Carver, Andy King, David Eveleigh, Gail Boyle, Jane Bradley, Dawn Dyer and Munawar Hussain were exceptionally supportive. Thanks too to the Rt. Rev. Declan Lang, Bishop of Clifton, for his kind permission to consult the archives of the Diocese of Clifton and to Canon J.A. Harding, Diocesan Archivist, and Gill Hogarth, Diocesan Librarian, for their time and advice and to all those of the Bristol Board, Ramgarhia Gurdwara Sri Guru Nanak Parkash Singh Sabha, the Sangat Singh Sabha Gurdwara, and the Shri Guru Singh Sabha, Bristol Central Mosque, Bristol Jamia Mosque, Easton Masjid (Mosque), Shahjalal Jame Mosque, Bristol and West Progressive Synagogue, the Bristol Hebrew Congregation, the Sanatan Deevya Mandal, the Polish Roman Catholic Church of our Lady of Ostrobrama, the Greek Orthodox Church of St Peter and St Paul for their hospitality and assistance, and to Tony Benn for his encouragement.

We of course retain full responsibility for whatever omissions and mistakes are contained in this book.

Madge Dresser
Reader in History at the University of the West of England.

Peter Fleming
Principal Lecturer in History at the University of the West of England.

Millerd's map of Bristol in 1673

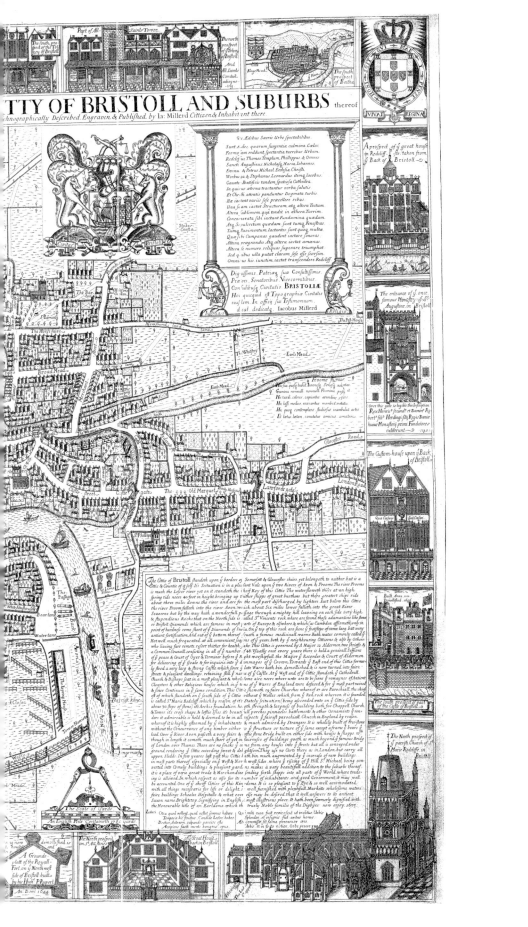

Figure 1 The depiction of Bristol from *The Mayor of Bristol's Calendar*, composed by the town clerk, Robert Ricart, from 1478/9, emphasises the town's Christian nature, with its churches, High Cross, and cross-shaped street pattern.

Introduction

This book investigates the activities of some of the different peoples who came to Bristol over the past thousand years – people coming from beyond England to earn a living, to escape persecution or to seek a new life. Bristol, like all cities, has long been a magnet for migrants, be they from the West Country or the West Indies, but unlike most others it has had a long and continuous history of immigration since Anglo-Saxon times. The place that rose during the Middle Ages to become one of England's top three cities gained international prominence during the 18th century as an important slaving port. Although its economy slowed in the 19th century, its diverse economic base meant it was able to enjoy relative prosperity throughout most of the modern period.

Some new arrivals in Bristol have been better placed than others to exploit the opportunities that the city has had to offer. The themes of economic survival, social dislocation, discrimination, and generational change are common to all the groups encountered in this book, but in our long view we have attempted to reveal important differences as well as crucial continuities. In examining a range of different ethnic minority groups in the city over this long period, we have considered their survival strategies and their relationship with the host or majority community. We have also explored the construction of identity: how the minorities saw themselves, how they were seen by others, and how they contributed to Bristol's developing, compound and complex sense of itself. Our aim has been to stimulate more research into the history of particular minority groups and to provide new insights into the wider history of both the city of Bristol and of the nation.

Our approach is uniquely wide-ranging, both in terms of its chronological spread and in its broad definition of ethnic minorities. In this book, we cover the city's history from very close to its beginnings until the watershed year of 2001, when the destruction of New York's World Trade Centre and the western powers' reactions ushered in a new and more complex period of ethnic relations, in Bristol as in the wider world. The people we have chosen to follow in our research are those non-English from within the British Isles itself – in other words, the Welsh, Irish and Scots – as well as those from further afield such as French Protestants, Eastern European Jews, Africans from the Caribbean and peoples from the Indian sub-continent. We were intrigued to see what continuities and differences might emerge when considering, in one place, such a wide range of divergent groups over such a long period. We were curious, too, to discover whether the experience of immigrants might have elements in common with that of English rural migrants to Bristol.

Although we have covered many different groups, we have simply not had the space to give some groups the coverage they deserve, especially in the 20th-century section. In particular, the Chinese, Italians and Greek Cypriot communities merit fuller treatment. A section on the travellers and their representation in the popular media would also have enriched this study, as would greater coverage of some of the most recently arrived groups in the city, such as the West Africans, the 'new' Jamaicans, the Kosovans and the Kurds. More work, too, needs to be done on the second and third generations of New Commonwealth immigrants, those who came to the city as children and those who were born 'Bristolian'. We hope the website which accompanies this book will develop as a resource to help redress these omissions.

We are aware, of course, that the very act of assigning people to ethnic categories can serve to distort our understanding of them, reifying and homogenising them, and in the process obscuring their full identity. For example, it proved difficult to fit in the experience of those of mixed racial or ethnic backgrounds when chapters are devoted to one or other minority group, or to feature individuals such as secularist and Christian Pakistanis who form separate minorities within a minority.

Ethnicity and Community

What precisely do we mean by ethnicity, ethnic minority or indeed by an ethnic community? 'Ethnic' comes from the Greek *ethnos* which, although it carries a range of meanings, generally refers to groups who usually have a common name, shared memories of a common past and certain cultural characteristics in common, be they religion, customs or language. They tend to claim a common ancestry, be attached to a common homeland, real or symbolic, and can organise as a group to affirm their identity.[1]

It is worth noting here that the word 'ethnic' was originally used to signal the difference between Christians and 'heathens'. This point perhaps explains the common use of the word 'ethnic' to imply a 'them' rather than an 'us'. Ethnic fashions or ethnic food, for example, are popularly taken to mean something not English. This disconnection of Englishness from ethnicity assumes that Englishness is the natural and timeless benchmark of all that is normal or proper. The sociologist Steve Fenton's observation that one cannot have ethnic minorities without an ethnic majority is a useful corrective here. It reminds us that the two are in constant interaction and that neither can be understood in isolation from the other.[2]

'Community' too, in this context, is a tricky term, one that implies values in common, shared experiences and shared markers of identity. However individuals are grouped into 'communities', there are always going to be differences within them, whether of class, gender, age, or religion. An ethnic community is no exception. Although it is easy to talk about ethnic communities as self-contained entities, most modern scholars agree that ethnic identity is something of a moveable feast. Those individuals we assign to particular ethnic categories are rarely as culturally – let alone biologically – homogeneous as these categories might suggest. Ethnicity is always being renegotiated according to the specific historical situation and, of course, it is far from being the only component of an individual's identity.[3]

Research and Sources

This book is the result of the Bristol England's Past for Everyone project (www.EnglandsPastForEveryone.org.uk/Bristol) and differs from most conventional academic histories in that it is the product of professional historians working with a group of volunteers. Volunteers have carried out many invaluable tasks under our guidance. Some have helped to identify and transcribe primary archival sources and a number have contributed their own individual research or collected oral testimonies, on the project's behalf. Others, who began their involvement by providing testimonies, have gone on to help locate contemporary, community-based records and extend the project's contacts with other people from ethnic minority backgrounds. All have brought their energy and specialist knowledge to the project and acquired a range of historical skills and insights in exchange.

Our research has of necessity employed an eclectic approach surveying a wide range of primary and secondary sources. Although its focus has been on Bristol, this book has drawn upon existing research on ethnic relations in other places and from other disciplines for ways of approaching our subject.[4]

The nature of the primary sources available to researchers changes greatly over the long period covered in this book, and inevitably this has influenced our account. Generally speaking, the further back one goes, the scantier the sources. In particular, personal testimony becomes rarer, to the point where, for the Middle Ages (in this book treated as from the 10th to the beginning of the

16th centuries) it is usually impossible to get any sense of people's individual personalities or aspirations. As we approach our own time we can do this more often, through more personal and imaginative accounts as well as bureaucratic ones. To this end, research for this book has utilised letters, diaries, autobiographies, plays, photographs and newspaper articles, as well as official documents.

We have done our best to ensure that the stories told here have come from a variety of voices. We have trawled popular accounts of the city's past as well as family genealogies; sociological surveys as well as academic histories. Official records have been read against the grain to see what they reveal about those who have been traditionally marginalised in such accounts but it is nonetheless difficult to conjure up a full picture of, say, the 19th-century Bristol Irish, when most of our evidence comes from often hostile external sources, such as newspaper and government reports. The availability of sources also varies according to the particular group we are examining, since some have produced more surviving records than others, due to differences in wealth, education and social position. In addition, a variety of cultural factors means that women tend to be under-represented in our sources, and so much of this story must be told through male eyes.

Oral interviews, both formal and informal, have helped us to flesh out the picture of 20th-century Bristol but we have used them, wherever possible, in conjunction with archival sources as various as census returns, community group reports and newly released police records. Although due care must be taken with oral testimony, since memory can play all sorts of tricks, it has proved invaluable in helping us meet with those whose experience would not otherwise be recorded and in enabling us to see how people make sense of their history and how they perceive their relationship with others.

Content and Structure

Bristol was founded by the Anglo-Saxons, probably at some time in the 10th century, at a bridging point of the Avon. By the Norman Conquest of 1066 it was a place of considerable importance, with its own mint. The Normans developed it further, building a castle and founding a number of religious houses, the most important of which was St Augustine's Abbey, now Bristol Cathedral.

Medieval Bristol's prosperity was based on trade, both internal to England, with Wales and Ireland, and with mainland Europe. The conversion of the river Frome into a deep-water harbour in the 1240s, accompanied by extensive draining of surrounding marshes and the extension of the Norman town wall to enclose the suburbs of Redcliffe and Temple south of the Avon, shows how wealthy Bristol had become by then, and also helped make possible further growth. From the 14th to the 18th centuries, Bristol was among England's wealthiest provincial cities. At the core of its later medieval economy were the export of wool and cloth, and the import of a great diversity of goods, among which one of the most lucrative was wine, coming mainly from English-held Gascony, in south-west France.

Bristol was badly hit by the Black Death of 1348, which killed perhaps a third of its population, but recovered sufficiently to be granted a charter in 1373 which established it as England's first provincial urban county. The town weathered another major blow in 1453, when England's defeat in the Hundred Years' War with France meant that Gascony fell under French rule. Bristol merchants reacted by developing their trade in Spanish and Portuguese wine, a connection that lasted well into the 20th century. The Reformation, beginning under Henry VIII (1509-1547), and the dissolution of the monasteries caused some disruption to Bristol's economic and cultural life. But, in 1542, the creation of the diocese of Bristol gave it its own bishop and a cathedral, thereby raising its status from town to city. A century later the English Civil War plunged Bristol into crisis, as the city was twice taken by storm and its inhabitants suffered greatly.

The city's fortunes changed for the better in the latter half of the 17th century, when it became a major participant in the development of England's trade with its colonies in America and the Caribbean.

For much of the 18th century this trade allowed Bristol to become England's second city. At the heart of Bristol's Atlantic economy was slavery, either in terms of the actual trade in African slaves or in the buying and selling of slave-produced goods. By the end of the century the position of England's premier provincial port-city was taken by Liverpool, and Bristol entered into a period of relative economic stagnation.

Bristol's economy has been characterised by diversity; while international trade has always been a mainstay, neither it nor any one manufacturing industry has ever eclipsed other sectors of the economy. During the late 18th- and 19th-century Industrial Revolution this meant that the city did not become dependent on any one industry; with a largely rural hinterland and relatively modest local coal deposits, it could no longer compete with the great Midlands or Northern industrial cities. Bristol entered the 20th century as a quietly prosperous provincial city, still dominating its hinterland, but no longer among the country's leading conurbations.

Figure 2 Bristol within its original town walls shown in this detail from Millerd's 1673 map. The street plan had probably changed little from the early Middle Ages.

Constraints imposed by the available evidence have meant that we have not been able to give the same degree of coverage to every century of this long and varied history. Over half of our period has been assigned just three chapters, with the remainder devoted to a period of a little over 300 years. Chapter 1 covers Bristol's first Jewish community, chapter 2 looks at medieval Bristol's other ethnic minorities, and chapter 3 takes this story down to the later 17th century. The next five chapters cover the long 18th century, which stretches from around 1688 to just after the Municipal Reform Act of 1835, when Bristol played host to French Protestant refugees (chapter 4) as well as continuing its time-honoured role as a second home for Welsh migrants (chapter 5). That period also saw an increased influx of Irish Catholics (chapter 6), Central and Eastern European Jews (chapter 7) and, thanks to the opening up of the slave-based Atlantic economy, a small but significant African presence (chapter 8).

With the partial exception of the Irish and the Welsh, Victorian and Edwardian Bristol did not witness major inflows of people from outside England and so only two chapters are devoted to the period between *c.*1837 and *c.*1910. Chapter 9 surveys mid-Victorian Bristol with special reference to Protestant immigrants and chapter 10 considers the experience and reception of the Irish, the Jews and others throughout the Victorian and Edwardian eras.

Chapter 11 offers an overview of 20th-century Bristol set against the break-up of the British Empire and the era of mass immigration from the New Commonwealth. Chapter 12 then discusses the experiences of African-Caribbean migrants, and their descendants in the post-war city. In Chapter 13, the arrival and experiences of Bristol's various South Asian communities in the aftermath of the British Raj are traced. Chapter 14 considers the changing image of refugees and asylum seekers in Bristol, paying particular attention to the city's post-war Polish community and more recent arrivals from Somalia. The conclusion outlines some of the main themes judged to have emerged from this study.

A note on racial terminology 'African-Caribbean', 'West Indian', and 'Black' community are used interchangeably in this book. 'Black' is sometimes used as a generic cover for all peoples who have experienced racial oppression, but in this book it is used to refer solely to people of African descent unless specified otherwise. To call someone 'black' using the lower case 'b' has colonialist associations so we have taken the course of capitalising the 'b' when referring to 'Black' people, and to maintain consistency have also capitalised the term 'White' as in 'White groups'. Terms such as 'negro' (18th to early 20th centuries), 'coloured' (19th- and 20th-century) and 'Negro' (*c.*1960s), which are today considered offensive, are used only when and as they occur in the historical record. So too, is the term 'mulatto', which in the 18th century referred to a person of dual African and European ancestry. We have also employed the (20th-century) term 'mixed race' where it seemed that the specific historical context demanded it.

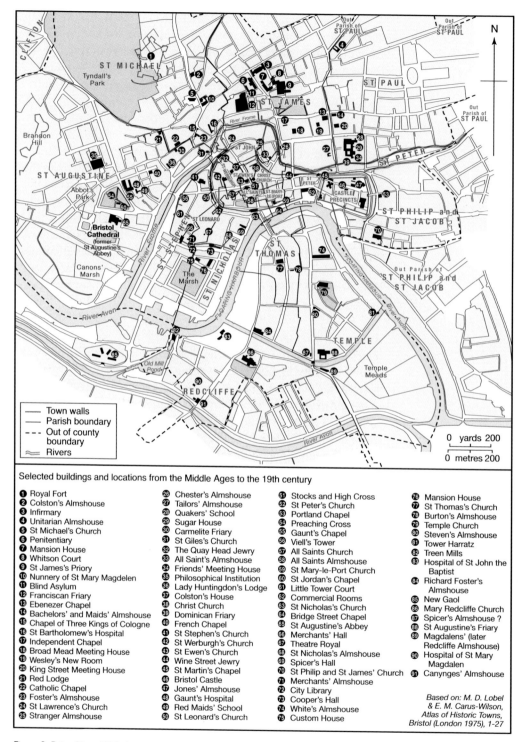

Town walls
Parish boundary
Out of county boundary
Rivers

Selected buildings and locations from the Middle Ages to the 19th century

❶ Royal Fort
❷ Colston's Almshouse
❸ Infirmary
❹ Unitarian Almshouse
❺ St Michael's Church
❻ Penitentiary
❼ Mansion House
❽ Whitson Court
❾ St James's Priory
❿ Nunnery of St Mary Magdelen
⓫ Blind Asylum
⓬ Franciscan Friary
⓭ Ebenezer Chapel
⓮ Bachelors' and Maids' Almshouse
⓯ Chapel of Three Kings of Cologne
⓰ St Bartholomew's Hospital
⓱ Independent Chapel
⓲ Broad Mead Meeting House
⓳ Wesley's New Room
⓴ King Street Meeting House
㉑ Red Lodge
㉒ Catholic Chapel
㉓ Foster's Almshouse
㉔ St Lawrence's Church
㉕ Stranger Almshouse

㉖ Chester's Almshouse
㉗ Tailors' Almshouse
㉘ Quakers' School
㉙ Sugar House
㉚ Carmelite Friary
㉛ St Giles's Church
㉜ The Quay Head Jewry
㉝ All Saint's Almshouse
㉞ Friends' Meeting House
㉟ Philosophical Institution
㊱ Lady Huntingdon's Lodge
㊲ Colston's House
㊳ Christ Church
㊴ Dominican Friary
㊵ French Chapel
㊶ St Stephen's Church
㊷ St Werburgh's Church
㊸ St Ewen's Church
㊹ Wine Street Jewry
㊺ St Martin's Chapel
㊻ Bristol Castle
㊼ Jones' Almshouse
㊽ Gaunt's Hospital
㊾ Red Maids' School
㊿ St Leonard's Church

51 Stocks and High Cross
52 St Peter's Church
53 Portland Chapel
54 Preaching Cross
55 Gaunt's Chapel
56 Viell's Tower
57 All Saints Church
58 All Saints Almshouse
59 St Mary-le-Port Church
60 St Jordan's Chapel
61 Little Tower Court
62 Commercial Rooms
63 St Nicholas's Church
64 Bridge Street Chapel
65 St Augustine's Abbey
66 Merchants' Hall
67 Theatre Royal
68 St Nicholas's Almshouse
69 Spicer's Hall
70 St Philip and St James' Church
71 Merchants' Almshouse
72 City Library
73 Cooper's Hall
74 White's Almshouse
75 Custom House

76 Mansion House
77 St Thomas's Church
78 Burton's Almshouse
79 Temple Church
80 Steven's Almshouse
81 Tower Harratz
82 Treen Mills
83 Hospital of St John the Baptist
84 Richard Foster's Almshouse
85 New Gaol
86 Mary Redcliffe Church
87 Spicer's Almshouse ?
88 St Augustine's Friary
89 Magdalens' (later Redcliffe Almshouse)
90 Hospital of St Mary Magdalen
91 Canynges' Almshouse

Based on: M. D. Lobel
& E. M. Carus-Wilson,
Atlas of Historic Towns,
Bristol (London 1975), 1–27

Figure 3 Bristol in c.1820 showing selected earlier features.

Figure 4 The remains of a
13th-century Jewish ritual
bath or *Mikveh* found in
2001 at Blossom's Inn,
City of London.

Chapter 1

The Bristol Jewry to 1290

FOUNDATION

The first Jews in England arrived from Normandy in the 11th century. As Jews in feudal society were precluded from ownership of land in fee (broadly equivalent to modern freehold), they were of necessity town-dwellers. However, urban life would seem to have been a natural choice, given its offer of *minyan* (the quorum of 10 male Jews over the age of 13 required for communal worship), *shohet* (the ritual butcher who ensures slaughtered animals are kosher), communal oven, school and cemetery, and a *mikveh* (ritual bath). They operated as bankers, lending money on interest, a practice, known as usury, which the Church formally discouraged among Christians. Jews lent money to both the Crown and its subjects, and the interest they accrued from the latter was heavily taxed. They were thus a very useful source of royal finance, and the Anglo-Norman kings perceived that it was in their own interest to protect them – and they needed protection. Many powerful magnates came to be indebted to them, raising the temptation of eradicating the debt by eradicating the creditor. In addition, not only did their religion not recognise the divinity of Christ, but they were also, as a people, believed to bear the responsibility for Christ's death. Consequently they were the victims of persecution, particularly vehement during periods of Christian religious excitement, such as the Crusades, from the late 11th to the early 13th centuries. Thus, England's Jews were at the king's mercy, effectively his property, tolerated so long as they served as royal milch cows, and vulnerable to attack from their Christian neighbours.[5]

Much of the surviving evidence for Jewish society in this period comes from financial and legal records, produced mainly by Christians, and so the picture that we can construct is a partial one, derived from often unsympathetic witnesses.

It has been assumed that Bristol was one of the early provincial Jewish communities, but the 1159 tax returns contain no reference to a Jewry (Jewish area) here. The earliest evidence from tax returns comes in 1194, by which time Bristol's Jewry was well established but not among the biggest: it ranked 13th out of 21 communities, its 15 members together paying £22 14s. 2d., a mere one per cent of the total Jewish tax-yield nationally. The Bristol Jewry was always among the smaller communities: it paid 3.5 per cent of the 1221

Jewish taxation in the country, 5 per cent in 1223, and only 0.3 per cent in 1239-42.[6]

Medieval Bristol's Jewish community was probably founded in the secure middle years of the reign of Henry II (1154-1189), when the Jews 'had been happy and respected'. The king had taxed the Jews heavily, but had also protected them. This was to change with his successors, and 'pogroms' (attacks on Jewish communities) became more common. Bristol's Jewry seems to have been spared these attacks until the 1260s, but was not immune from other pressures. The Jews' business activities came under closer royal scrutiny. From the 1190s a special government department, the Exchequer of the Jews, was established to supervise Jewish money-lending, and by 1220 Bristol had joined those towns which kept a chest, *archa*, in which was kept a copy of each credit transaction. Taxation increased to punitive levels under King John (1199-1216), and in 1210 he resorted to outright extortion. He ordered a general captivity in Bristol Castle of all the wealthier Jews in England. One rich Londoner was hanged and another Jew had his eyes plucked out. Many poor Jews fled the country. On the channel ports a special watch was kept, but from Bristol escape by boat to Ireland would have been easier.[7]

Attitudes changed after John's death, when the Regency Council of the boy-king Henry III realised the danger of killing the goose that lays the golden egg. In 1218 the sheriffs were commanded to proclaim 'throughout their lands that we have assured the Jews our peace'. The right of Jews to reside at Bristol in a self-governing community was formally confirmed, and 24 of the town's most prominent citizens were made personally responsible for their security. In 1215 the Fourth Lateran Council (a general assembly of the Western Church), enacted that Jews had to wear a badge of yellow taffeta depicting the two tablets of stone that carried the Ten Commandments. This was part of its efforts to minimise their contact with Christians. However, in England the Council of Regency permitted individuals, and even whole communities, to obtain dispensations on payment of a fine. Significantly, the papal legate complained that the Regency Council was unduly protective of the English Jews.[8]

Attempts by the Church to interfere with the king's Jews were rigorously resisted by the Council of Regency. It responded quickly when Bishop Sylvester of Worcester, whose diocese included Bristol, sought to interfere with the taking of interest. Walter de Beauchamp was ordered to restrain the bishop, 'for our Jews are no concern of his. You shall not permit them to be impleaded in any episcopal court on account of any debt'. Bishop William de Blois (1218-36) sought to maintain the church policy of isolating Jews

Figure 5 Writ of Henry III ordering officials of Bristol to extract all bonds of Jews and Jewesses who had not paid their taxes from the Bristol chest and to deliver them to the Justices of the Jews in Westminster, dated 10 July 1271. The officials to whom the writ was sent were the chirographers who kept records of the bonds (i.e. securities for money lent by the Jews) and the constable of Bristol Castle. This royal order, found in the archives of Westminster Abbey, was in effect cancelling the debts owed to the Jews.

from their Christian neighbours, by forbidding Christian women to stay overnight in Jewish households and the employment of Christians as wet-nurses by Jews. This tells us much about popular attitudes. Bishop Walter de Cantilupe (1237-56) went further and ordered that 'such Christians as consult Jews about their life or actions shall be brought before the bishops to be punished'. Such recourse to Jewish soothsayers again reflects the popular view of Jews as sorcerers and masters of the occult, although many were doctors, with high, even international, reputations.[9]

However, the motive for royal toleration remained the same, and under Henry III royal taxation practically bankrupted the English Jewry. The expropriations began in 1239 and lasted until 1258. Henry's policy also put indirect pressure on those who had borrowed from the Jews, since to pay their taxes the latter were often forced to call in their loans. This hit the knightly class particularly hard, and partly as a result many of them backed Simon de Montfort's reform movement from 1258. When open warfare erupted in 1263, the Jewries and their records or *archae* were amongst the principal targets of Simon de Montfort's baronial forces. At Bristol the *archae* were burned and the Jewry plundered.[10]

Edward I succeeded his father, Henry III, in 1272. As prince, Edward had been instrumental in introducing the Provisions of the Jewry in 1271, which prevented Jews from making loans secured on land. As king, he was first of all responsible for the Statute of the Jewry in 1275, which prevented Jews from charging interest on loans. This was a major blow, since money-lending had, out of necessity, been their main source of income.[11]

If 1275 was a bad year for English Jews generally, it was particularly so for the Bristol Jewry. In that year two incidents occurred that suggest that relations between Jews and Christians were at breaking point. Bishop Giffard of Worcester excommunicated the Bristol Jews, forbidding 'all traffic with such wicked Jews'; their alleged offence had been to subject a chaplain of St Peter's

Adam of Bristol

There developed in medieval Europe a collection of stories in which Jews were portrayed desecrating the consecrated Host, as the body of Christ, and torturing and murdering Christian boys, in a blasphemous imitation of Christ's crucifixion. There is no evidence that any such things actually happened, but these stories were widely circulated and provided further impetus to violent attacks on Jewish communities. The earliest of the European ritual child murder, or bloodguilt, accusations was raised at Norwich in 1144, where the Jewry was accused of crucifying the 12-year-old William. His cult, as St William, child martyr, became widely celebrated, and emulated. In 1158 fishermen on the Severn at Gloucester found a boy's corpse with presumed marks of martyrdom. Gloucester Abbey's monks tried to generate a local cult around the 'martyr', but with little success (Jessop & James, 1896; Hillaby 1994-6, 69-109; McCulloh 1997, 698-740; Trachtenberg, 1943).

The Gloucester story may have influenced Bristol's own crucifixion legend. This related to events in Henry II's reign (1155-89) but was probably composed between 1216 and the relocation of the Jewry to Winch Street between 1264 and 1275. The story goes that Adam, young son of William the Welshman, resident of St Mary Redcliffe parish, is seduced into entering the house of Samuel the Jew by the offer of apples. When Samuel crucifies him, the house shakes with a voice declaring, in Hebrew, 'I am the God of Abraham and of Isaac and Jacob, who thou hast for a fourth time nailed to a cross'. Samuel, we are informed, crucified three boys the previous year. On hearing this voice in Hebrew, his wife cries out, 'We have sinned and done wrong', and promises to be baptised the next day. Enraged, Samuel slaughters both his wife and son, who had resolved to join his mother in baptism. An Irish priest discovers the crime, and buries Adam in Ireland. The tale is written in Latin as dialogue, with detailed musical directions; this and other internal evidence suggests that it is a play script for a performance staged by Franciscan friars at St Mary Redcliffe on the Feast of the Assumption of the Virgin Mary (15 August).

The story was probably composed in Bristol, since it displays detailed knowledge of local

Samuel crucifying Adam, from the sole extant copy of the tale, in a 14th-century manuscript in the British Library.

features. While it is extremely inflammatory, with its detailed depiction of horrendous tortures inflicted on Adam, its incidental details reveal close interaction between Jews and Christians, reflecting the contemporary Church's concern that there was too much friendly contact between the two groups. So, while this story seems intended to arouse hatred against the Jews, it may, ironically, provide evidence of an unexpectedly high level of integration between Bristol's lay Christians and Jews.

The tale also provides intriguing evidence for 13th-century Bristol's multiethnic and multilingual culture. Adam is the son of Welsh migrants, and his murder is discovered by a passing Irish priest. Adam speaks English and French. The Jews speak English, French and Hebrew; the priest speaks Irish, French, Latin and English, but his Irish companions cannot understand English. The Jews' Christian neighbours speak English but, apparently, are ignorant of Hebrew (Stacey, 2007).

Church, who had attempted to administer the Holy Eucharist to a sick person in the Jewry, to 'iniquitous insults, blasphemous and injurious, upon the most holy body of our Saviour'. The other incident was even more serious. In this, 22 men and women were alleged to have attacked the town's Jews, robbing and burning their houses. The leader of the attack was William Giffard, the former sheriff of Norfolk and Suffolk, who was heavily indebted to three Bristol Jews, Preciosa, Aaron and Isaac. His aim in leading the raid seems to have been to destroy the evidence of his debts. The following year, 1276, Bristol Castle played host to a number of local Jews who had not paid the latest round of onerous taxes.[12]

By now, England's Jewish community was being bled dry by the king, and it is likely that an increasing number were driven to crime. Given their traditional occupation, a particular temptation was coin-clipping, whereby the edges of silver coins were clipped and melted down. This was a capital offence. In 1278-9 many Jews were accused of this felony. Investigations and prosecutions lasted several years. In 1283, all Jewish householders, some 600, were imprisoned on coin-clipping charges. In London alone, some 293 Jews were hanged. At Bristol, Hak le Pretre, Moses of Kent, and Cresse were amongst the victims, hanged outside Bristol Castle, as was Benedict of Winchester.[13]

Not all Jewish coin-clippers suffered the death penalty. Aaron of Ireland, son of Benjamin of Colchester, went to the Bristol shop of Robert of Arras, goldsmith, and offered him a silver plate, before the eyes of many Christians. Having weighed it, Robert accused Aaron of offering a plate from coin clippings. Aaron snatched it back, ran off with it to Bristol Bridge, followed by many Christians, and threw the plate into the Avon. Being charged, he refused trial by the customary jury of Christians with Jews, and was committed to Hereford gaol. Three friends put up 2s. each, and Aaron forfeited a property in Colchester, worth 8s. a year, and promised to abjure Bristol town, following which he was released.[14]

On 18 July 1290 came the final act, the Edict of Expulsion. The Jews were no longer a significant source of royal income, and were intensely unpopular among most Christians. Their expulsion would therefore help to increase support for Edward during a time of increasing demands for contributions towards the financing of his wars. All unconverted Jews had to leave the realm by 1 November. Any remaining would be subject to the death penalty. They could take their cash and personal property, but all bonds for debts were to be left behind. No Jews were to be 'injured, harmed, damaged or grieved' on their journeys to the ports. It has been estimated that some 2,500, many of whose families had been living in England for over three generations, were expelled

(England's population at this time was probably between three and four million). The enquiry into the property of the expelled Bristol Jews reveals how the community had shrunk by 1290: only five are recorded as holding houses or land, and only eight as holding bonds. At least one Bristol Jew, 'Menrok, a convert', remained in the town. However, on conversion he lost his property, which passed to Walter le Menn. Edward I received less than £2,000 from the sale of Jewish houses and other property. On the other hand, Parliament voted him a larger grant of money than any of his predecessors had ever received.[15]

BRISTOL'S JEWISH COMMUNITY

Medieval Bristol had two successive Jewries, that is, the area of Jewish occupation: not a ghetto, since Jews and Christians lived side by side. The town's first Jewry was at the Quay Head, around what was formerly Jewry Lane. It thus formed part of the town defences, between St John's Gate at the end of Broad Street and St Giles' Gate at the end of Small Street. This was a highly vulnerable site, on the edge of the Anglo-Norman town and some 500 metres from the royal castle, but this would have seemed less important if, as seems likely, it was founded during the peaceful reign of Henry II.[16]

After the attack by Simon de Montfort's supporters, the quayside Jewry was abandoned for a more secure quarter in Winch Street (present-day Wine Street) close to the gates of the royal castle, where it was in existence by 1275. Jewish houses were constructed on the north side of Winch Street, between the town wall to the north and castle ditch to the east. Here lived Benedict of Winchester, Isaac son of Josce of Caerleon, and another Isaac, father of Cresse. 'In the same street' Hak le Pretre had held two plots. Josce of Caerleon lived even closer to the castle, in 'the street next the castle', later Narrow Winch Street, inside the Old Gate. So did Moses of Kent, whose house was 'outside the castle'. This new Jewry was established with royal assistance, for its houses were held directly of the king. Furthermore, Hak's two plots of land in Winch Street were 'rebuilt by the Constable (of the castle)' for the king. As we have seen, even here, virtually next to the castle, the Jews were far from safe.[17]

Excavations in 1975-6 in Peter Street uncovered an exceptionally well-preserved three-wick bronze lamp, one of the very few examples of the English medieval Jewry's material culture to have survived. Identified as a Sabbath lamp, it would have been lit by the wife above the table on Friday evenings and the eve of festivals,

Figure 6 A detail from Millerd's 1673 map of Bristol, showing the site of the Quay Head Jewry.

Built Anno 1110
Demollyhed 1656

The fouth profpect of Caftle
of the Caftle of Briftoll
Avon flu

Figure 7 Bristol Castle, from Millerd's map of Bristol, 1673. By Millerd's time the castle had been demolished, but this is probably a reasonably accurate depiction of the keep.

Figure 8 The Sabbath Lamp from Peter Street. This oddly shaped copper alloy object is a 13th-century lamp with three spouts to hold wicks. It is thought to have been used by Jews on their Sabbath. The lamp was so efficient that once lit it stayed alight all day – re-lighting it would have been considered work and against the conventions of a day of rest.

to symbolise the light of religion that such occasions bring to the Jewish family. The precise find site would have fronted Narrow Winch Street, on the south side, whereas the documented buildings already referred to were on the north.[18]

For the Jewish people as a whole, freedom to control the internal lives of their local communities was of great symbolic importance. Self government was achieved through the *kehila* (community council), and expressed through its institutions, such as the cemetery (*bet hayim*, House of Life, or *bet olam*, House of Eternity), with its associated *bet tohorah*, or place for washing corpses, and the synagogue, which functioned as a place of assembly, prayer, study (reflected in the Latin medieval term, *scola Judeorum*), and *kosher* food preparation. The communal cemetery was at the very heart of the community; its establishment could precede the building of a synagogue, as religious services could be held in any private house. Only in 1177 were provincial Jewries granted a licence to have their own cemeteries, outside the town walls. Previously, dead Jews had been carried to London for burial at the Cripplegate cemetery.[19]

Bristol's Jewish cemetery was on Brandon Hill (see figure 10). A deed of 1235-6 refers to one croft at Clifton 'against the Jews cemetery', and another, undated, deed records that after the Expulsion Josce of Reigny paid 6s. 8d., for 'the Jewish cemetery next to Brandon Hill'. Jewish tombstones were found in 1844, when construction was begun on the Queen Elizabeth's Hospital School on the north slope (the plot purchased was still called the 'Jews' churchyard'), apparently with Hebrew inscriptions, but they were destroyed soon afterwards and not recorded. These discoveries are of particular interest, as Brandon Hill is the only place in England where Jewish tombstones have been found. Elsewhere, they were sold off after the Expulsion, with the surrounding stone walls. Brandon Hill was evidently too remote to have been subject to such attention.[20]

In nearby Jacob's Well Road a small rock-cut chamber with two stone steps contains a wellhead. The lintel above has part of an inscription, of which only one Hebrew character (*chet*) can be read with confidence. Given its proximity to the medieval cemetery, this is almost certainly a Jewish medieval monument. It has been suggested that the well was used as a *mikveh*, or ritual bath used principally for female purification, but its distance from the Jewry, some 1,600m, and the terrain on Brandon Hill, rule out its use by the women, as they would have been highly vulnerable to unwelcome attention, or even attack, on their regular monthly visits. More probably it was a *bet tohorah*, a ritual bath associated with burial rites. Jacob's Well, it seems, offered provisions for ritual purification, whether of the corpse itself or of those who were deemed impure through contact with it.[21]

Figure 9 The well on Jacob's Well Road lies beneath a modern structure, so its true character will only be understood if it is ever excavated.

Medieval Bristol had three synagogues. To avoid inflaming public opinion, synagogues were usually constructed out of sight, to the rear of the patron's house. Bristol's first synagogue remained etched on the civic memory, for William Worcestre refers to it six times in his *Topography* of the town of 1480. 'The wall of the Jewish temple' was 'at the very start of the Head of the Quay'. 'By the old temple of Jews', he tells us, 'be great vaults under the highest wall of Bristol and the old Church of Saint Giles was builded over the vaults in the way going by Saint Lawrence Lane in to Small Street'. The synagogue wall was 'near the stone entry gate to Small Street'. This description is confirmed by John Leland, over sixty years later, who noted the remains of a 'temple' where St Lawrence Church then stood, 'and thereby in the same lane dwelled the Jews, and their temple, or synagogue, is yet seen there, and now is a warehouse'. The Jewry, one must assume, lay behind the town wall.[22]

In the new Jewry were two synagogues. The first, carefully designated 'the old synagogue', was 'opposite St Peter's', a vulnerable site given the fate of the London synagogue, which was closed because 'the continuous wailing, howling and loud lamentation of the Jews' disturbed the neighbouring friars. The second, on the north side of Winch Street, 'adjoining' one of Hak's two plots, was held by the community on a 20-year lease dated Easter 1285. Within the town wall, there should have been adequate privacy.[23]

Jewish Society in Medieval Bristol

Residents of the Bristol Jewry between 1159 and 1194 included
Berachyah (Benedict), a royal tax collector who died in 1184
leaving a widow, Leah and two sons, Mosse (Moses) and Jose
(Joseph). His death caused problems for his family: the king
claimed heavy death duties from this wealthy man's widow, which
the family struggled to pay; in addition, Leah was in dispute over
her inheritance with Mosse, who was her step-son. Joseph followed
his father as a tax collector, and was probably lending money to the
Somerset gentry in the early 13th century.[24]

Figure 10 Bristol in
the later Middle Ages
(*c*.1300-1500), showing
town walls, major roads,
castle, churches, and
religious houses.

Both male and female Jews engaged in money-lending: in 1265
John de Wodestock mortgaged land and rent in Winch Street to
Preciosa, daughter of Aaron of Kingston, for a debt of £1 13s. 4d.
Prohibitions against Jews securing loans on land affected Preciosa
and other Bristol Jews in the 1270s. Another Bristol Jew, Hagin,

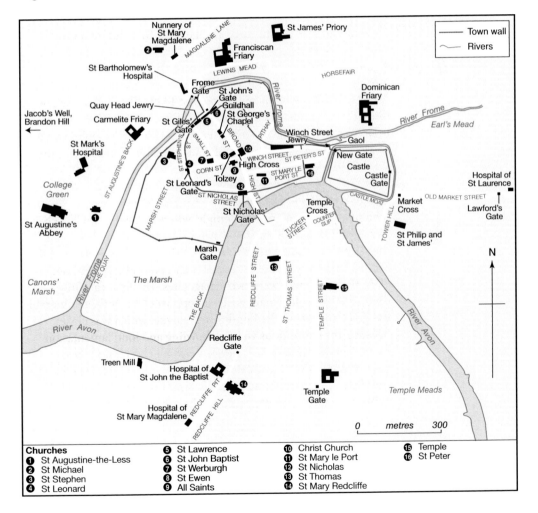

son of Isaac, may have tried to pass himself off as a Christian, adopting the name Benedict Bateman, and was the subject of investigation in 1272.[25]

Bristol's Jews appear to have been highly mobile. Isaac, joint chirographer (keeper of the *archa*) from 1253, was the son of Jose, a wealthy Jew from Caerleon, who had bought three houses in or near the Winch Street Jewry. In 1274 he and his fellow chirographer, Isaac le Prestre, were found guilty of forging a bond, were fined, and expelled from office, but Isaac continued to live in Winch Street and both he and his father appeared as parties in a debt dispute in 1283. He was among those expelled in 1290. Another Bristol Jew evidently with Welsh interests was Cok of Striguil (Chepstow). In 1283 Moses of Kent (a native of Canterbury), Benedict of Winchester, and Aaron of Ireland (who actually came from Colchester) were all Bristol Jews accused of coin-clipping, and Manser (Manasseh), son of Solomon of Calais, accused a Christian of breaking into his Bristol house.[26]

CONCLUSION

Medieval Bristol's Jews, like those of England generally, found themselves in an increasingly difficult position, squeezed by royal expropriations and subjected to periodic violence by some of their Christian neighbours. Their position as moneylenders, one of the roots of this hostility, had been forced upon them. The other source of hostility, the imputation upon all Jews of guilt for the death of Christ, was further compounded by libellous fantasies of ritual infanticide and desecration of the Host. Some of the stock images of modern anti-semitism had their birth in this period, and Bristol, unfortunately, played its part in this process. By the time of their expulsion from England in 1290, Jewish communities had already been financially ruined and severely depleted. And yet, despite all these pressures, for most of its hundred years of recorded existence the Bristol Jewry apparently maintained itself as a vibrant community. Jewish law united all its members, making them responsible for one another and transforming them into a tight political organisation, able to forge commercial, social and intellectual links with other Jewries.

Chapter 2

Ethnic Minorities in the Middle Ages

Figure 11 St Wulfstan depicted in 19th-century stained glass from Worcester Cathedral.

MIGRATION BEFORE THE 15TH CENTURY

Medieval Bristol was a frontier town. Wales lay just across the Severn, and the Bristol Channel gave relatively easy access to Ireland. When Bristol was founded both of these regions were independent of England, and to varying degrees hostile. One of Bristol's earliest appearances in the documentary record is in connection with its trade with Ireland. St Wulfstan, bishop of Worcester (1008-1095), whose diocese then included Bristol, was shocked to find young male and female slaves tied together in long rows in the town's market, waiting to be shipped to the Viking city of Dublin. While St Wulfstan managed to eradicate this trade, despite some local resistance, other commodities continued to be shipped in great number between the two settlements.[27]

Commerce turned to conquest in 1167. By 1171 Henry II was claiming lordship over the whole of Ireland. Dublin was given to Bristolians to colonise, and the new charters of the major Irish towns were modelled on the liberties enjoyed by Bristol. While neither Henry nor any of his medieval successors made their claims of lordship effective throughout the island, the south-eastern coastal strip, from Dublin to Cork, remained the core of English lordship in Ireland. This was also the part of Ireland closest to Bristol, and from the 1170s the town's merchants were trading not with the subjects of foreign kings, but with English and Welsh settlers and their descendants, some of whom would have been their own kinsmen. 'Irish Mead', a Bristol place name since at least the 1160s, was a constant reminder of these connections.[28]

Bristol had been the base for English forays into Wales even before the Norman Conquest, and its strategic position made it a vital border strongpoint during the Anglo-Norman conquest of South-East Wales of the 11th and 12th centuries. Thereafter, water-borne trade between Bristol and English settlements along the South Wales coast and the Wye Valley became, like the Irish trade, a staple of the town's economy.[29]

The sea connected Bristol with a third front in England's expanding empire, France. When Henry of Anjou became Henry II in 1154, the rich vineyards of Gascony came under English rule. Well placed to exploit this new market, Bristol was, by the 13th century, importing about 3,000 tuns of wine a year mainly from

Names, People and Places

Bristol property deeds survive in considerable numbers from the 13th century, and these, combined with early 14th-century taxation documents, lists of office holders and central government records, allow us to identify a large number of Bristolians for the period c. 1200 to c. 1350. Many of them have toponymic surnames – that is, names that denote a place or region. An example of an individual who bore, apparently, both a toponymic and a physical description is John le Lung (Long) de Kerdyff (Cardiff), merchant of Bristol, who was a civic office holder of the town in the 1280s and '90s, and had been among those accused of attacking the Bristol Jews in 1275.

There are problems with this approach, however. The surname le Fraunceys/French and its variants originally meant 'the French(man)', and at least 13 separate individuals bearing the name have been found in 14th-century Bristol, but were they all of French origin, or had this become a family name?

Of course, not every immigrant had a toponymic surname that betrayed his or her origins. For example, John le Veys and Catherine, his wife, were Flemings who had lived in Ireland, where John had traded as an alien merchant, and by 1309 were established in Bristol. In the 1320s John de Treye, Reiner de Berfray and John Roundel were granted royal protection as Frenchmen who were now resident with wives and households in Bristol.

However, where toponymic names are found in this period the likelihood is that they do relate to their bearers' place of birth. Based on this assumption, the analysis of Bristol surnames reveals some interesting trends. Including Fraunceys, there were 33 individuals bearing surnames relating to places in northern France or the Netherlands, and 27 and 10 relating respectively to Welsh and Irish origins. Despite the strong trade ties between Gascony and Bristol, no place names from Gascony are evident. Nor does there appear to have been a Gascon community in Bristol, so those aliens who settled in Bristol seem not to have arrived as a direct consequence of the wool-wine trade.

The results for Wales and Ireland are much more in line with expectations based on Bristol's western trade routes: the Welsh towns are all along the south coast or the Wye valley, while the Irish towns are all along the south or central east coast. The scarcity of Celtic names among this group is noteworthy. With few exceptions, there

The medieval Welsh depicted in the 'Laws of Hywel Dda' (a native Welsh law code), in a 13th-century manuscript.

are no obviously Gaelic or Welsh names. While such appellations as *Hiberniensis* (Irishman) or 'le Walse' may conceal a Gaelic or Welsh identity, most of the bearers of these surnames have the usual Anglo-Norman Christian names, such as John, William or Thomas. The exceptions all relate to the 'Welsh' group. The one 'pure' Welsh name was possessed by Cradoc, a servant, and it is perhaps significant that the single unmistakeable Welshman is also the sole example of a servant among our group. Other names belonging to members of the burgess class show a mixture of Celtic and Anglo-Norman elements. Notably absent before the mid-14th century is any evidence of Celtic patronymics, that is, to give a Welsh example, the use of *ap/b*, derived from *mab* (son). This absence is particularly striking given the frequency with which such names are found in 15th-century Bristol.

References

Taxation: Fuller, 222-78; Franklin, 29-31.
Deeds: BRO & TNA, various; Elrington; *CPR, 1272-81*, 24, 107. Office holders: Latimer (1903), 108-37.
French surnames: *CPR, 1301-7*, 347; *CPR, 1324-27*, 41, 55, 252; *1348-50*, 338-9; *1313-17*, 35, 68, 133-4, 143-4, 489, 605; TNA SC8/120/5988.
Celtic surnames: *CPR, 1313-16*, 444, 605; BRO 00859/2, P.AS/D/HS/E/1.

Bordeaux. In return, Bristol exported first wool and then, from the 14th century, cloth.[30]

Alien merchants were not a significant feature of Bristol's overseas trade. In both the periods from 1324 to 1329 and 1478 to 1482 Bristol accounted for less than one per cent of total English overseas trade carried by aliens, and in the latter period only 4.1 per cent of the port's overseas trade was in alien hands. Therefore, we should not expect to find a large community of alien merchants in medieval Bristol.[31]

THE 15TH CENTURY

Only from the very end of the 14th century does the surviving documentation allow us to begin to piece together a more detailed picture of Bristol's ethnic minorities. Licences granting permission to reside in England, wills, and the records of taxes imposed on aliens are among the new forms of evidence that now appear.

Figure 12 Mayors of later medieval Irish towns: the elite of the English settlers in Ireland, from the Waterford Charter Roll.

The Irish

From the mid-14th century England's Irish colonies deteriorated
to a state of near anarchy. Already suffering from an economic
depression, large numbers abandoned Ireland in search of better
prospects in England and Wales. The effects were felt in Bristol:
in 1381/2 the Royal Council was petitioned to take more effective
action to restore peace in Ireland in order to stem the flow of Irish
refugees that was afflicting Bristol and Cornwall. The Crown's reaction to this influx was to issue periodic orders that all Irish living in
England and Wales should return home, but it also sold licences of
exemption to individuals, allowing them to remain.[32]

We know of 11 Bristol Irish who bought licences after the
first order to return was issued in 1394. There were surely far
more Irish in Bristol at this time, and it is likely that the rest
either returned or became 'illegal immigrants', hoping that they
would escape official notice. The licensees were probably among
the more prominent of the Bristol Irish. At least three held civic
office: Walter Seymour and John Preston were sheriffs in 1392/3
and 1397/8 respectively, while John Sely, a merchant, was mayor
in 1410/11.[33]

Seven Bristol Irish bought licences in 1413, two of them
substantial cloth merchants. John Aylward was active from at
least 1390 until the 1420s. Nicholas Devenyssh was mayor in
1436. While classed as an Irishman, Nicholas came from a long
line of Bristol Devenysshes, a family probably originating in
Devon. Nicholas's son and grandson were officials of the town's
Tolzey Court; both were probably born in England, but another
Devenyssh, John, was taxed as an alien in 1440 and so was presumably born in Ireland. The family had clearly put down roots
either side of the Irish Sea.[34]

This does not exhaust the list of prominent Bristol Irishmen
at the turn of the 14th and 15th centuries. John Toky of Limerick
traded cloth and hides between Ireland and Flanders until 1382,
when he began to be known as John Banbury; about the same time
he established himself in Bristol, where he prospered. He was bailiff
in 1389/90, sheriff in 1391/2 and mayor in 1397/8, and in 1397 he
sat for Bristol in Parliament. When he died in 1404/5, he asked to
be buried in Bristol, even though he had maintained links with his
birthplace. We can never know Banbury's reasons for adopting an
'English' name, but it may well be that he thought it more acceptable to the Bristolians among whom he made his home.[35]

In the 1420s Robert Londe, master in Bristol's Newgate school,
produced some Latin translation exercises for his pupils, among
which was this: 'To Bristol, the which is a port town, come more

Figure 13 The Bristol mayor-making ceremony: the new mayor is sworn in at the Guildhall, surrounded by councillors and civic officers, from *The Mayor of Bristol's Calendar*, composed by the town clerk, Robert Ricart, from 1478/9.

strangers than to Coventry, the which is not a port town, notwithstanding that both be equally good.'[36]

He knew of what he wrote, since as an Irish-born priest he had once been a 'stranger'. Londe lived in Bristol from at least 1419 until his death in 1462, but he was not allowed to forget his foreign origins: as an Irishman he had to purchase a licence to remain in 1430 when his compatriots were ordered to leave England, and in 1440/1 he had to pay a tax on aliens, despite being a subject of the king of England.[37]

By 1440 the English parliamentary class's growing xenophobia, combined with the Crown's desperate need for money to sustain its failing military efforts in France, produced the first alien subsidy,

Figure 14 Brass of Robert
Londe, from St Peter's
church, 1462. A picture of
respectability, but perhaps
not fully accepted as
a loyal subject by the
English Crown.

effectively a poll tax on those born outside the territories over
which the king claimed lordship. The Irish were classed as aliens
for the purposes of this first subsidy, although in subsequent
grants they were exempted, as were those born within the king's
allegiance in France. Specifically exempted from the beginning
were the Welsh.[38]

The Bristol returns to this subsidy give lists of names, divided
between householders and non-householders, the latter mainly
servants and chaplains, and were made over the period 1440 to
1441. They indicate that around eight per cent of Bristol's population of a little under 10,000 were born outside England and Wales.
Of these, the bulk were probably Irish, and of English descent. Of
131 householders assessed, only one, Edmund Broun, shared his
name with a civic office-holder, and this man, a bailiff in 1421/2,
rose no higher. Only around one third were householders; if most
of the assessed were Irish, it follows that most Bristol Irish were of
humble means.[39]

The inclusion of the Irish among those 'aliens' forced to pay
the 1440 subsidy must be seen in the context of widespread anti-
Irish feeling in England, not least in Bristol. In 1439 the Irish had
been banned from membership of the civic governing body, the
Common Council, and from the guilds of hoopers, fletchers and
bowyers. Discrimination against the Irish was motivated by English
difficulties in Ireland and by the mid-century economic depression
and the protectionist reaction it prompted. One consequence in
Bristol was that in 1455 the mayor and Common Council imposed
differential fees for apprentices entering the freedom (thereby
being able to trade freely as full citizens), depending on whether
or not they were born within the king's allegiance: those who had
been paid the customary two shillings; those who had not paid
104*s.*, a sum, one suspects, designed to deter such individuals from
trading in Bristol altogether.[40]

Later that same year an attempt to impose the higher fee on an
Irish-born apprentice provoked a major dispute with the town's
Irish population. In 1455 the Irish-born Bristol burgess Henry May
presented Richard May, his apprentice of seven years, to the mayor
and the chamberlains, but they refused to allow him membership
of the freedom without payment of the higher fee, which May
refused. Henry took the mayor and chamberlains to the court of
Chancery for their refusal to admit his apprentice. Meanwhile,
Bristol's leaders had raised a considerable sum of money in an
effort to secure an Act at the Westminster Parliament, apparently to
sanction their discrimination against Irish burgesses. In response,
Bristol's Irish community organised a levy with which to finance
their lobbying at Parliament against the bill. The lobbyists, together

Figures 15a and b An extract from the 1440/1 tax on aliens in Bristol, for St Michael's parish, with the original leather pouch in which it was kept. 'Galfridus Sligo', presumably Irish, and 'Henry Lokier ducheman' are fourth and sixth on the list respectively.

with Henry May, were ejected from the freedom of Bristol. Further litigation followed, but the mayor and Common Council seem to have failed to secure their Act. The case shows that there was a significant degree of cohesion and self-identity within the Irish community: within two months of the start of the dispute Bristol's Irish had organised and funded what appears to have been a successful lobbying operation at Westminster against the Act.[41]

The Welsh

In 1400 Owain Glyndŵr's rebellion against English rule broke out in North Wales, and for the next eight years Wales was convulsed by violence. Disturbances and tension continued until 1413. The position of the many Welsh living in England was generally very difficult, and they had to cope with discrimination and suspicion. However, there is very little evidence of this within Bristol, perhaps in part because most Welsh migrants came from South Wales, where there was less support for Glyndŵr.[42]

Welshmen held high civic office in Bristol during and immediately after the rebellion. David Ruddock was bailiff in 1411/2 and sheriff in 1419/20. James Cokkes was bailiff in 1406/7, sheriff in 1409/10 and mayor in 1419/20. The other bailiff in 1406/7 was David Dudbrook, alias ap Adam, who was a common councillor until 1422 and a Bristol MP in 1411. David's elder brother Robert was sheriff in 1400/1 and mayor in 1404/5. Thomas Yonge, alias Mere, was bailiff in 1402/3, sheriff in 1407/8 and MP in 1414. In 1407 Yonge's marriage to Joan, widow of the prominent merchant

Figure 16 Bristol's first sheriff, appointed after the granting of the 1373 charter, flanked by two sergeants, as depicted in Ricart's *Mayor of Bristol's Calendar*.

John Canynges, placed him at the heart of Bristol's civic and commercial elite. Bristol's accommodating attitude was not shared by the Crown: in 1413 Cokkes, David Dudbrook and Yonge were among the eight Bristol Welsh purchasing licences to remain in England following the royal proclamation ordering the Welsh back to Wales.

In contrast to the situation in earlier centuries, Welsh personal names occur with great frequency in the 15th-century Bristol records at all levels of society. Among the parties to Bristol Tolzey Court actions in 1480/1 were 30 individuals bearing Welsh names who appeared on 46 separate occasions in about 90 cases. Between 1390 and 1525 high civic office (bailiff, sheriff or mayor) was held 39 times by 22 men with Welsh names, or known to be of Welsh origin, a figure that represents around 10 per cent of the total number of office-holders for that period.[43]

Early Tudor Bristol displays a particularly strong Welsh presence among the governing elite. With the accession in 1485 of Henry VII, a king conscious of his Welsh roots and mindful of the part the Welsh had played in his triumph, the promotion of Welshmen to civic office in Bristol might not seem remarkable, but this generation of Bristol Welsh had begun to hold civic office

Figure 17 Richard ap Meryk's name from a contemporary document. He is described as a merchant of Bristol.

before August 1485. The Vaghans were particularly important in this context. They had links with South and West Wales and had been represented in Bristol since at least 1405, but it was Henry Vaghan who was at the centre of their Bristol network. Active in Bristol from at least 1467, he has been described as early Tudor Bristol's 'most successful and respected merchant'. Bailiff in 1469/70, sheriff in 1477/8 and thrice mayor in the 1480s and '90s, he was also MP in 1487 and 1497, and constable of the Bristol staple in 1491. At least five other Vaghans held civic office in early Tudor Bristol. They were joined by several ap Howells, Rhyses, Joneses, a Griffith, Williams, Edwards, Ap Merick and a Davies. Among these, Richard ap Meryk is of particular interest. He was twice pardoned by the king. In his pardon of 1495 he described himself as Richard Meryk of Bristol, merchant, alias A Meryk, alias ap Meryk; in his pardon of 1499 he was called, simply, Richard Amerik. His name's movement from Welsh patronymic, Richard ap Meurig, to English surname, Meryk, may well reflect his own transition from a Welsh to an English cultural community.[44]

Of course, we cannot assume that everyone with a Welsh name was culturally 'Welsh', in that they identified themselves as Welsh rather than English, and only rarely is it possible to demonstrate an unmistakable connection with Wales. Two examples are Thomas Jones, a burgess who made his will in 1496, asking to be buried in his Bristol parish church of St Nicholas, but leaving bequests to a number of churches in Monmouthshire, and the Bristol merchant Richard Vaghan, who in his will of 1507 asked to be buried in St Stephen's, next to his former wives Margery and Cecily, in their recently constructed tomb, but who also provided for prayers to be said for his soul in the parish church of Aberystwyth, 'wherein I was Christened'.[45]

Immigrants from Continental Europe

In 1435 the duke of Burgundy ended his alliance with the English and allied himself with the French. The following year Burgundian subjects living in England – mostly Flemings – were given the choice between swearing an oath of loyalty to the king or expulsion. The names of the oath takers were recorded, along with their place of origin. Twenty-six Bristol aliens took the oath. They all came either from the Low Countries or from the Rhine Valley, and this region probably provided the majority of 15th-century Bristol's alien population.[46]

The alien subsidy returns of 1455 and 1458 are the only ones which systematically give the nationalities of those assessed, and the combined results are given in the following table:[47]

Table 1 Nationalities given in Bristol Alien Subsidy Returns, 1455 & 1458 Combined

	Householder	*Non-householder*	*Total*
Breton	1	2	3
Dutch	1	5	6
Flemish	7	4	11
Frenchman	0	1	1
Iceland	0	16	16
Picard?	1	3	4
Zeelander	0	1	1
Total	10	32	42

The subsidies suggest that Bristol's true alien population was a mere half of one per cent of its total population of approximately 10,000. Bristol's alien population appears even more insignificant when compared with London's, which in 1483 may have accounted for about six per cent of its population, not counting Irish. Most of Bristol's small alien population was composed of Dutch and Flemings, but there was very little direct trade between Bristol and the Low Countries, so aliens from this region had probably arrived from London or an east-coast port. This may therefore be an example of 'step-migration', or movement away from the port of entry towards another destination in several stages. Their emigration was probably prompted by a combination of disorder at home and greater opportunities in England. The Flemings, at least, seem on average more highly skilled than the other immigrants, and perhaps more so than the average Bristol craftsman (they had long enjoyed a reputation for being innovators in textiles and brewing), and the higher incidence of house-holding among the Flemish alien subsidy payers may support this speculation.[48]

The near absence of French from the 1455 and 1458 alien subsidies might be partially explained by the fact that those born in former English possessions in France would have been exempt from the tax. However, while Bristol had a thriving trade with Gascony before 1453, there are few references to French residents in early 15th-century Bristol. A rare example is provided by William de la Motte, alias Guylliam de la Motte of Bristol, late of Conket, Brittany, merchant, who was languishing in Bristol's gaol in 1442 for some unspecified offence. A small number of refugees appeared in Bristol after the loss of France. They included Moses

Figure 18 Sebastian Cabot in later life; he was the son of John Cabot (Giovanni Caboto), the Italian explorer who arrived in Bristol in 1495/6 before embarking on his voyage to Newfoundland in 1497. His family, including Sebastian, continued to live in their house in St Nicholas Street until at least 1499.

Conterayn (who received letters of denization allowing him to become a subject of the king of England in 1461), Bernard Bensyn and William Lombard, formerly merchants of Bordeaux. The last may be identical with the William Lombard of St Mary-le-Port parish, assessed as an alien in 1441, and buried in St Nicholas's church in 1488. Merchants tended not to be based in foreign ports, but to work through agents, or factors, who could be locals. This may have been the case with Jordan Sprynge, who was working in Bristol for a French merchant in 1458.[49]

Neither does there appear to have been a significant Spanish or Portuguese presence. However, Mark William, mayor and MP for Bristol in the early 15th century, was also known as Spaynell, and appears to have been of Spanish origin. His adoption of an English-sounding alias, however, reminds us of the possibility of there being other aliens who disappeared behind an adopted name.[50]

There is some evidence for alien occupations. Among those who swore the 1436 oath were two goldsmiths, a leatherworker and a tailor. Some of the aliens listed in the subsidy returns are either given occupational descriptions or surnames that suggest an occupation. There are two brewers of beer, the new-fangled Flemish innovation that would eventually supplant ale, two tailors, a pinner, pointmaker (maker of laces for securing clothing), shearman, bellmaker, leatherworker, goldsmith, smith and, possibly, herdsman. Of 107 individuals given occupational descriptions in the 1441 alien subsidy returns, the largest group – 25 – were leatherworkers. There were two large households of Dutch leatherworkers in All Saints parish, one headed by Olffe Ducheman, with three alien leatherworker servants, the other by Garard Ducheman, who had four alien leatherworker servants. The next largest groups were 14 priests and 11 tailors.

Tiny though it was, Bristol's alien population was still regarded as a problem by the civic authorities. In 1450 the tailors, goldsmiths and cordwainers, whether aliens or natives, were prohibited from taking on alien apprentices or journeymen, and any current alien apprentices and journeymen were ordered to leave forthwith. The ordinance of 1455 that imposed a higher fee on any apprentice born outside England and Wales seeking admittance to the freedom has already been mentioned, as has the 1479 ordinance of the guild of bowyers and fletchers (makers of bows and arrows) restricting apprenticeships to those who were not Irish or aliens. In the same year the fullers placed restrictions on 'foreign' men coming into the craft. In these cases, the motive seems to have been the protection of employment opportunities for the English and Welsh.[51]

Icelanders

The most surprising aspect of the post 1440/1 alien subsidy returns is that the single largest group is made up of Icelanders, all of whom were non-householders. They are only ever identified by their first names ('Snorry Iseland', 'Helgy Iseland', 'Haraldus Iseland' etc), without any occupational designation, strongly suggesting that they were servants. This suspicion is confirmed by a remarkable return of 1484, which lists 49 Icelandic servants. Ten are described as 'Icelandic boy', followed by 36 described as 'Icelandic servant', and one is not described but his master paid the standard rate of 2s. for a servant. Only two servants are named, William Yslond and John Yslond. William Yslond had received denizen status and was shipping cloth from Bristol to Lisbon in 1492, and so was evidently a servant of the superior sort in 1484, as was, probably, his compatriot John.[52]

From the 1430s to the 1470s Bristol was heavily involved in England's Icelandic trade. Icelanders were reliant on imports for the necessities of life, and in this period suffered serious poverty. There is ample evidence from both English and Icelandic-Danish sources of trade in a very particular commodity between the two countries: child labour. English merchants kidnapped Icelandic children, or persuaded their parents to sell them, to work as servants in English households and workshops, supposedly in virtual slave conditions. A 1462 ordinance of the Bristol Weavers' Guild probably relates to this trade. It complains that many weavers:[53]

> … daily receive and put in occupation of the said craft strangers, aliens, and others not born under the king's allegiance, and for their singular profit, provoke and stir divers merchants and others to bring into this town of Bristol people of divers countries not born under the king's allegiance but rebellious, which be sold to them as it were heathen people, and through the continuance thereof in default of correction it has caused that such strangers and aliens be greatly multiplied and increased within the town of Bristol, and that the king's liege people born within this said town and other parts of this his realm be vagrants and unoccupied, and may not have their labour for their living …[54]

The Ordinance also suggests the sort of work they were put to: to be a threat to native textile workers they would have to have been employed in the industry, presumably at low or non-existent wages. In addition, few of the masters named in the 1484 subsidy return appear to have had any connection with the Icelandic trade, which confirms the Weavers' allegation that merchants sold on

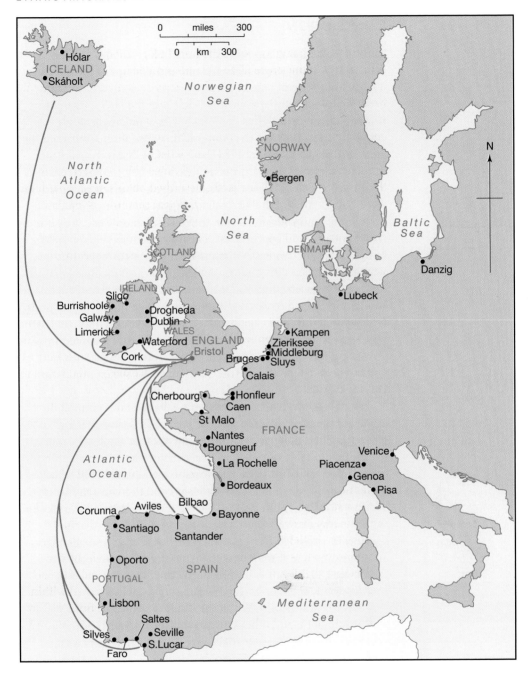

Figure 19 Immigration from Europe into Bristol in the Middle Ages.

their human cargoes to craftsmen. That so many Icelandic servants should appear in Bristol in the mid-1480s, at a time when the Icelandic trade was declining, suggests that the bulk of these, those not described as 'boys', had been in Bristol for some time. Bristol's 17th- and 18th-century slaving activities are notorious, but its exploitation of bonded labour evidently has a much longer history.

CONCLUSION

In the 15th century, and probably long before, Bristol's major immigrant groups came from Ireland and Wales. For much of the Middle Ages Bristol's immigrants from those areas seem to have been predominantly of English stock. From the later 14th century this was changing as far as the Welsh were concerned. There was evidently an influx of Irish economic or political refugees from the later 14th century, and most of these were probably much more humble than the Welsh burgesses who were beginning to make their mark. Personal name evidence suggests that few of these Irish were Gaelic. Anti-Irish discrimination was therefore not focused exclusively on the Gaels, nor on the lower classes, since the poor could not aspire to apprenticeships, guild membership, or a place in the Common Council, which is where the local legislation would have taken effect. However, the records of medieval Bristol's local courts have all but disappeared, and it is here where we would have hoped to catch glimpses of the lives of the town's poor. Official discrimination against the Irish at local and national level was part of a broader prejudice against outsiders, prompted by growing English national consciousness, foreign policy disasters and economic depression. This affected Bristol's alien population to varying degrees.

The only group which seems to have escaped discrimination, at least at the burgess level, was the Welsh. This is surprising, given that they suffered discrimination in other English border towns, that Glyndŵr's rebellion was a major blow to Anglo-Welsh assimilation, and that Bristol appears to have played host to an increasing proportion of native Welsh – and therefore probably Welsh-speaking – immigrants. Why the Welsh should have escaped the antipathy shown towards the Irish (to the extent of being specifically excluded from measures aimed at Irish and aliens) is an interesting question. While the Anglo-Irish, and even some of the newer English settlers, were Gaelic speakers and had adopted Irish customs, those who came to Bristol presumably also spoke English, or Hiberno-English. Bristol's ethnic Welsh population was presumably also bi-lingual, in English and Welsh. If the vast majority of the Bristol Irish were of English descent, and an increasing number of the Bristol Welsh were Celts, this seems to have mattered little to the town's English elite. Was Bristol's proximity to Wales a factor? Was South-East Wales so firmly part of Bristol's hinterland that English Bristolians did not recognise any material difference between themselves and their neighbours across the Severn?

Chapter 3

Ethnic Minorities, 1500–1685

In this period political events both within the British Isles and in Continental Europe had important effects on Bristol's ethnic identity. The Reformation, beginning in Germany in 1517, came to create a new class of migrant, the Protestant religious refugee. In the 1530s and 1540s Wales was brought within the administrative structures of the English state, and Welsh society and culture were opened up to greater English influence, a development that most of the Welsh elite warmly embraced, although Protestantism made slow progress in the west and the central uplands. The increasing Anglicisation also encouraged the disappearance of distinctions between those of Celtic and settler stock, subsumed into one 'Welsh' identity.

The final adoption of Protestantism as the official religion of England, embodied in the Church of England, added confessional to ethnic differences as a further barrier between English and Gael in Ireland, where the population remained overwhelmingly Catholic. In 1594 an uprising broke out against English rule in Ireland and this turned into a nine-years' war, with the rebels led by Hugh O'Neill, the Gaelic earl of Tyrone. This had a devastating impact on the Irish economy. The effects were felt in Bristol, which not only acted as a major port of embarkation for English armies, but also played unwilling host to Irish refugees. The war coincided with a period of famine in both countries. Similarly, the Irish revolt of 1641 came after economic depression; it was the catalyst that plunged all three kingdoms – England, Ireland and Scotland – into war, and Bristol had to contend with an influx of Protestant Irish refugees from the fighting across the water.

Later 16th-century France was riven by religious wars between Protestants (who came to be known as Huguenots) and Catholics, but by the terms of the Edict of Nantes (1598) the former were guaranteed a certain degree of security. The Edict's revocation in 1685 led to the emergence of a significant Huguenot community in Bristol, and this date is taken as the end point of this chapter. Bristol played host to a small number of Continental Protestants before 1685, mainly from the German lands of the Holy Roman Emperor and Spain's territories in the Low Countries.

Figure 20 Hoefnagel's map of Bristol, 1581.

THE WELSH

The Welsh continued to be Bristol's biggest ethnic minority and seem to have met no more discrimination than in previous centuries. Welsh surnames were borne by about 15 per cent of civic office holders (sheriffs and mayors) in the 16th century, falling to seven per cent in the period 1600 to 1685, and by a little over eight per cent of the new entrants to the freedom recorded in the Burgess Books for 1557 to 1590. However, the twin processes of cultural Anglicisation and social assimilation, together with the long history of their settlement in Bristol, make it more difficult to identify Welsh men and women in this period. There were still real differences, nevertheless, between English and Welsh, at least in Tudor Bristol. In the 1530s Thomas Jones of Bristol, brother and executor of William Jones of Newport, claimed in the course of a case in Chancery that the latter had requested that his children be brought to Bristol, 'to the intent to have his children brought up according to the manner & conditions of the nurture of England'. If true, then this statement demonstrates that there was a significant difference between an English upbringing, of the sort available in Bristol, and that found in Newport, surely one of the most Anglicised of Welsh towns.[55]

Despite the Welsh elite's necessary adoption of English as their language of business, Welsh remained the mother tongue of their humbler compatriots. Welsh was spoken in Tudor Bristol. In 1549 a commission investigating corruption at the Bristol mint examined a Bristol shoemaker, Jenkin Dee, who related how he had been given information by the wife of one of the mint officials, who had spoken to him in Welsh, which he could understand. In 1651 Roger Bay, a Bristol tailor, acted as interpreter for a monoglot Welsh-speaker from Monmouthshire testifying before one of the city's courts.[56]

In addition to apprenticeship, burgess status could also be acquired through purchase (by payment of a 'redemption' fine) or by marriage to a freeman's daughter or widow. Entry by marriage was far more common than by purchase and probably more important than apprenticeship as a means of entry into Bristol society. Parish registers begin to survive from the latter half of the 16th century, and these provide valuable evidence. In the parish of St Augustine's the Less, for example, in the three years between 1663 and 1666, six parishioners married Welsh brides, three from Cardiff, one from Cowbridge (Glam.) and two from Monmouthshire. Marriage licence bonds are extant from 1637, giving the names and places of residence of bride and groom. These furnish many examples of marriages between Welsh and Bristolians at all levels of society. In most of these cases, it is the groom who is Welsh, and the geographical distribution is, as expected, focused on South-East Wales, with Monmouthshire and Cardiff featuring particularly strongly.[57]

Wills provide further evidence of Bristolians who had been born in Wales. In his will of 1529 the Bristol merchant John Thomas requested burial in his local church of St Werburgh's, but he bequeathed £10 to buy land in Abergavenny which would support annual prayers to be said there for his soul and the souls of his parents. The saddler Edward Thomas was a parishioner of St Thomas, Bristol, but in 1545 he probably made his will in Mounton, Pembrokeshire, where he asked to be buried; he had a shop in Pembroke and held the advowson (right to appoint the priest in charge of the church) of Castlemartin in the same county, as well as property in Monmouthshire. David Jones made his will in 1598 and asked to be buried in his parish church of St Nicholas, but his bequests to St Ishmael's in Carmarthenshire show that he had not forgotten his Welsh origins.[58]

Apprentices

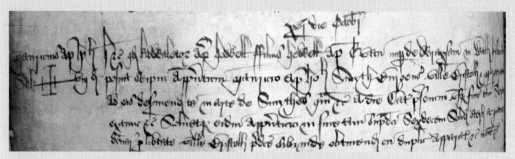

A page from a Bristol Apprentice Book. Kadwaletor ap Howell is apprenticed to Maurice ap Howell, smith and burgess of Bristol.

The institution of apprenticeship provided training, education and socialisation for young men – and a few young women – leading, in many but far from all cases, to entry into the freedom as a burgess. Apprenticeships usually lasted for seven years from around the age of 14. In Bristol they were recorded in the 'Apprentice Books', which named parents or guardian, sometimes occupation, and the master, together with his trade. These survive from 1532. In the period 1532 to 1552 a total of 3,139 apprentices were registered, of whom 766 came from within Bristol, and 456 from Wales. Welsh apprentices therefore constituted 14.5 per cent overall, but 19.2 per cent of non-Bristolians (for distribution see table)

County	No. of Apprentices	
Anglesey	3	(0.6%)
Brecon	40	(8.7%)
Caernarfon	7	(1.5%)
Cardigan	3	(0.6%)
Carmarthen	29	(6.3%)
Denbigh	20	(4.3%)
Flint	1	(0.2%)
Glamorgan	72	(15.7%)
Merioneth	3	(0.6%)
Monmouth	168	(36.8%)
Montgomery	17	(3.7%)
Pembroke	84	(18.4%)
Radnor	9	(1.9%)

Unsurprisingly, most came from South-East and South Wales. 280 (61.4 per cent) came from Brecon, Glamorgan and Monmouthshire. Surprisingly, since it contained one of the three largest towns in Wales, only 26 came from Carmarthenshire whereas 84 came from Pembrokeshire in the far west. Regional distribution within Pembrokeshire perhaps accounts for this. Of the 78 apprentices whose place of origin can be identified, only four came from the largely Welsh-speaking north. The rest came from the Anglophone area south of the so-called 'Landsker', the linguistic boundary. This was also where Pembrokeshire's larger towns were located, and it had easier communications with Bristol.

How did prospective apprentices and masters make contact? Cases like that of Thomas, son of Richard Rogers of Tenby, apprenticed to Thomas ap Gwillyam, tanner, and his wife Alice in 1536, suggest a previous Welsh connection might matter. Between 1532 and 1552, 325 Bristol masters, 28 per cent of whom had Welsh names, retained Welsh apprentices, and 77 of these took on a Welsh apprentice more than once. In some instances the apprentices were drawn from the same area, and sometimes the master had a Welsh name as well; in 14 cases the master shared his surname with one of his apprentices. These examples indicate some form of prior connection, either familial or commercial. In general, however, the lack of an exact correlation between the family and ethnic background of the majority of masters and apprentices strongly suggests that there was no general desire for Welsh youngsters to be apprenticed within an ex-patriot community: there was no Welsh ghetto in early-modern Bristol.

Not all Welsh apprentices finished their term and entered the freedom as independent craftsmen or traders. Many were either unwilling or unable to complete, and most probably left Bristol to practise their skills elsewhere. Naturally, there were success stories among those who stayed. Edward Sandy of Cadoxton, near Cardiff, apprenticed his son Walter to the Bristol merchant William Challoner in 1611. Walter entered the freedom in 1627 and married into the Challoner family. He was a member of the Common Council from 1640, treasurer of the Merchant Venturers in 1645-6, sheriff in 1646-7, and alderman for St Stephen's ward from 1656. He made use of his Welsh contacts as one of the founders of the Ynyspenllwch iron works in the Swansea Valley.

Spencer Dimmock* and Jinx Newly

* research as part of a project on medieval Welsh towns, directed by Ralph Griffiths and funded by the Board of Celtic Studies, University of Wales.

Sources
Hollis; Ralph & Hardwick; Ralph (1992); Lang & McGregor, 48; Nott, 253-4.

Figure 21 A depiction of Irish mercenaries, by Albrecht Dürer, 1521. Their appearance seems to have struck this widely-travelled German artist as strange and exotic. Would they have had the same effect on an English observer?

THE IRISH

Irish migrants appear in the sources described above, but in smaller numbers. Irish apprentices constituted only around six per cent of Bristol apprentices indentured between 1532 and 1542. They constituted fewer than 2 per cent of 17th-century merchant apprentices.[59]

However, most Irish migrants to Bristol in this period came in unfortunate, even tragic circumstances. From the mid-1590s, and again after 1641, Irish refugees appeared in great numbers. Irish vagrancy had been perceived as a problem in England long before the 1590s, and in 1587 the mayor was ordered by the Privy Council to provide food and lodging for Irish vagrants being transported from London back to Ireland, via Bristol. Within a few years poor Irish were coming directly to Bristol in significant numbers. In 1628 the mayor described the situation to the Privy Council in these words:[60]

> … the scarcity of Corn in his Majesty's Realm of Ireland is such at this present as the poor people of the said Realm are enforced for the avoiding of famine to come over into this Kingdom, and are now very offensive in all the western parts, especially in the said City of Bristol, the number of the said poor … being like daily to increase …

The parish registers of St Augustine the Less bring home what this meant in human terms. Between 1597 and 1629, 12

Figure 22 An Irish feast, from John Derricke, *The Image of Ireland* (1581). This outsider's view of the Gaelic Irish portrays them as wild and uncouth.

burials are recorded of poor Irish; in 1629 these made up six out of 18 burials. The plight of some of the Irish is indicated by such descriptions as, 'a poor young man that came out from Ireland, who died in the street'; two other deceased Irish were buried anonymously, their names unknown. Another burial was of 'Harry Harden an Irish man that was executed for his offence above [St] Michael's Hill'. The reaction of Bristol Corporation was to ship as many refugees back to Ireland as possible. The sum of one shilling per head was allowed for the passage, and the total number of Irish returned may have reached over a thousand. For its part, the Crown ordered the mayor to take bonds from all ship's masters that they would not transport refugees out of Ireland. At the same time, the government ban on the export of grain to Ireland was not helping the situation, and in 1629 the mayor successfully petitioned the Privy Council for Bristol merchants to be allowed to resume this trade.[61]

Bristol was once again beset with Irish refugees 12 years later, but the reaction to this influx, at both the civic and parish level, appears to have been rather different. The Irish revolt that began in November 1641 was seen as a Catholic rebellion, supported by France and Spain, and those of its victims who found their way to Bristol were characterised not as vagrant Irish but as good Protestants who had suffered for their religion. Sympathy would have been increased by the fact that some of them had come from Bristol in the first place, or had relatives in the city. In 1618-19 King James had ordered the mayor to encourage 'good Bristol

Protestants' to settle in Waterford, which had received a new charter. The response was disappointing, but Bristolians had been settling in Ireland for centuries, so that the failure of this initiative does not necessarily mean that all the refugees in the 1640s were outsiders. In 1642 approximately 400 Protestant Irish refugees arrived in Bristol. They were given a sympathetic reception. The Corporation rose to the challenge with generosity, as this example from the mayor's audits shows:[62]

> Item paid £2 unto Peter Spurrier by Mr Mayor's order and is given with Elizabeth Nethercott a poor Fatherless and Motherless child which came out of Ireland which is bound Apprentice to the said Spurrier and his wife for 12 years, to learn to make buttons.

This was matched by the generosity of the parishes. While the St Augustine the Less burial register tells its melancholy story, with six Irish interred between 1642 and 1645, including 'a poor Irish child in the Jews Church yard' (presumably Brandon Hill), several sets of churchwardens' accounts provide plentiful evidence of help rendered to the living. Particularly noticeable are payments made to ministers of religion and their wives: these occur, for example, in the accounts for the churches of Sts Philip and James, St Mary Redcliffe, and All Saints'. St Mary's account for 1642 is graphic: 'To the minister driven by the rebels out of Ireland …To a poor minister that came out of Ireland … To a minister stripped of his estate by the rebels in Ireland', and, 'To certain Protestants stripped by the Rebels in Ireland … To some poor English driven out of Ireland'. This last entry indicates that some of these refugees had not been so long in Ireland as to lose their English cultural identity. Churchwardens usually employed such phrases as a 'poor man that came from Ireland', 'a poor woman Margaret that came from Ireland', or 'several distressed people out of Ireland'; rarely did they refer to 'poor Irish'. Bristol's generosity is all the more remarkable in light of the desperate privations it suffered during the course of the civil wars, when the city was twice taken by storm.

A number of Irish refugees went on to establish themselves in Bristol. William Pearson, a barber, William Freeman and John Iles had been business partners in Ireland, and in 1650 they were all three living in Bristol, possibly in the same house; William Smith had lived in Limerick before moving to Bristol in 1642, where he was still settled in 1651, while Jonathan Blackwell, a Bristol vintner by 1654, and his brother Joseph, then living in London, had been Irish landowners before 1642. Bristol's sympathetic attitude to Protestant, 'respectable' Irish is the more notable when compared with the activities of some of its merchants in the mid-17th century, who were involved in the transportation to the Caribbean and American colonies of Catholic Irish vagabonds and 'Tories' (supporters of the Royalist cause), there to labour in appalling conditions as forced labour. Bristolians' sympathy towards Protestant refugees in their city is also apparent in the case of Continental immigrants.[63]

Figure 23 A Tudor subsidy return for Bristol: the return for January 1523.

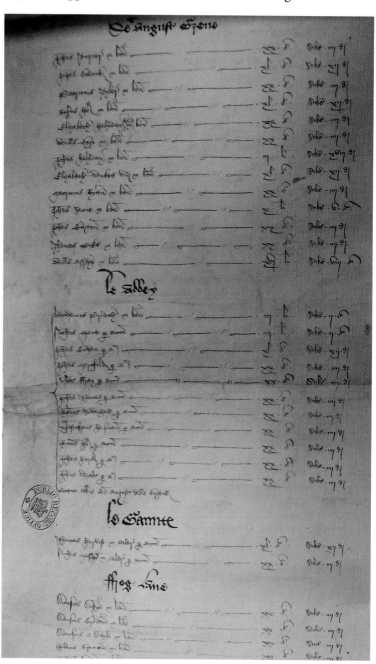

ALIENS

The Tudor subsidies, levied from 1514, generally discriminated against aliens by charging them double the rate of taxation, and consequently in the returns of taxpayers those born outside the allegiance of the English Crown can be identified.

The 1520s returns reveal that, while most of the assessed were of relatively humble means, two were relatively wealthy: Angeretus Nogay had goods assessed at £12, while Francesco Borsa was assessed at £30 in goods, and had two servants, the Englishman Thomas Wotton and James Hobbard, a Frenchman, who was in receipt of £1 6s. *per annum* in wages. Peter Gareyte, a Dutchman assessed at £2 in goods, also had a servant, John Gillam, to whom he paid £1 10s. *per annum.* Others, such as the Frenchman John Mottons, were servants to English masters: in Mottons's case, this was James Brown, who had three other, indigenous, servants. Not all aliens were caught by the subsidy collectors: two Portuguese merchants, Aries Fernandes and Anthony Fonso, were described as being from Bristol in the middle years of the 16th century, when they were trading in woad and sugar, and, as we shall see, there was a community of Portuguese Jews who are also absent from the subsidy returns.[64]

Sometimes it is possible to put a little more flesh on the bones. Francesco Borsa was evidently well established in his parish of All Saints. In 1525 he witnessed a property deed involving one of his neighbours; he was a trustee of the parish's Halleway chantry in 1530, and in 1537-8 he was churchwarden. Peter Charitas received letters of denization in January 1524, as Peres Carytas of Bristol, from Condom in Gascony; he may be identical with the 'Petrus Charite', haberdasher, who, with his wife Agnes, was taking on apprentices in the later 1530s. Peter Demetrius, assessed in 1571, may be identical with the man of the same name who received letters of denization the same year, described as from the dominions of the king of Spain.[65]

Dirick Dirrickson senior and junior were admitted to the freedom as dyers in 1579 on payment of £20: that they entered together, by redemption, suggests that they may have been relatively new arrivals. One of them may have been the Dirick Dirrickson from the dominion of Philip, king of Spain, who was granted letters of denization in 1573. Dirick Dirrickson senior and junior were assessed as aliens in Trinity Ward in 1581, but only one Dirick Dirrickson was assessed in Trinity Ward in 1590, so Dirrickson senior had presumably died. At around the same time Dirick Dirrickson of Bristol was trading with Spain in Dutch ships. This might have been the same man as Derrick Derrickson the dyer

Bristol Aliens in the 16th Century

Surviving returns for Bristol identify resident alien taxpayers for the 1520s, 1540s, and the period from 1571 to 1590. These returns give the street or ward in which the taxpayer lived, and this information has been plotted on the figures below.

Immediately apparent from these maps is how few aliens were assessed. There seems not to have been any substantial increase in their numbers since the 15th century. Nor was there an alien 'ghetto': the small size of Bristol's alien community hardly allowed for the formation of

a 'foreign quarter' in any case. The origins of these aliens offer few surprises. Most are French (including Bretons) or Dutch (including Flemings and Germans). There are a few interesting exceptions. Simon a Portingall and Anthony Dies were Portuguese, Francis Ryvera either from the Iberian peninsula or Italy, while Francesco Borsa was an Italian. Angeretus Nogay, 'denizen', had presumably acquired a letter of denization from the Crown, giving him approximately the same standing as a native-born English subject, but he

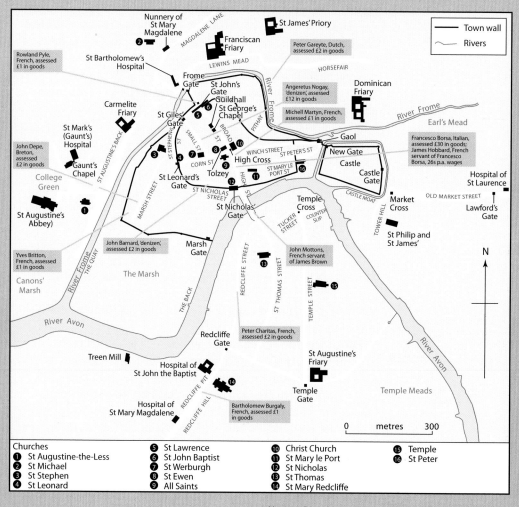

Aliens in Bristol, as recorded in Tudor subsidy returns: the 1520s.

was still noted by the subsidy collectors. A letter of denization from the Crown and a parliamentary act of Naturalisation were the two ways one could become an English subject.

Nogay and Borsa were among the very small number of wealthy Bristol aliens. The spelling of personal names might vary in this period, even for the English-born, and Bristol scribes sometimes mangled foreign names, so it is seldom possible to make a positive identification between those individuals recorded on the subsidy returns and those

appearing in other records, but in a few cases we are able to make reasonably confident identifications, and arrive at basic biographies for some of the city's aliens. Borsa, for example, became a leading member of his parish of All Saints', while the life story of Philip Scapulis, assessed in 1571 and 1581, can be reconstructed to some degree, and yields some fascinating details.

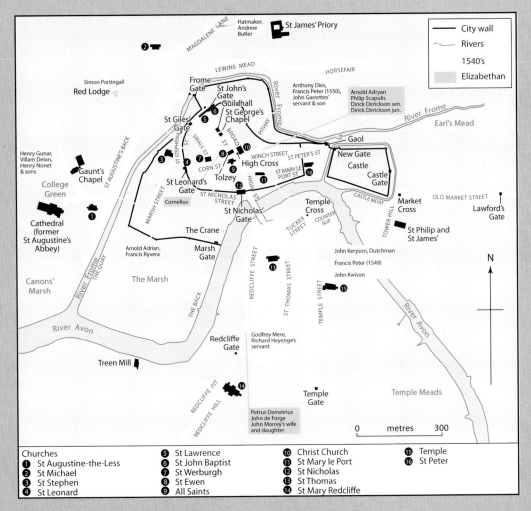

Aliens in Bristol, as recorded in Tudor subsidy returns: the 1540s, and 1571 to 1590.

who made his will in 1596. He wished to be buried at St Peter's in Bristol, where his father and mother were buried. He left bequests to his sister Anne Nicholas in Delft and her two children, as well as bequests to the fabric of St Peter's, and to the companies of dyers and tailors. He appointed his wife, Annes, as his sole executor, and as his overseers, 'my very loving friends' John Webbe and Richard Smith, both future mayors.[66]

Philip Scapulis was assessed in Trinity Ward in 1571 and 1581. Describing himself as a stationer, 'borne in Germany in the ancient city of Trier', he was living in Wine Street when he made his will in 1589. He asked to be buried in Holy Trinity church, 'before the pew wherein I was wont to kneel'; he left several bequests to named poor and incapacitated Bristolians, and 10s. to a woman, '... who did dwell with me in London and did there nurse me a child in my house dwelling now in Bristol ...'. He also gave 6d. to each of 'fifty poor men or women that be known to be true Protestants ...'. He rewarded his gardener and two maids; his (second?) wife Elizabeth was his executor. One overseer, Hugh Harvey, was a schoolmaster and scrivener, the other was a hooper; to both, he left his bows, arrows and quivers to be shared between them. He also remembered his godson, Philip the son of Anthony Symons, tailor. To Richard Fourde, stationer, sometime his apprentice, he left his equipment for making paste board, while one of his two long riding swords was left to a neighbour. The will was proved in 1590. Trier Protestants had been subjected to intense persecution, and this was doubtless what prompted Scapulis to move to England. He was established in Bristol by 1558, from which year until 1565 he and his (first?) wife Mary took on five apprentice bookbinders and stationers. In the 1570s he had acted as overseer to the wills of two other Wine Street residents, Arnold Adrianson, burgess and basket maker, and his wife Katherine. The former is presumably identical with Arnold Adryan, assessed in St Nicholas Street in 1550, and in Trinity Ward (which included Wine Street) in 1571. Their house was to go to their eldest son, Adrian, and in the event of his death to their second son, Cornelius.[67]

The Dirricksons, Scapulis and the Adriansons evidently ended their lives as comfortable, well-connected members of Bristol's elite. There were doubtless many more who came to Bristol from the continent, or whose parents had done so, and who found fortune in the city. While the entries in the Burgess Books do not state the origins of new burgesses, names such as Cornelius Freyling, Robert Autill, Aulerus de la Beeke, Peter Demastres, and Cornelius Keve certainly suggest Continental origins.[68]

Both Scapulis and Dirrickson made wills that were strongly Protestant in tone. While Continental Protestants may have come to Bristol to escape religious persecution, economic imperatives doubtless also played their part – Scapulis, after all, may initially have come to London as a Protestant refugee from the persecutions in Trier, and so presumably there were other reasons that brought him to Bristol. The Adriansons bought their house in Wine Street from William Pepwell, whom Arnold described as a gentleman of Thornbury in his will, and the activities of this individual provide one example of the means – and perhaps motives – by which some aliens came to England. In the 1530s Pepwell was a Bristol merchant operating in Spain, and in 1530 he was among the founders of the Andalusia Company, an association of English merchants in the Iberian trade. He was also an agent for Thomas Cromwell, sending him intelligence reports and on one occasion offering to kidnap two Irishmen whom he suspected of being in the pay of the Emperor. By 1542 he was back in Bristol, as sheriff, and he was mayor in 1557-8 and 1567-8. His relevance to us, however, lies in his link with France. In 1544, 17 French miners from the town of Croys acquired letters of denization: all of them were employed in English royal mines, by virtue of a commission issued to William Pepwell. The letters do not indicate where these mines were located, but in his will of 1571 Pepwell left one ton of lead to a servant, and so these French miners may have worked the Mendip lead mines. There would have been no shortage of local labour, and so it may be that these Frenchmen were specialists, their introduction part of an effort to revive a stagnant industry.[69]

Jews

Jews would not be officially tolerated in England until the 1650s, but in 1556 the Portuguese merchant Tomaz Fernandes revealed to the Lisbon Inquisition the existence of a small Jewish community in Bristol, centred on the household of his uncle, Henrique Nuñes, a physician, and the latter's wife, Beatriz Fernandes. According to Tomaz, the family were settled in Bristol between 1545 and 1555, when they moved to France, probably as the result of the more repressive regime under Queen Mary (1553-1558). Iberian Jews had been importing Bristol cloth in the 15th century. In 1492 and 1497, respectively, the Jews of Spain and Portugal were given a stark choice: either convert or leave. Many of those who converted were Marranos, or crypto-Jews, ostensibly Christian but maintaining their Jewish religion in secret. Life for the Portuguese Marranos became more difficult after 1540, when the Inquisition began its work. The establishment of the Bristol community was doubtless a response to this new situation. Including himself, Tomaz named 14 members of the community, among whom were merchants, sailors, and a surgeon, Pero Vaz. The Nuñes house accommodated a synagogue, and the Bristol Jews strictly observed the Sabbath and festivals; at the heart of religious life was Beatriz, who gave religious instruction, obtained kosher food and baked *matzoth*. The community was in contact with its London counterpart, and thereby with the intellectual life of the European Jewish Diaspora.[70]

In 1581 the Royal Mining Company invited to England a Bohemian (Czech) Jewish metallurgist and mining engineer, Joachim Gaunse. Gaunse helped to transform the English copper smelting industry, and accompanied Sir Walter Raleigh's 1584 expedition to Virginia. By 1589 he had settled in Bristol. Here he seems to have lived for a while unhampered, giving Hebrew lessons to those who wished to read the Old Testament in its original language, until a minister, the Reverend Richard Curteys, trapped him into denying the divinity of Jesus Christ. He was brought before the mayor, who then passed him on to the Privy Council. After this Gaunse disappears from the historical record.[71]

Africans

The other new element in Bristol's immigrant population was its black Africans. The first known reference to a black African in the city occurs in a witness statement made in 1580, but referring to events about twenty years earlier, which mentions a 'blacke moore' employed by the wealthy merchant Sir John Young to guard the garden of his Bristol house. Thereafter, there are intriguing references to 'blackamores' or 'negroes' in parish records: Joan Smyth, Peter, and Mary, a servant to William Edmonds, buried in Sts Philip and James's churchyard in 1603, 1610 and 1632 respectively; Katherine, who had worked at the *Horsehead Tavern* in Christmas Street, buried at Christchurch in 1612; Francis, a merchant's servant buried at the Broadmead Baptist chapel in 1640; and Solomon, a slave belonging to William Hayman, and William, 'son of a black', baptised in St Augustine's the Less in 1631 and 1684 respectively.

There are also occasional references in other contexts: in 1651 two unnamed Africans are recorded in Bristol, having been taken from a Portuguese ship by privateers and then purchased by the prominent Bristol merchant Robert Yeamans, while Titus Blackmore was among the possessions of Humphrey Hooke in 1677. Dinah Black, described as a 'servant', although actually probably a black slave, had been baptised and had spent five years in the Bristol household of Dorothy Smith before her mistress forced her onto a ship bound for the West Indies; she was rescued, and returned to Smith's house, but her mistress refused to take her back. Her case came before the Court of Aldermen in 1667, where it was decreed that Dinah Black should be free to earn her living in Bristol until the next quarter sessions, the record of which has not survived. Just outside Bristol, Cattelena, a 'single negro woman', died in Almondsbury in 1625, reportedly leaving an estate of £6. Neither Cattelena nor Katherine of the *Horsehead Tavern* seems to have been a slave, although those described as 'servants' may well have been.

As we have seen, Bristolians were involved in what appears to have been an Icelandic slave trade in the 15th century, but their participation in the African slave trade may date back to the time of Robert Thorne, who was active in the Spanish slaving port of Seville in the first half of the 16th century. In any case, Bristolians were regularly participating in slaving voyages between Africa and the Caribbean by the 1640s. Bristol's first black population probably owed its existence to both the English and the Iberian slave trades.[72]

CONCLUSION

Bristol's ethnic minority population in this period was drawn largely from those regions from which most of the town's medieval immigrants originated: Wales and Ireland, with a smattering of Continental Europeans. As with the earlier period, there is no indication of discrimination against the Welsh – although, as ever, this may have occurred but been unrecorded – but there is evidence for hostility towards the Irish. From the Reformation this is suffused with anti-Catholicism, and from this point it would seem that religion was regarded as at least as important as nationality in determining an immigrant's acceptability. The new religious dimension is apparent in the welcome extended to Protestant refugees, whether from Ireland or the Netherlands. Protestant Bristol's acceptance of its Portuguese Jews was surely far less warm, but the fact that the community could exist for a decade, until central government policy forced it out, and that a prominent Jew could establish himself in the Elizabethan city, suggests a certain degree of tolerance. The complexity of attitudes towards ethnicity is also apparent from the black experience in this period, with, apparently, both free and enslaved Africans present in the city. The new elements of religious refugees and Africans would both become markedly more significant after 1685.

Chapter 4

Religion and Refugees, 1685–1835

For our purposes, England's 'long 18th century' opens in 1685 when France began to persecute its Protestant subjects, thus precipitating a flow of religious refugees throughout the world. The century also saw the incorporation of Scotland into the new entity of 'Great Britain' in 1707, and the absorption of Ireland into the 'United Kingdom' in 1801. It ended with the partial modernisation of local government in 1835.[73]

During that time, family lineage, locality and religion more often than ethnicity were the means by which people expressed their identities. Generally speaking, society was still very parochial, and most people did not venture much beyond the parish of their birth. Localism, although under pressure from the centralising tendencies of an emerging capitalist economy, was still intense, in Bristol as elsewhere, and here at the beginning of the period 'strangers' and 'foreigners' were terms still routinely used to refer to those from outside Bristol's city gates. The Corporation and the guilds continued to act as strict gatekeepers. In the 1720s, Daniel Defoe condemned Bristol Corporation's practice of preventing outsiders from trading in the city as particularly tyrannical, characteristically narrow-minded and ultimately self-defeating. At this time Bristol's civic culture was essentially Anglican, elitist and inward-looking, but as the century progressed it came under increasing pressure from population increase, economic growth and the rise of the city's professional middle classes. However, while trading restrictions on 'foreigners' were gradually eased, civic discrimination against outsiders would persist.[74]

MIGRATION, IMMIGRATION AND DIFFERENCE

Wealth and religion were crucial factors influencing the degree to which outsiders found acceptance among Bristol's burgesses; ethnicity was another, but not necessarily the most important. English newcomers who happened to be poor, or Catholics, could experience far greater hostility than wealthy, Protestant foreigners. Incomers from surrounding English counties might be 'repatriated' if thought likely to be a burden on the rates, in much the same way as Irish refugees were from the 16th to the 19th centuries. The Kingswood miners, 'the most neglected, degraded and reckless community in the kingdom', who worked the surface coal pits on

Figure 24 This fine statue of William III in Bristol's Queen Square was erected to symbolise the triumph of the Protestant Established Church, although the artist, Michael Rysbrack (1736), was himself a Catholic.

the outskirts of the city, were often represented as essentially different from ordinary citizens, and as less than human. Blackened by coal dust and feared for their propensity to violence, they were routinely demonised, portrayed as 'savage Natives', who 'earth'd like Worms in subterranean Holes' and characterised by the Bristol elite in much the same way as enslaved Africans. Even Bristol-born paupers were treated in ways somewhat reminiscent of the demeaning regulations imposed on Jews in medieval Europe and elsewhere, being periodically made to wear parish badges which publicly proclaimed their destitute status.[75]

Religious Difference

The assertively Protestant nature of Georgian Bristol's official culture is expressed through the magnificent statue of William III in the centre of Queen Square (fig. 24). Although the work of the Catholic Flemish artist, Michael Rysbrack, it was commissioned in 1732 by Bristol Whig merchants to celebrate a triumphant Protestantism: this 'King Billy' had vanquished the Catholic James II at the battle of the Boyne in 1690, an event to this day commemorated by Ulster Protestants in Orange Parades.[76]

Freedom of conscience and tolerance of public worship by Dissenting Christians and even non-Christians such as Jews became enshrined in the new constitution from 1689. However, British tolerance did not initially extend to Roman Catholics. From 1688 and for much of the following century, Catholics in England and Wales were unable to own land, hold a mass, or teach their religion, let alone participate in political life. By the 18th century, the fevered celebrations of Guy Fawkes night in Bristol as elsewhere remind us of the widespread fear that Catholics and other supporters of the Catholic King James and his Stuart line might again attempt to subvert the kingdom by violent means. These fears, although exaggerated, were not groundless, as the Jacobites actually attempted this in 1715 and 1745. By then, the Jacobites, whose ally was Louis XIV, were seen as the crypto-Catholic supporters of unlimited royal and papal power.

Under this mask of 'anti-popery' lurked uglier, more tribal motives – a contempt for the Irish poor, a hatred of the French, a suspicion of the Welsh, and a puritanical dislike and suspicion of anyone different. At the end of 1688, a Bristol mob burnt and looted the house of a 'Romanist' harness maker in Castle Street and 'wrought great havoc' on two other dwellings in King Street inhabited by Catholics. Such sectarian violence would periodically resurface in the city right up to 1829, when the Catholic Emancipation Act gave Catholics equal rights.[77]

Unsurprisingly then, the minority groups who were most accepted in Bristol in this period were those who shared the Protestant values of their hosts, especially those who had the skills most needed by an expanding capitalist economy. Although sheer labour power was also required, the demand for it was unstable and, when times were hard, the host community would batten down the hatches and look first to its own. In 1826, Bristol's mayor complained during a year of acute unemployment about 'the number of foreign seamen, blackmen and men of colour' who were competing with 'native' Bristolians for jobs. Those groups who were more educated, used to a regular work discipline and in posses-sion of either technical skills or trading contacts, would prove to be the most likely to prosper. In a mercantile city such as Bristol, economic self-sufficiency was the key to social acceptance.[78]

Patriotism in Times of War

External political factors could threaten such acceptance. Throughout this period, England was frequently at war and during invasion scares and threatened conspiracies, foreigners in Bristol were vulnerable to scapegoating. In the aftermath of the Jacobite Rebellion of 1745, amid reports of French privateers harassing Bristol-bound ships, Mr Dominique, the impresario of a troupe of travelling players, felt compelled to appeal in the local press for people to attend his show in Stokes Croft and explicitly to deny any personal French connection:[79]

> being sensible that he has suffered greatly in the opinion of the Town this Winter, by being supposed to be the Master of a French Company at a Time when an unnatural Rebellion is supported by France against his Majesty's Crown and Dignity [he assures]… the Publick that not one person of his whole company is of that Nation; that he himself is born in Switzerland, Madam Garman of Amsterdam, Mr. Jonno of Milan and that all the rest are natives of Great Britain.[80]

By the time of the French Revolution in 1789, there was some support for French émigrés fleeing the Terror, but as the Revolutionary and Napoleonic wars followed an intense loyalism was demanded of Bristolians and all aliens residing in the city had to obtain a special licence. French fencing masters, miniature painters, clergymen and others found they were the objects of general suspicion, scrutiny, and even, on occasion, wrongful arrest.[81]

THE HUGUENOTS

Against this background we can return to the beginning of our period to discuss one particular group of foreign immigrants, the Huguenots. Some had settled in cosmopolitan London from at least 1680, but the great wave of Huguenot refugees dates from the revocation of the Edict of Nantes in 1685. It has been estimated that as many as 50,000 Huguenots came to England out of the two million thought to have fled France.[82]

Most Huguenots fled to London or Plymouth. Only around 400 to 500 are known to have come to Bristol. This would represent about 2.5 per cent of Bristol's 20,000 population. The influx occasioned both alarm and compassion. In 1681, the mayor, Thomas Earle, bridling at having to raise funds for their relief at the behest of the central government, complained in a letter that the refugees' 'great number and poverty renders us utterly at a loss how to dispose of them, having more of our own people than we can keep at work …'. By contrast, some Anglicans and Dissenters within the city, as in Britain generally, welcomed them as victims of Catholic oppression, raising funds for those whose harrowing and often heroic stories of resistance and escape inspired their sympathy.[83]

The Bonnets' was one among many such stories. Although prohibited from leaving France, Daniel Bonnet and his wife, so the family tradition goes, posed as vegetable sellers in order to complete a 50-mile trek to the west coast from where they hoped to sail to England. The coast was under heavy surveillance and the Bonnets hid their two small children in panniers slung on their donkey and admonished them to be quiet at all costs. As they approached the coast, a soldier demanded to know what they were carrying and casually thrust his bayonet into one of the panniers. The distraught parents had to wait until they were out of sight before they could attend to their child. Happily they discovered their child, though stabbed through the calf, had managed to keep silent and the family were able to make their escape to Bristol.[84]

Those refugees first arriving in Bristol came, like the Bonnets, from the coastal region just to the south of Brittany: Poitou, Aunis and Saintonge. In Poitou alone, there had been 38,000 forced conversions to Catholicism in the period up to 1682. The following year, Bristol Quakers recorded visiting and distributing relief to some 50 refugees, who camped out in St James' Churchyard, whilst others formed a small colony just outside Lawford's Gate, unable to find work or too sick to seek it. The Quakers' vivid report, one torn page of which survives in the Bristol Record Office, records their encounter at Lawford's Gate with people like 'James Blondeau a sickly man [and] his wife being sick now in her bed with a little

Figure 25 Map of Early Modern France.

daughter'. They met Peter Lucas, an unemployed weaver, his wife and two toddlers, describing them as being 'in great want [Peter Lucas] being not able to get enough for to maintain his family'. Peter Lievre, another weaver and his brother, a blacksmith, were also unable to find employment as were two youths known only as 'Luminal' and 'Consel'.[85]

Refugee numbers increased sharply after 1685. A significant minority were well-educated people, such as the silversmith Solomon L'Egaré who had been away at college when he first heard that his family had been forced to flee from Lyon. L'Egaré disguised himself as a peasant and fled to Geneva before being re-united with them in Bristol. However, a third of the 152 heads of families recorded in Bristol were textile workers and another third seamen: although the port was expanding, work was not always available for Bristolians let alone foreigners. Even some skilled craftsmen had difficulty finding employment. Although the mayor complained about the expense caused by these refugees, in 1687 the bishop of Bristol, Sir John Trelawney, generously helped them to secure the loan of the Lord Mayor's Chapel (St Mark's) for their French language services.[86]

Figure 26 St Mark's chapel, built in 1230, is owned by the city of Bristol and known as the Lord Mayor's chapel. The corporation lent it for the use of Huguenot refugees in the early 18th century as an expression of Protestant solidarity and goodwill.

Not every prominent Bristolian was so liberal. In 1693, Sir John Knight, Tory MP for Bristol and its former mayor, spoke in the Commons against a bill to naturalise foreign Protestant refugees. Much reprinted (and some say written) by his political allies, it anticipates Enoch Powell's 'Rivers of Blood' speech of three centuries later. Knight warned of the dangers immigration posed to national identity and expressed himself unwilling to 'sacrifice our *English* Liberties to a number of Mercenary Foreigners'. He heaped contempt upon the Dutch, but saved his special invective for the French, whom he likened to 'a plague of frogs', and in a much-quoted passage he ended by declaring, '… let us first Kick the Bill out of the HOUSE, and then Foreigners out of the Kingdom'. Knight's views represent well entrenched, but not unchallenged, opinion in Bristol and beyond. His speech played on the anxieties of the host population and the worries that foreign workers would displace English ones, especially acute when bad harvests or cyclical downturns in trade made life hard for the common people.[87]

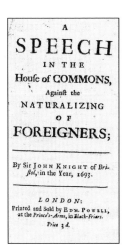

A

SPEECH

IN THE

Houſe of COMMONS,

Againſt the

NATURALIZING

O F

FOREIGNERS;

By Sir J O H N K N I G H T of Bri-
ſtol, in the Year, 1693.

L O N D O N:
Printed and Sold by E D M. P O W E L L,
at the Prince's-Arms, in Black-Friars.
Price 3 d.

Figure 27 Title page
from Sir John Knight's
speech against foreigners.
Knight, mayor of Bristol
in 1690 was also MP for
the city 1690-1695 and is
best known for his 1693
speech to the Commons
which opposed awarding
naturalised status to
foreign-born Protestants,
and attacked foreigners in
no uncertain terms.

Huguenots and Transnationalism

The small but well organised Huguenot elite were particularly well-placed to take advantage of the burgeoning transatlantic trade. The time was propitious. The sugar revolution in the Caribbean in the 1680s began to boost the profit potential of slave plantations and with it the whole of the Atlantic economy. Most of these wealthier Huguenots came from La Rochelle and had already been engaged in Atlantic trade. Many of their co-religionists had sought refuge in Holland or in the British colonies in North America and the Caribbean. In an era during which personal ties were so crucial to successful trade, Bristol Huguenots were able to make the most of their far-flung network of family and friends. They saw themselves as part of a 'Protestant International' whose world also embraced 'the Dutch republic, British Isles … and the American colonies'. Thus, the Huguenots helped to plug Bristol into an international trading community which further stimulated the city's growth. A number of Huguenot weavers and other workers left Bristol to seek work in London, Dublin or America. Solomon L'Egaré's family, for example, moved to Massachusetts, whilst Solomon himself become a distinguished silversmith in Charleston, South Carolina; his work is still much sought after.[88]

When Stephen Peloquin arrived in Bristol in the mid-1680s as a religious refugee, he was a young man probably in his twenties, and, unlike most Huguenots, his was a wealthy family. He accompanied his father, Etienne, a merchant from La Rochelle, and his extended family which included his mother, sister, brother, nephew and brother-in-law. Along with the money that they were able to smuggle out, the Peloquins brought trading contacts, know-how and a stern Calvinist work ethic. They were also linked by marriage to the wealthy D'Harriets clan of New York. They traded in tobacco with other Peloquins in Maryland, and Stephen was part of a trading consortium with his brother-in-law Augustus Jay of New York and some of Jay's New York Dutch associates (Jay himself was the son of Pierre Jay, who had fled to Bristol in the 1680s). Their firm traded in commodities in America, Bristol and Barbados and also invested in some privateering ventures in Dutch Surinam. In 1693, within a decade or so of his arrival, Stephen was taken up by Bristol's lord mayor and became a freeman of the city. This was an important step in his acceptance into the merchant elite, but acceptance was only ever partial: it may have been his Quaker-like refusal to take an oath that prevented him from becoming a member of the Society of Merchant Venturers four years later. His will of 1730 showed that he was wealthy enough to leave a house in Queen Square to his wife, £1,200 to each of his two sons, David and John, and £1,000 to his daughters Marianne and Judith.[89]

Figure 28 Portrait of Henry Cruger, MP for Bristol in 1774 and the grandson of John Cruger, by Gilbert Stuart (c.1781). Stuart (1755–1828) was an American painter who also worked in England. One of his portraits of George Washington, used on the dollar bill, is said to bear some resemblance to the likeness he made of Cruger.

Another Huguenot merchant was John Cruger, whose family, like many others, fled to the Netherlands and from there to New York. Cruger, already a slave trader, was involved in the Bristol and West India trade and set up offices in Bristol. Other first generation Bristol Huguenot merchants, like Louis Casamajor, John Roy (later King), and Daniel Goisin, were also involved in the New York, African and/or the West Indian trades. Daniel Goisin and his son and namesake were sugar merchants, as were Louis Casamajor and Jacob Peloquin, Stephen Peloquin senior's nephew. All of these families amassed property in Bristol; John King, for example, was involved in the early development of the docks at Sea Mills, Daniel Goisin had land in Westbury-on-Trym and both Peloquin and Goisin had property in Queen Square.[90]

The records of one of England's first private banks, Hoare's of London, strongly indicate that Bristol Huguenots were involved in the early development of English banking. Daniel and Lewis Casamajor are mentioned as transacting business with Hoare's, and by 1721 'Goisin and Son' had a Hoare's account which shows the firm to be drawing monies from a variety of Bristol merchants including the Harfords, the Farrs and Richard Champion, apparently to invest in London firms or lend to others at interest. By 1724 the turnover of the account was £13,000.[91]

The engagement of Huguenots in Bristol's industrial development is harder to document. Pierre Lucas, probably the same man found languishing outside Lawford's Gate in 1693, seems to

Figure 29 This brass crown, dating from the early 1700s, was probably used as a ceremonial piece for trades processions in Bristol. It was made by Francis Billo, who is thought to have been a Bristol Huguenot.

have made a respectable livelihood as a serge maker and vinegar manufacturer in St Philip's and Jacob's parish, in whose church he was buried. Another probable Huguenot, Francis Billo, a brazier later renowned for his metal chandeliers, was admitted in 1720 as a burgess to the city, after convincing the Corporation to accept 'a brass cistern and fountain of his own workmanship' in lieu of the £15 fee usually required for this privilege.[92]

The Huguenots quickly assimilated into Bristol's population, but their wills indicate that some of the first generation suffered a sense of social isolation and dislocation, with a telling number of these documents being 'translated from the French'. Even Stephen Peloquin retained his distinctively Huguenot identity throughout his life. Both his wives, Suzanne Challes (d. 1701) and Francoise Jay (d. 1742), were fellow refugees from La Rochelle, and to the end of his days he was determined to reclaim the rents due to him from his French properties. A leading member of Bristol's French-language Protestant church, he described himself in his will as 'a native of La Rochell [*sic*] in the Kingdom of France, now living in the City of Bristoll in England, where it has pleased Divine Providence to give me grace to refuge [*sic*] myself'. It was no accident that Peloquin and others had pushed in the Bristol Council for a more liberal attitude towards the naturalisation of foreign Protestants.[93]

Vanishing Huguenots

Thanks in part to the emigration of those whom the local economy could not absorb and in part to their own industry, Bristol Huguenots appear increasingly assimilated into the majority population. The Society of Merchant Venturers not only admitted Huguenots by the 1720s but promoted James La Roche and Casamajor to high office. The city helped the community establish its own chapel in Orchard Street in 1726. There were a number of Bristol lord mayors and MPs of Huguenot origin, including La Roche (1750) and David Peloquin (1751). Henry Cruger, whose father (also Henry) is buried in Bristol Cathedral, was the grandson of the John Cruger already mentioned. Born in New York, Henry Jr was sent by his father to Bristol where he became a partner in the family trading firm of Cruger and Mallard. In 1774, he became Whig MP for Bristol with Edmund Burke and, although later a New York State Senator, Cruger retained his membership of Bristol Corporation until his death. Although Stephen Peloquin II had been a staunch Calvinist, his children, like Pierre LaRoche and Daniel Goisin, began to step up the social ladder into the Anglican elite. David Peloquin was both alderman and lord mayor in the 18th century and reportedly left some £80,000 on his death to his

Figure 30 The Huguenot chapel on Orchard Street (now demolished) first built in the early 18th century.

Figure 31 Portrait of David Peloquin, Huguenot refugee and merchant, and mayor of Bristol in 1751. By an unknown artist, it now hangs with that of his wife in the office of Bristol Charities.

Figure 32 Portrait of Mary Ann Peloquin (d. 1778). Artist unknown.

'sister of the half blood' Mary Anne (whose mother was Stephen's second wife). It was Mary Ann who eventually inherited the bulk of the family fortune, as her sibling predeceased her. She famously left £19,000 to the poor of the city in a charity which still functions today in her name.[94]

By the mid-1700s the French church at St Mark's was beginning to lose its adherents and the wealthier Huguenots attended St Stephen's and St Nicholas's churches in Bristol's old merchant quarter, where some of their memorials can still be seen. Those lower down the social scale, the lesser merchants and manufacturers and cloth workers, went to church in the less elegant parish of Sts Philip and Jacob. The victualler Daniel Raoul, probably the son of another Huguenot refugee, lived in this parish. While no merchant prince, Raoul was wealthy enough to leave his son £200 and his stock and house. He entrusted his orphaned granddaughter Elizabeth Rogers into the guardianship of Thomas Evans of the City of Bristol and Peter Powell Jr. rather than to others of Huguenot origin, illustrating that assimilation was happening in the middling ranks. We do not know how many of these later Huguenots retained a sense of their non-English ancestry but their mixing reminds us of the plasticity of 'ethnic' identity.[95]

The Huguenots embodied the Protestant values of hard work and strong family life. Their puritanical lifestyle complemented their trading traditions and they benefited from having a well-educated and wealthy elite within their ranks. Overall, their values meshed well with those of middling English or Welsh Protestants, and Bristol could count itself culturally as well as economically enriched by their presence.

Chapter 5

The Welsh in the 18th Century

The Welsh constituted the largest immigrant group in Bristol until the 1960s and are certainly the oldest. This chapter will consider what economic and cultural forces drew the Welsh to Bristol in the long 18th century and assess their impact on the city. It will also explore how they were perceived by their fellow residents, and the extent to which Bristol Welsh of second and subsequent generations retained their ethnic identity.

WHO WERE THE BRISTOL WELSH?

The Welsh, as we have seen, have been moving to Bristol since the city's earliest days. Before 1750, Bristol was the major urban centre for a largely undeveloped South Wales and it is mainly from the south and west of Wales that most of Bristol's Welsh inhabitants seem to have come. Of the city's 16,500 inhabitants listed in 1696, some 20 per cent had Welsh surnames, nearly three times the proportion in London at that time. This proportion probably declined as Swansea displaced Bristol as 'the Welsh metropolis', and Bristol experienced a huge influx of people from its English hinterlands, but, as late as 1825, a contemporary observer estimated that at least 10 per cent of Bristolians had Welsh surnames. Of course, Welsh surnames did not always indicate an active Welsh identity,

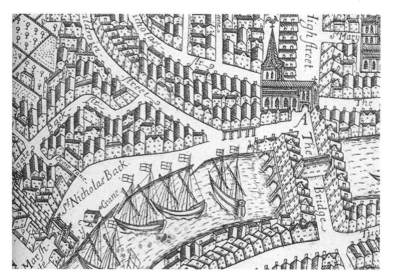

Figure 33 Detail of James Millerd's map of Bristol (1673) showing the Back, later known as Welsh Back, the quayside on the north side of the Avon.

but these figures still attest to the strong and longstanding links between Wales and Bristol.[96]

Welsh workers came to Bristol as both seasonal workers and permanent migrants. A trawl of Welsh names in the Bristol Record Office suggests that people of Welsh origin were represented at most levels of society. Many intermarried with English Bristolians and assimilated into the host community completely, but some, as we shall see, retained links with family and friends in their country of origin and a consciousness of their Welsh identity.[97]

The Welsh were mainly economic migrants. Whilst some came to be prosperous merchants, many others were servants, traders and craftsmen with a growing minority of professional men appearing by the end of the century. Wales was exploited for labour and raw materials by its neighbour, attracting increasing amounts of industrial investment from Bristol as the century progressed. Until the mid-18th century Bristolians had, as Daniel Defoe observed, 'the whole trade of South Wales, as it were, to themselves and the greatest part of [that of] North Wales'. Until the late 1700s, Bristol's economic life centred around market days and two annual fairs in early September (St James's Fair) and early March (Temple Fair) which were among the largest in the country. These were

Figure 34 Detail of an anonymous 18th-century painting of the Broad Quay at Bristol, showing a man in a red Monmouth cap, an item first produced in Wales and widely copied in Bristol. Careful examination of the painting as a whole shows at least two dockside workers wearing such caps. Painting shown also, figure 60.

popular with Welsh traders. Wales supplied much of Bristol's food supply, particularly livestock, fish and dairy products. With the goods came the people who brought them. Welsh drovers from Glamorgan, Pembrokeshire and Carmarthenshire took their black cattle on small boats across the Severn before driving them into Bristol's cattle market in St Thomas Street.[98]

The Bristol quayside on the north bank of the Avon, known today as Welsh Back (figure 33), was the particular locus of Welsh trade and migration in the city. An early description of 'The Back', as it was then known, comes from William Goldwin's *Poetical Description of Bristol* of 1712, where his characterisation of the largely Welsh-speaking traders and drovers there, bringing their stock off the boats, leaves readers in no doubt of their distinctive language and dress:[99]

> For here the Wallian Fleets, like *Noah's* Ark,
> With Couplets stuff'd, a Medley-stock debark;
> O'er which the chatt'ring Tribe in dapper Dress
> Quick broken Tones in gutt'ral Words express.[100]

The Welsh market which, by 1776, had its own dedicated market building designed by Thomas Paty, lasted into the next century. The antiquary George Weare Braikenridge recalls that, in the 1820s, it was still 'much frequented by the Welsh who come up by the traders and many of whom keep the market erected for the Welsh and called the goose market'. Rental records of the Welsh market from 1776 show that the vast majority of traders in the Welsh

Figures 35 and 36 Sample page from the 'Welch Market Book' held in the Bristol Record Office. This book contains the names of the various Welsh traders (mostly women) who traded on the Welsh Back in Bristol in the 18th and early 19th centuries.

Figure 37 Houses on Bristol Back near the end of King Street drawn by Hugh O'Neill, 1823. The old pub, the *Llandoger Trow*, is on the left.

market were women with recognisably Welsh names. Aside from foodstuffs, wool and leather were also imported from Wales, and the latter was traded in the Leather Market, just behind Welsh Back. Bristol was the place to which wealthy Welsh people resorted for 'every article of consumption both in and out of the house', first at its markets and increasingly at its shops.[101]

A growing army of innkeepers and lodging house keepers, money lenders and prostitutes, some of whom were themselves from Wales or of Welsh origin, serviced or fleeced the drovers, traders and mariners who came to the Back. Among the taverns on the Back were the *Llandoger Trow,* probably named after Llandogo in the Wye Valley between Chepstow and Monmouth, and the flat-bottomed barges used on that river, the *Newport Boat*, the *Chepstow Boat*, and the *Brockwar Boat*, all names redolent of the Welsh trade, although the reputed favourite of Welsh traders was the *White Hart*, which served *metheglin*, a type of Welsh mead.[102]

Those who came to trade on market days were not, by definition, immigrants, and so we have to look elsewhere for evidence of

Figure 38 An anonymous 19th-century depiction of the Welsh Market in Bristol Back.

Welsh settlers. There are no trade directories before 1776, but by then only two of the eight people listed on Welsh Back have Welsh names. A perusal of newspaper announcements and wills shows a sprinkling of Welsh tradesmen on the Back or nearby. Thus, by the middle of the century John Griffiths had a china and glass ware-house, whilst Thomas Llewellin made a good living as a fishmonger and owned property. His son, a butter dealer on the Back, inherited his father's business and by 1765 announced his opening of a larger shop 'during the Fish and Butter Season' nearby, where among

Figure 39 The Old Custom House on Bristol Back, from a watercolour by Thomas L. Rowbotham (1825). Dating from 1666, it is the tallest and most ornate building in the drawing. It was abandoned in 1710 when a grander Custom House was erected in nearby Queen Square.

other wares, 'fine pickled Tenby oysters and sturgeon' would be sold. Other apparently Welsh tradesmen fanned out from the Back to the centre of the city. In 1754 Evans and Co. opened a linen-drapery and haberdashery shop in Castle Street whilst Edward Morgan had a woollen drapery business in the High Street.[103]

Apprenticeship records afford us a glimpse of the backgrounds of those fortunate enough to gain entry into Bristol's trading community. Although, as in earlier times, the overwhelming majority of apprentices came from the surrounding English counties of Gloucestershire, Somerset, Wiltshire and Herefordshire, they also reveal a stream of Welsh boys coming to serve mainly English masters and their wives. Before 1750 the proportion fluctuated at around 10 per cent of all the apprentices in the years sampled but rose to 20 per cent in 1759 before declining again in the 1770s. These apprenticeships were for skilled work such as hoopers, tobacconists, apothecaries, soapboilers, shipwrights, brassfounders, and anchorsmiths. Of those coming from West Wales in the 18th century (some 400), two thirds came from Pembrokeshire, with just under a third from Carmarthenshire and only a dozen from Cardiganshire, a pattern broadly similar to that found in earlier centuries.[104]

Although many of these apprentices served English masters, 25 had the same surname as their master which, given the distribution pattern of names in West Wales, might well indicate a family relationship. In 43 cases both the apprentice and master had names that were common in West Wales, suggesting that apprentice and

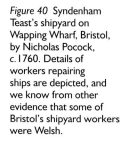

Figure 40 Syndenham Teast's shipyard on Wapping Wharf, Bristol, by Nicholas Pocock, *c.*1760. Details of workers repairing ships are depicted, and we know from other evidence that some of Bristol's shipyard workers were Welsh.

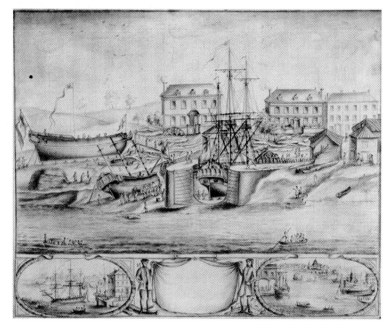

master were connected by family or friends. By this calculation, nearly a quarter of apprentices from West Wales might have been related to their masters. As we shall see, a number of poor Welsh apprentices were assisted by a Bristol-Welsh association. Similar research remains to be done on Bristol apprentices from Glamorganshire, but preliminary findings suggest that more apprentices came from West Wales than Glamorganshire and that the Glamorgan apprentices contained a number of former seamen and labourers and seem to have been from less genteel backgrounds than those from Pembrokeshire.[105]

In some cases, immigrant workers clustered around employers who were either of a similar origin or who had key workers who recommended their compatriots. The shipbuilder Richard Tombs (whose name suggests a Monmouthshire origin) seems to have been such an employer. In 1759, he and William Tombs Jr (possibly his father or brother) took on apprentices from Glamorgan. Over thirty years later, in 1792, Richard Tombs presented a bill to the Welsh-born Bristol slave trader James Rogers for work done on Rogers' slave ship *The Crescent*. Of the 65 men his bill lists as having worked on the job, 18 have Welsh names, and one of them, Thomas Gedrych from Cardiff, had been apprenticed by Tombs seven years before.[106]

HOW WELSH WERE THE BRISTOL WELSH?

The Welsh were not a uniform group, but varied along lines of class, geography, religion, and political orientation. Most Welsh migrants to Bristol appear to have come from the lowlands of Glamorgan, Monmouthshire and Pembrokeshire, which were in terms of religion, agriculture and trade more like a West Country shire than the more distinctively Welsh uplands where a more exclusively pastoral economy held sway.

The propertied Welsh elite in Bristol tended to be Anglican and English-speaking. From what we can tell from wills and other genealogical evidence, Bristol's early 18th-century Welsh elite and prosperous middling ranks were largely assimilated into the host population, although some retained links through property holdings and family with Wales. Inter-marriage with established English families in the city appears to have been common. That quintessentially Bristol merchant (and slave trader) Isaac Hobhouse (1685-1763) was the son of Anne Madox of Glamorgan (1722) and John Hobhouse of Minehead.[107]

However, it is impossible to discern much about the ethnic identity of the Bristol Welsh. The grocer William Morgan's 1702 will makes no mention of Welsh property, family, friends or business associates, nor do the wills of three wealthy central Bristol shop-owners by the name of Morgan. On the other hand, a contemporary and near neighbour of these men, the mercer Anthony Morgan, definitely did retain Welsh links, and possibly Jacobite sympathies, bequeathing in his will £20 '… to the parish church of Llannelli in the county of Brecon …'.[108]

Sir William Lewis, mayor of Bristol in 1702 and knighted by Queen Anne the following year, was the son of a Pembrokeshire man and had served as apprentice to the Bristol soapboiler Richard Benson. His son or grandson, also Sir William Lewis of Bristol, appears to have expanded the family property portfolio, owning land in Pembroke, Radnor and Monmouth as well as in Bristol. We know that this younger Sir John Lewis retained an attachment to Wales as he bequeathed money to build a schoolroom and pay a schoolmaster in Lampeter and to help two poor families there.[109]

These trends continued into the mid-century. A number of wills reveal links with Monmouthshire and suggest a concentration of Welsh in the victualling and innkeeping trades. Both Thomas and his nephew Seth Williams, for example, were Bristol innkeepers, and his son John was an upholsterer in the city. John owned lands in Monmouth and Bristol, including tenements near the Welsh Back and the Cattle market. The victuallers George Jones

Figure 41 South and West Wales, showing English and Welsh-speaking areas.

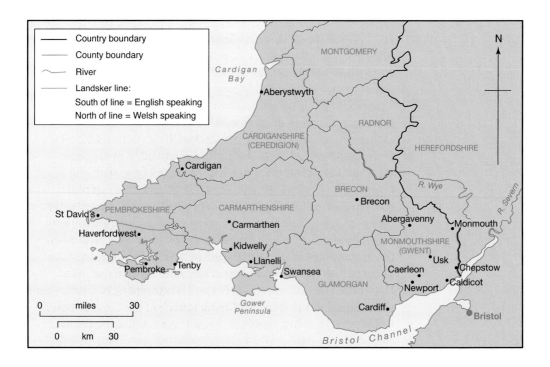

of St Stephen and Thomas Pritchard of St James also remembered their Monmouthshire family in their wills, as did the brewer Richard Llewellin, who named his properties in Magdalen Lane near St James's church 'Llewellin Court' and 'Pembroke Court', and left a bequest to his brother in Haverfordwest. The Bristol widow Mary Lewis named a sister in Swansea and a Bristol godson with a Welsh name (Thomas Llewellin) in her will of 1745, while Dorothy White, the widow of a Bristol weaver from Tenby, appointed a female relative in Tenby as her sole executor.[110]

One of the ways the Welsh elite in Bristol negotiated their dual Welsh and Bristol identity was to establish, in 1754, a Bristol Branch of The Society of Ancient Britons. The Society had originally been established in London both as a Loyalist group, at a time when the Welsh were still subject to charges of Jacobitism, and as a charitable group assisting poor Welsh apprentices. The Bristol branch was inaugurated in February 1754 with a meeting at the *Nag's Head* tavern in Wine Street to discuss the 'revival of that ancient feast' of St David's; it is uncertain whether or not we can assume from this that St David's Day (1 March) had once been celebrated in Bristol but had since been neglected. Aside from the reference to St David's Day, there do not appear to be any specifically Welsh cultural activities connected with the Bristol Society of Ancient Britons. Established around the same time as other Bristol civic societies, most of which, like the Society of Ancient Britons, assisted apprentice boys and lying-in women (who had just had a baby), it should also be seen as a counterpart of the Gloucestershire, Somersetshire and Wiltshire Societies which flourished to foster links between Bristolians of similar geographical origins; it can also be compared with civic charities like the Bristol Royal Infirmary, on whose ceremonies it closely modelled its own.[111]

In 1765 the *Bristol Journal* reported that the St David's Day meeting and procession began at the Exchange, proceeded to St Stephens church and then to the Merchant-Tailors' Hall where 'elegant entertainment took place'. While by 1772 the annual feast had been moved to the middle of March, apparently to avoid clashing with the opening of Temple Fair, the fact that the Society's presidents from the late 1760s increasingly bore Welsh names suggests no dilution of Welsh identity. As apprenticeship waned, the Society shifted its attention to 'poor distressed women in childbed' resident in Bristol and by 1780 had claimed to have helped 1,860 such women, which seems to indicate that the Society had grown considerably since its inception. However, there seems to be no mention of a Bristol branch of the London-based Cymmrodorion Society which was much more oriented towards the celebration of Welsh culture.[112]

The last quarter of the 18th century saw the rise of the professional middle classes in the city, and by then Welsh school masters, surgeons, and dissenting ministers regularly appear in the newspapers and directories. These were not typical of the mass of Welsh settlers, who came from below the middling ranks. These labourers and artisans would have been more 'foreign' in terms of language and manners, but they rarely left wills or any other written records, and so it is difficult to know very much about them as individuals. What evidence does survive suggests that they tended to be well absorbed if not completely assimilated into the host population within a few generations, so that at this level the sense of Welsh identity would only have been renewed by successive waves of migrants. Whilst the wealthiest merchants and wealthier tradesmen lived in College Green, the less prosperous Welsh seem to have lived in the outer parishes of Bristol where non-conformity was also strongest: St James, St Mary Redcliffe, St Philip and James and Temple.[113]

WELSH WORSHIP IN BRISTOL

The Welsh were overwhelmingly Protestant, and although Welsh names abound amongst those baptised in Bristol's Anglican churches between 1754 and 1812, the town's Welsh population was popularly supposed at the time to be more 'Chapel' than 'Church'. The chapel (be it Dissenting or Methodist) was one institution which helped Welsh migrants affirm their Welsh identity, but individual chapels varied in their Welshness and in any case offered their members an alternative identity as part of the non-conformist 'Protestant international'.[114]

The relationship between Bristol and Welsh Dissenters goes back to the 1600s. An entire congregation in Llanfaches in Monmouthshire had fled to Bristol in 1653 and Welsh Quakers had come to the city to support the city's Quakers when they were being persecuted by Bristol authorities later in the century. Pembrokeshire and Carmarthenshire Quakers paid the apprentice fees of some West Wales apprentices in Bristol in the early 1700s.[115]

All five non-conformist chapels surveyed in Bristol between 1715 and 1729 had worshippers with country votes in Wales. The Welsh and Bristol Quakers were in constant contact with each other throughout the 18th century for practical as well as religious reasons. For example, sometime before 1709, a relation of the Lloyds of Dolobran, Montgomeryshire, suggested that a local ironworker, John Thomas, contact a fellow Quaker in Bristol to find work. He did so and later went on to become the technical

Figure 42 One of Bristol's Welsh chapels (now demolished) at Castle Precinct, Bristol, *c.*1822.

innovator and personal assistant to Abraham Darby at the Baptist Mills Brass Works and Thomas's previous Bristol employer, Edward Lloyd, became a partner in the same firm.[116]

The Bristol Baptist College under the dynamic leadership of the Brecknockshire-born Divine Hugh Evans (and later his Bristol-born son Caleb) attracted Welsh students. Under Caleb, who succeeded his father as principal, the college continued to foster a radical spirit that was to challenge the pro-slavery culture of Bristol's Anglican and Presbyterian elite. Universalist and internationalist in their missionary work, the college attracted such men as Thomas Llewelyn (*c.*1720–1783) whose promotion of the Welsh Bible encouraged Welsh identity. The General Baptist minister in Bristol, John Evans (1767–1827), was one of a coterie of Welsh Baptists who combined progressive politics with a love of Welsh culture.

The Welsh Calvinistic Methodists was founded in 1798 in Merchant Street, and by 1822 a Welsh-language (Independent) chapel was opened to cater for the increasing number of the Welsh labouring poor who had previously used the premises of friendly local Quakers. Many Welsh in the city were attracted by evangelical Christianity. In 1738 an Anglican preacher named Morgan preached to Kingswood miners and by the mid-1740s John Cennick's small group of Awakened Christians, mainly from dissenting backgrounds, included several with Welsh names; Cennick himself was descended from Czech refugees.[117]

The Moravians and Methodists with their emphasis on hymn singing and emotional fellowship proved especially attractive to the Welsh and drew people from Wales into Bristol to be closer to the preachers there, such as Ruth Jenkins from Pembrokeshire and Margaret Davies from Haverfordwest. The Methodist leader Howell Davies (1717?–1770) was converted by Howel Harris and preached in Bristol. Charles and John Wesley had a number of Welsh among their coterie. One of the more singular cases is that of Jane Morris, the daughter of a Welsh-speaking Anglican cleric in St David's who was struck blind as a child. She learned to speak English, came to visit her sister in Bristol and found in the Moravian church with its musical traditions, communal rituals and living quarters both spiritual fulfilment and a sense of belonging.[118]

HOW WERE THE WELSH REGARDED?

We are immediately faced with a paradox here. On the one hand, there are centuries of intermarriage between natives of Bristol and Wales. We have seen, too, that men of Welsh descent held high civic office. By the later 18th century the Powells, the Protheroes and the Meylers, all prominent merchants involved in the sugar or slave trade, were amongst the leading families in the city. On the other hand, there was some sense of popular antagonism against foreigners in general and to some extent the Welsh labouring poor were considered 'foreign'. Before 1745 some were suspected of Jacobite sympathies, and there were indeed pockets of Catholicism and Stuart loyalism in Wales in the first half of this period.

The Bristol dramatist and comedian John Hippisley raised laughs from his Bristol audiences with his 1733 play *A Journey to Bristol or The Honest Welch-man*, which seems to have been first staged at his theatre in Jacob's Well Road. Its very title exploited the usual characterisation of the Welsh as sly, untruthful and voluble.[119]

Hippisley, who protested in a later London edition that he did not mean to cause offence by his portrayal of the Welshman of the title, admitted nonetheless that he 'introduced him only for the sake of the Humour and drew his character from Nature and observation'. 'Davy Shenkins' [whose very name made fun of the Welsh pronunciation of the name Jenkins] was played by Hippisley himself. The surviving edition of the play which was clearly toned down from the original, showed Davy as amiable and honest but not overly bright. Shamelessly exploited by his unpleasant boss, a tight-fisted and jealous Bristol merchant, Davy mangles the English language, sings in Welsh and shows his ignorance of city ways at every turn.[120]

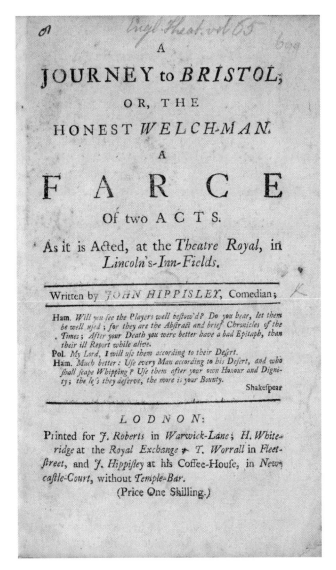

A

JOURNEY to *BRISTOL*;

OR, THE

HONEST *WELCH-MAN.*

A

F A R C E

Of two A C T S.

As it is Acted, at the *Theatre Royal*, in *Lincoln's-Inn-Fields.*

Written by *JOHN HIPPISLEY*, Comedian;

Ham. *Will you fee the Players well beftow'd? Do you hear, let them be well ufed ; for they are the Abftract and brief Chronicles of the Times; After your Death you were better have a bad Epitaph, than their ill Report whole alive.*
Pol. *My Lord, I will ufe them according to their Defert.*
Ham. *Much better: Ufe every Man according to his Defert, and who fhall fcape Whipping? Ufe them after your own Honour and Dignity; the le's they deferve, the more is your Bounty.*
Shakefpear

L O D N O N:

Printed for *J. Roberts* in *Warwick-Lane*; H. Whiteridge at the *Royal Exchange* ✦ *T. Worrall* in *Fleetftreet*, and *J. Hippifley* at his Coffee-Houfe, in *Newcaftle-Court*, without *Temple-Bar.*

(Price One Shilling.)

The very fact that Hippisley felt obliged to revise the play and include an apologetic preamble is revealing in itself. It suggests he had been confident about what Bristol audiences might find funny but that he had not reckoned on striking such a raw nerve amongst those with Welsh connections. Stereotyped though it was, his characterisation of Shenkins does seem to have been directly related to some of the contemporary issues relating to the Welsh poor in Bristol: their imperfect grasp of English, their illiteracy, and their vulnerability to exploitation and scapegoating. But there are also sly references to shoddy Welsh goods and horse dealing.

The fraudulent exploitation of the poor rural migrant, in life as on stage, was even more likely when that migrant could neither speak nor read English. Such an occurrence was documented in 1699, when a Bristol magistrate heard the case of one Morgan Davy of Eatton in Monmouthshire. This Davy had come with a friend to the Bristol area to seek harvest work. Speaking no English and as illiterate as the fictional Shenkins, he, too, was treated as an easy mark by his Bristol employer who had paid his English-speaking friend but had refused to pay him.[121]

During times of stress, the Welsh, along with other outsiders, were vulnerable to suspicion and stereotyping. Hippisley makes this point by having Shenkins terrified of being wrongly blamed for being a member of an actual extortionist gang which had threatened arson attacks in Bristol shortly before his play was written. When a Welshman was amongst those named in a pederasty scandal at the Bristol Baptist College, one pamphleteer claimed in 1756 that a 'Bristol-man' would never have been 'guilty of such a black offence'.[122]

The stationing in Bristol of militias from Wales did not usually do much for Welsh-English community relations. In 1762 affrays broke out in 'a house of ill fame in Marsh-Street' over 'a girl of the Town' involving Welsh militia members and local sailors. The following month, a Welsh speaking resident of the city was nearly killed by four members of the Welsh militia when he overheard them plotting in Welsh to leave a public house in Broadmead without paying for their drinks. That same night the violence spread to Nicholas Street near the Back where English butchers and the militia clashed, and one of the butchers was killed. Welsh militias brought in to guard French prisoners of war and to suppress anti-catholic rioters in 1780 were, one senses, also unpopular in the city, the Anglesey militia reportedly leaving the city 'to the no small joy of the inhabitants'.[123]

By the end of our period, Wales was industrialising and absorbing some of the labour it might otherwise have exported to Bristol. Nevertheless the 1841 census shows a continuing inflow of Welsh workers into Bristol. Their Protestantism enabled them to assimilate more easily into the city than their Irish counterparts.

Chapter 6

The Irish, 1685–1835

Two of Georgian Bristol's most famous MPs were Irishmen — Robert Nugent and Edmund Burke. Edmund Burke's barrister brother Richard was Recorder (Judge) of Bristol for many years, while Francis Danby, the much admired member of the 'Bristol School of painting', hailed from Wexford. Men of substance like the merchant John Shadwell and the slaving merchant Noblett Ruddock were linked to Cork, and Ruddock was grand enough to specify that he wished to be buried in his father's family vault in County Cork if he died in Ireland and in his mother's family vault should he die in Bristol. But these Irishmen were at least nominally Protestant. By contrast, most of Bristol's Irish inhabitants were Catholic and of decidedly modest means. The stereotype of the Bristol Irish in this period is of a rough community, prone to drunkenness, crime and disorder. There is some truth to this image, but it is only a half-truth that needs to be critically examined and put into context.[124]

BRISTOL'S IRISH MIGRANTS

Most Irish migrants to Bristol came from Cork, Dublin and Waterford and, although their numbers swelled to some 4,000 in 1851, they were a much smaller presence before the great famine of 1846. Nevertheless, they were, as we shall see, a source of increasing disquiet.

Figure 44 Postcard showing Edmund Burke's statue in Bristol's city centre, *c.*1900.

Colston Avenue, Bristol.

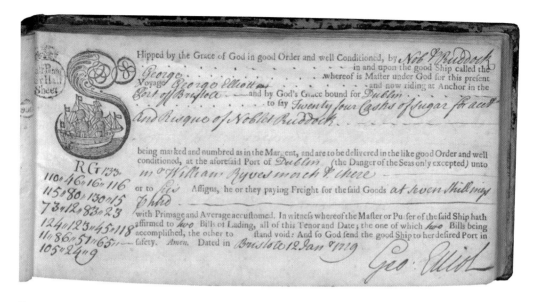

Figure 45 This 1719 bill of lading, documenting the receipt of cargo aboard a ship, refers to the Irish Bristol merchant Noblett Ruddock.

In his 1735 report on religion in Bristol, Thomas Secker, then bishop of Bristol, stated there were very few Catholics of any nationality in Bristol. By 1766, his successor, Bishop Thomas Newton mentions a colony of 'some hundreds' of Irish in the quayside parish of St Stephen's alone, describing them as 'a poor wretched set with no persons of rank or note among them', mainly 'Irish sailors and their wives or females of a worst denomination'. Newton's blanket characterisation of these people as 'mean' and 'low' 'wretches' obliterates them as individuals and obscures the fact that some Irish in the city, such as Thomas Kelly of Wexford, Michael Casey and James Moore, mariners from Cork, had managed to scrape together some small amount of property to leave to their families and friends, while others like the victualler James Kennedy or Thomas Flaherty, who leased land in Henbury, were modestly wealthy.[125]

Of the 18 'Papists' listed in the Temple parish for that same year, only three had Irish names: John Mackey a middle-aged cooper, Richard Macvoy, a weaver in his mid-thirties and John Fitzonil, a young sailor, all of whom had been resident in the parish for two years or less. The other parishes with significant Catholic numbers, perhaps some 100 in all, were St James and Sts Philip and Jacob, but we do not know how many of these were Irish sailors or Flemish brass workers. But perhaps we should not take these numbers at face value. Given the official hostility to Catholics on the part of the Anglicans, the transient nature of the mariner community, and the widely held assumption that the Irish controlled much of the smuggling trade then rife in the Bristol Channel, it is possible that not all the Irish in Bristol would have cared to be recorded as such.[126]

Popular anxiety about the criminality of these economic migrants was fanned by press reports. The lives of the Bristol Irish were ignored by the press except when crime and disorder were involved, in which case the suspect's Irishness was pointedly made explicit. When Irish people were executed in the city, such as 'the stout seaman' Jeremiah Hayes, a 'native of Ireland' hanged in 1749 for a brutal murder, it was noted with additional if implicit disapproval that he died without renouncing his Catholic faith. It was all too easy to make scapegoats of the Irish for unsolved crimes. There was the notorious case of the son of an impoverished Irish doctor named Powers, who on a visit to Bristol in 1730 was wrongly accused of a recent spate of unsolved arson attacks. Since it was evidently thought that one of the gang involved was Irish, he, being Irish, was seen to fit the bill. Summarily arrested, he was taken to Newgate prison where he was chained in a dungeon (the 'pit') for a year. Although eventually acquitted, he was made to pay costs to his gaoler.[127]

Figure 46. Great Britain and Ireland.

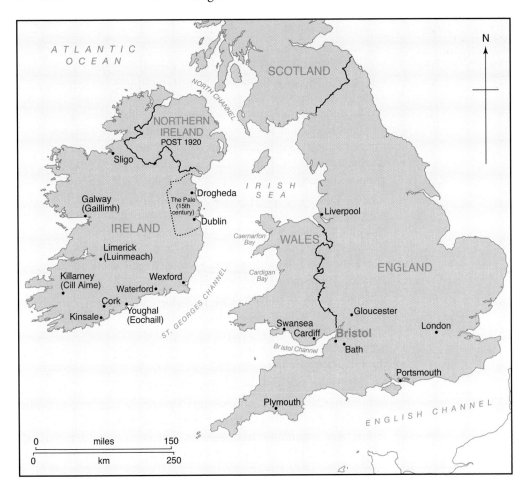

Both the tough reputation of Bristol's Irish migrants and the anti-Irish prejudice of the Bristol authorities was lampooned in Christopher Anstey's 1756 picaresque satire, *Memoirs of the Noted Buckhorse* in which the hero Buckhorse (loosely based on a real life boxer and man about town, John Smith) was called to Bristol where he hoped to reclaim some money owned to him. Charged with assault after a violent encounter in Marsh Street, he came before the mayor, 'who to do him justice, was a very good kind of man, and mortally hated the Irish' and 'who suspecting Buckhorse to be of that nation' asked his nationality and failing to get an answer asked where he was staying:

> … In Marsh-street, Sir, replied Buckhorse, at the Harp and Crown. Ay, I knew, said the Mayor … I should make him confess; I know these Irish Fellows by their Look: You are guilty, Sirrah, of this Assault, that's plain. Ho, ho, says the Mayor, this Fellow is set on by the Colliers to burn the City … Constable, carry him down to Bridewell. Ay, a Papist, an Irish Papist, to be sure, says the Mayor …[128]

The Bristol establishment's view of 'Irish Papists' had been established since Cromwell and was strengthened by the city's support of 'King Billy's' suppression of the Stuart forces in Ireland. Wolfe Tone's United Irishmen might have combined Protestants and Catholics in an attempt to throw off the English yoke, but the image of the Irish as a dangerous insurrectionary force was no doubt confirmed in 1798 when his alliance with the French and his support for a plan to burn Bristol were made known. Soon afterwards, two purported leading lights of the United Irishmen were arrested in a lodging house in Queen Square, where they had been 'residing for some weeks'.[129]

Ireland's colonial relationship with England had produced an exploitative and underdeveloped system of agriculture and land tenure, which spawned a particularly downtrodden and often desperate poor. Unlike the Huguenots or even the Jews, the Irish peasantry did not come with the skills needed to flourish in an emerging capitalist economy. They spoke Gaelic, they were peasants, not urban traders or craftsmen, and they were less literate than the English rural poor. As poor and exploited as English rural workers were in this period, their counterparts in Ireland were much worse off. Subject to periodic famines, these abjectly destitute people routinely came to England to seek jobs or to take advantage of the poor relief available here, for in Ireland there was no such provision. This caused resentment amongst Bristol ratepayers as early as 1740, and the poor law authorities did their

Figure 47 Marsh Street, by Hugh O'Neill, 1823, showing St Stephen's church in the background. Marsh Street, notorious for its many taverns, was where many Irish migrants lived.

utmost to send back those who could not obtain work. These migrants, unskilled and hungry, would work for less than their English counterparts and the Bristol press nervously reported the influx of Irish poor undercutting wages elsewhere in the country.[130]

The Irish competed with the English poor for the worst jobs in the city. Very few Irish Catholics were taken on as apprentices: John Wheeler of County Cork was the only Irish apprentice out of the 245 lads taken on by Bristol masters in 1725 and James Bonbonous, also of Cork, was the only one of 197 apprentices taken on in 1735, and given his name and that of his master (Joseph Daltera), he was probably of Huguenot origin. By contrast, most of the 37 taverns said to be in Marsh Street alone were reputedly in Irish hands, although this is probably an over-estimate as a number seem to have been owned by those of Welsh or English origin. These taverns were notorious for their 'music, dancing, rioting, drunkenness and profane swearing', and as sites, as Thomas

Clarkson discovered, for the practice of 'crimping', whereby a sailor was enticed with credit to get drunk and make merry and then threatened with debtors' prison if he did not sign to serve on a slaving voyage.[131]

Irish sailors and masters worked alongside English mariners aboard Bristol ships, including slavers. A small proportion of slave ship masters between 1770 and 1807 had Irish names and Irish mariners and surgeons served aboard Bristol slave ships. One slave-ship master, John Kennedy, made some nine voyages in that period for his employer William Rogers, and comes across from his letters as a vicious brute. He was described by another Bristol Irishman, the mariner Neal O'Donel, who had the misfortune of serving under him, as a 'man of very bad character, a gambler and remarkably letizious [litigious] [and] a trikey and troublesome fellow'. Kennedy, who mistreated both his crew and those Africans he enslaved, was also at odds with the Irish ship's surgeon Matthew Neely, a man whom O'Donel defended as 'an honest man' and who was himself appalled by Kennedy's treatment of the slaves.[132]

One famous Bristol Irishman was Patrick Cotter, later known as Patrick O'Brien, the so-called 'Bristol Giant'. Cotter, a bricklayer from Kinsale, was an easy mark for 'the avarice of a showman', being some eight feet tall. He was brought to England at 18 under some sort of indenture to an unscrupulous captain of an Irish trader. When he found Cotter less tractable than he wished, the captain accused him of a fictitious debt and Cotter was put into custody, fearfully anticipating a stay in debtors' prison. A Bristol hosier, William Watt, reportedly discovered this 'immense sized person', 'howling most woefully' in the corner of a sponging house in Taylor's Court off Broad Street. Having learned of his plight, Watt was said to have stood Cotter's bail, and ensured that he was no longer legally under his old employer's power. Under Watt, he was kitted out in 'a large gold-lace hat and red coat and a waist-coat trimm'd in gold' and packaged as the 'Irish giant the lineal descendant of the old and puissant King Bryan Boreau'. Watt's management enabled Cotter to pursue a successful career exhibiting himself at Temple and St James's fairs. By his early forties he had enough money to retire from a life he reportedly found 'exceedingly irksome to his feelings'. He lived on Hotwells Road, an area of Irish settlement, and he ensured that his body would be buried deep in the stone doorway of the Trenchard Street Catholic Chapel to foil body snatchers in search of a medical curiosity. Despite his Catholicism, his nationality and his size, he was in some respects well integrated into Bristol life, being a member of a Bristol Freemasons' lodge and an enthusiastic attender of the Theatre Royal. He created a romantic Irish brand which, combined

Figure 48 Etching of Patrick Cotter and his tailor John Rankin by the caricaturist John Kay, 1808.

with his affable nature, made him an unthreatening Irishman, who was held in affectionate but somewhat patronising regard by his English chroniclers.[133]

The employment patterns of the Irish women who came to Bristol remain obscure. The early Catholic chapel registers begun late in the 18th century show an increasing number of Irish women but do not specify occupations. The 1767 return of Papists suggests that the majority of those in St Stephen's worked as traders and casual workers. One, Ann Malone, was an earthenware seller near the Quay on St Augustine's Back, another, Elizabeth Kennady, was cited as a school mistress in Milk Street near Castle Green, which given the area probably meant she ran a very small dame school. We can assume that outside the central district, with its distinct Irish community, isolated servant women worked in the great houses but, because of the absence of census material indicating occupational status before 1851, we have no idea how many worked in the mines and iron manufactories to the east of the city or as agricultural workers further out.[134]

Figure 49 Cleansing the floating harbour by Thomas L. Rowbotham, 1828.

Although they made up only a small proportion of the city's manual workforce, Irish navvies laboured alongside English ones on the cleaning and then the reconstruction of Bristol's floating

harbour. When, in 1809, their task was completed and a celebratory feast organised in Hotwells for the thousand workers involved, it quickly degenerated into a drunken affray split along ethnic lines. Fighting spread to Prince Street when the Irish reportedly went back to Marsh Street to fetch their shillelaghs or cudgels.[135]

The ending of the Napoleonic wars in 1815 saw a huge increase in poverty as troops returned home in search of work. This coincided with the increased movement of impoverished Irish vagrants into England and Wales, with Bristol becoming (along with Liverpool) one of their two main entry points. An increasing proportion of Irish in Bristol were vagrants, most coming from 'the mountainous parts of Kerry and the barren tracts of Cork' after finishing harvest work in Limerick. They competed with harvest workers in Gloucestershire and South Wales and with workers within the city for jobs, and, whilst the Irish certainly did not cause the growing slum problem, they certainly exacerbated the pressure on housing. The tiny courts and alleys of the centre of town were filled with the transient poor in overcrowded conditions and the Irish vagrants were amongst the most wretched. As more Irish poor came into Bristol, ethnic tension grew. *The Times* reported in 1817 that 'a sergeant of the Irish Militia', then quartered in Bristol, was stabbed in an unprovoked attack in St James's churchyard by two men expressing anti-Irish sentiments.[136]

The extreme poverty which beset both English and Irish labourers in the first decades of the 19th century predisposed a few to revolutionary acts, and a Bristol carpenter, Richard Bradburn, was one of the 'Cato Street conspirators', who in 1820, a year after the Peterloo massacre, plotted to murder the entire Cabinet. Bradburn was transported for life to New South Wales for his part in the conspiracy. As *The Bristol Mirror* noted, with more sympathy than one might expect: 'He is an Irishman by birth, and had been possessed of some property, but by unforeseen misfortunes became reduced to poverty and was a long time without work or the means of subsisting his family, which consisted of a wife and two children.'[137]

But sympathy was tempered by the economic burdens which increasing numbers of Irish migrants brought to the city. That same year, James Johnson, who had just left his post as the Deputy-Governor of the Bristol Corporation of the Poor, published *An Address to the Inhabitants of Bristol on the subject of Poor Rates with a View to their Reduction* … Johnson discussed both English and Irish poor but was particularly exercised by recent legislation which obliged local authorities to maintain destitute vagrants, find them work or give them free transport back to Ireland. According to Johnson, this was a recipe for fraud: 'I do not think, however,

Figure 50 'St John's Bridge', as seen from the back of the *Adam & Eve*, Lewin's Mead, 1821, by Hugh O'Neill. This seemingly picturesque scene at the top of what is now Colston Street was actually one of urban deprivation. The houses where many Irish lived were densely packed and the river was an open sewer.

notwithstanding the great numbers that have applied for these three years past, that more than a dozen ever engaged in the employment afforded them'. In 1824, the Bristol MP Henry Bright presented a petition from Bristol's Poor Law authority complaining of the expenses incurred by the transportation of Irish paupers.[138]

CATHOLIC EMANCIPATION

It was against this backdrop that in the 1820s Bristol considered the question of Catholic emancipation. A few progressive Dissenters argued that banishing the mass of Irish Catholics into 'a political Siberia' was not the way to effect positive change in the country. Others argued that religious restrictions were driving 'half-starved Irish labourers into England' by fostering misgovernment in Ireland. But, alarmed by the militant rhetoric of Daniel O'Connell and the Catholic Association in Ireland, and fearful of the influx of Irish poor into the city, Bristol public opinion in the city was overwhelmingly against Catholic emancipation. In the run-up to the parliamentary vote on the Catholic Emancipation Bill of 1829, public disputations were held between prominent Protestant divines and the city's two Catholic priests, one of whom, the Bristol-born Father O'Farrell, was of Irish extraction. Feelings were running high. The extravagantly anti-Catholic rhetoric employed by the more militantly Protestant non-conformist ministers painted Catholic practice in Ireland in such dark colours that it could not but affect public sentiments towards the Irish themselves. In 1828 a 'well attended' general meeting of 'the Bristol and Clifton Association for the Moral and Religious Improvement of Ireland' decided the only way to improve the country was to convert the Catholics there.[139]

> **I'd be a Catholic** [to be sung to the air of 'I'd be a Butterfly']
>
> I'd be a Catholic born in old Erin
> Where naught but Religion and Loyalty grows;
> I'd Gladden Shiel and O'Connell with Cheering,
> And follow Jack Lawless wherever he goes,
> I would stand up for the Catholic faction
> Sharpen their pikes and muster their men
> Kill all that we could in a state of inaction
> But when rang'd to meet us we'd turn back again.
> … Our priests they must drive on the people to plunder,
> And give absolution for every crime
> Say Nothing but force can keep Protestants under,
> And if we will use it, that now is the time …

This verse, which is from *The Bristol Gazette*, 30 October 1828, represents Irish Catholics as uniformly violent and dangerous to English interests.

Religious sectarianism was thus infused with ethnic tensions. In February 1829 a demonstration against Catholic emancipation which attracted between 10,000 and 35,000 people into Queen

Figure 51 Host Street, Bristol. Formerly known as Horse Street, this quayside street in St Stephen's parish was associated with the Irish poor.

Square must have caused some trepidation amongst the Irish population. In April 1829 a mob of some 300 people attacked the recently opened St Joseph's chapel in Trenchard Street, throwing stones and breaking its windows before going on to Host Street to attack the Irish Papists. Further unrest accompanied the passage of the Catholic Emancipation Act, and Bristol's Irish were widely blamed for much of the violence during the Bristol Reform Act Riots of 1831, a riot which destroyed much of Queen Square.[140]

Bristol authorities attempted to send as many vagrants back to Ireland as possible, but ratepayers balked at the cost, and there were further criticisms that those seeking seasonal work were exploiting the system to get a free ride home. There was some truth to this, with gangs of workers giving their wages to one of their number for safekeeping and then declaring themselves destitute. Little evidence survives to give us the Irish poor's side of the story, but that vagrants were working the system shows that they did establish informal strategies for mutual support, although not in the way Bristol's ratepayers would have hoped. The additional suspicion that many poor Irish workers intended to stay permanently in the country was also confirmed in 1833 by the Report of the House of Commons Select Committee on Irish Vagrants, which found that many Irish migrants absconded before being sent back home. Worse still, they found that in 'places like Marshfield, near Bristol', corrupt officials allowed Irish paupers to stay on fraudulent grounds.[141]

The values of self-reliance, thrift and sobriety, which fostered success in the urban capitalist economy, did not mesh easily with the culture of mutuality, generosity and convivial drinking associated with the largely rural Irish poor. Also, unlike the Huguenots and the Welsh, Bristol's Irish Catholics did not yet have a large core of wealthy and influential people who might exercise patronage and influence on their behalf. However, after emancipation, Bristol's largely Irish Catholic community slowly began building its own communal institutions. A charity school was set up towards the end of the century (where the famous Australian actor Barry Sullivan went to school in the late 1820s) and plans were made in 1834 to erect a new church, although it initially foundered because of financial mismanagement on the part of the priest, Dr Edgeworth. This nascent infrastructure would be sorely tested by the potato famine of the 1840s, the impact of which will be addressed in a later chapter.

Chapter 7

The Black Presence, 1688–1835

The Huguenots, Irish and Welsh were, whatever their differences, near neighbours of the English. But the two groups discussed in this and the next chapter, Africans (or those of African descent) and Jews (mainly from Central and Eastern Europe), were perceived at the time as altogether more 'foreign'. The aim of these chapters is to consider how and why people from these groups came to the city, how they were treated and what their impact was on the city's identity.

As already established, Bristolians had been engaged in trade with the West African coast since at least the 1500s. 'Brize-yo', literally 'children of Bristol', was reportedly the name first given to the English by the Neyo people of what is now the Ivory Coast.[142]

Figure 52 Britain and the Atlantic slave-based economy, *c.*1660s–*c.*1807.

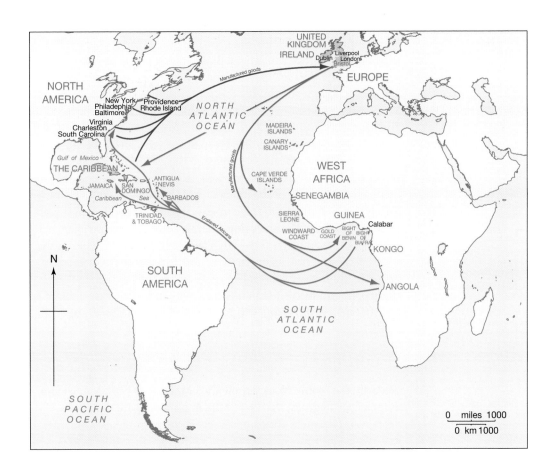

Figures 53a and b These 18th- and 19th-century tobacco trade cards attest to the link between Bristol and African slave labour.

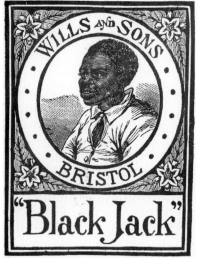

Bristolians were also involved in at least the early colonisation of the Caribbean and North America, and from the 17th century in the setting up of slave plantations there. British plantations initially depended on indentured and forced White labour from Bristol, the West Country and Ireland, but soon enslaved Africans replaced them in vastly greater numbers. Bristol famously became Britain's second slaving port for much of the 18th century, eclipsing even London and Liverpool in this regard during the 1720s and '30s. Yet despite transporting over a half a million enslaved Africans to America from around 1698 to 1807, of whom an estimated 90,000 perished *en route*, Bristol ships brought few Africans to Bristol itself.

Enslaved Africans largely by-passed the city, being shipped directly from Africa to the Americas. Bristol's slave trade was a relatively minor part of the port's export trade, although Bristol was hugely dependent on the trade in slave-produced goods and thereby an integral part of the emerging Atlantic slave economy. Sugar refining, for example, was the city's largest industry throughout the 1700s; its distilleries, its brass, glass, and gun manufactories and its textile trade were substantially geared for 'the Guinea market' (figure 52) and its earliest banks and insurance firms were funded by 'African', 'West Indian', 'Virginian' and 'Carolina' merchants.

BLACK RESIDENTS IN THE ERA OF SLAVERY

Nevertheless, some Black people did come to the port. Some came as 'privilege negroes', that is, as human bonuses paid to a ship's captain or first mate after a profitable slaving voyage. Some came as enslaved servants directly from the Caribbean, whilst others

Figure 54 Detail from Samuel and Nathaniel Buck 'The South East Prospect of the City of Bristol', *c.*1734 showing caricatured Black servant with employer.

had won their freedom by serving in the armed forces. A few came as emissaries from West African trading ports. Although it has been claimed that there was a community of perhaps as many as 15,000 Africans in London during our period, we have been able to document the existence of only just over 100 in Bristol. There were undoubtedly more people of African descent in Bristol than this, but how many more awaits further research and will probably never be properly ascertained. Records, especially for the early part of the century, are scarce and, because of the racialised stigma of slavery, family historians have until recently proved reluctant to explore this aspect of their ancestry.[143]

Figures 55a, b and c Grave of Scipio Africanus (d. 1720), servant to the Earl of Suffolk, in Henbury churchyard. Replicas of the headstone (top) and footstone are shown below.

The best-known Africans who came to Bristol before the abolition of the British slave trade in 1807 were 'Scipio Africanus' (d. 1720),

and 'Pero' (1740-1818) who served as a personal servant to John
Pinney, an important Bristol merchant, after years on his master's
Nevis plantation (a footbridge erected by the City Council in 1999
was named in his honour). A number of servants of African or
'mulatto' background were employed at various times in Pinney's
Bristol household. Kate Coker, a 'negro woman servant', accompanied
Pinney's children from Nevis to England in 1778 and was later manu-
mitted or freed. So, too, was Frances Coker, a trained seamstress who
worked as servant and companion to John Pinney's wife.[144]

Black servants were baptised and buried in various Anglican
churches in the city and accepted as members of the Baptist,
Moravian and Methodist congregations throughout this period.
In the later 18th century, Frances Coker was described by an elder
of the Broadmead Baptist church as giving 'a most intelligent and
pleasing account of the work of God upon her soul' when she was
accepted as a candidate for baptism there. Black Ned, a child of 12,
was reportedly buried in the city's Quaker burial ground in 1778.[145]

Not all Black people in Bristol in this era were servants or
enslaved. Free Black sailors, from both West Africa and the
Caribbean, served aboard Bristol ships (including slavers). We
know something of John Quaqua (or Quaco) who married a
local Bristol woman, had a family in Princess Amelia Court and
paid poor rates in the mid-18th century. Peter Stephens, another

Figure 56 This document
records that John Quaco,
a free Black sailor in
Bristol in 1763, was
entitled to a pension
from the Bristol Society
of Merchant Venturers.

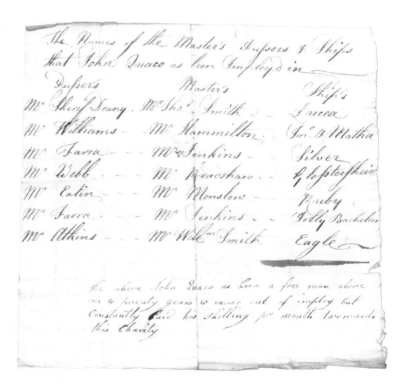

mariner, lived in Marsh Street in the 1770s and John Dean served aboard Bristol slave ships and testified to the anti-slavery campaigner Thomas Clarkson in 1788.[146]

West African trading partners of British slave merchants occasionally sent their sons to England to learn English and book-keeping, and at least one came 'to take shipping at Bristol' in 1759. In 1774 two young kinsmen of an important Ifik slave trader (Ephraim Robin John) of Old Calabar (now in Nigeria) escaped as stowaways to Bristol, having previously been tricked into slavery and taken to Virginia. At first held captive, they eventually obtained assistance from one of their kinsmen's Bristol trading partners (the slave trader, Thomas Jones), and received hospitality and religious instruction from Charles and John Wesley and other local Methodists, before returning to Calabar. By 1786 John Wesley had personally baptised at least one person of African origin in Bristol whose occupation is unknown but whose piety impressed Wesley and the whole congregation. Robert Southey remarked that the mixed-raced children of wealthy planters were sometimes sent to be schooled in Bristol, and Brother Franks, 'a negro', was recorded as a member of Bristol's Freemasons in 1782, where his colour was not to be mentioned on pain of a fine.[147]

Black men also served in the British military during this period. William Cheeseman, who enlisted in Bristol for the British army in 1814, was an African-American who later served in the Worcester Militia. Between 1792 and 1815, 20 to 30 of the French prisoners of war who were kept in Stapleton prison near Bristol were Black sailors from the Caribbean, and many, including the cook Louis Theodore, captured off the *San Pedro*, were recruited into His Majesty's service between 1805 and 1806.[148]

Only a year after Waterloo soldiers and sailors poured back into the country looking for work and flooding the job market, and, as we have seen, Bristol's mayor complained about the 'foreign seamen, blackmen and men of colour' then in Bristol looking for work. In 1820, an employer advertised in a Bristol newspaper the virtues of 'a man of colour' who worked as a porter or warehouseman for seven years and with whom he 'would not part', 'had he [had] further occasion for his services'. This may well have been Henry Saunders, who was reported in 1821 as arriving in Bath from Bristol looking for work and,[149] '… on descending from the coach in Horse Street, a mean-dressed youth asked him if he could tell him of any man of colour who wanted a situation as he knew of a good one. Saunders quite delighted, informed him that he wanted a place …' The youth, who seems to have targeted Saunders partly on account of his race, then made an unsuccessful attempt to make off with Saunders' gold watch.[150]

A few Black people worked in what we would today call 'the entertainment industry'. Black musicians, portrayed as lodging in Clifton in Smollett's 1771 novel *Humphrey Clinker*, were much in demand in the regiments and one well-known tavern keeper specifically advertised for Black horn players for a patriotic show he was staging during the Napoleonic wars. At the less salubrious end of the trade were circuses and fairs. Economic necessity or simple coercion drove some Africans to appear in 'menageries' and travelling freak shows. 'A savage Ethiopian' was reportedly on display in Bristol during the St James's fair in 1780 and in 1811 a Khosian woman from South Africa, Saarjite Baartman, the 'Hottentot Venus', could be viewed at the Horsefair in Bristol on payment of a shilling. Acting was another way to gain a living, but Black actors faced particular problems. Othello was a perennial on the Bristol stage, but such was the strength of racialist feeling in some quarters that even the thought of a White actor 'blacking up' in order to play Othello caused revulsion, especially with regards to scenes with Desdemona.[151]

Unlike London, where there was an established Black community, most Black Bristolians were socially isolated as servants in private homes. Inter-racial liaisons, whilst they did occur, happened mainly amongst free seamen and local women, and seem to have been limited in number. They were certainly not acceptable in 'polite' society. Thus when the immigration of Black servants ceased after Emancipation, Bristol's small Black population appears to have dwindled into insignificance.

BEFORE AND AFTER EMANCIPATION

Slavery informed and poisoned attitudes towards Black people in general. Both the fact that enslaved Africans did not own property and their legal status *as* property, profoundly lowered the status of all 'people of colour'. Added to this, the spectre of violent slave resistance had been a constant motif in the local press and a source of constant anxiety to planter interests throughout the period. White Bristolians may have been more receptive than most to anti-Black views, given their extensive contact with Jamaica (where slave resistance was fiercest) and the considerable influence of the pro-slavery lobby in the city.

Poverty was another factor in shaping attitudes. Unemployment was the scourge of the poor during the early industrial period and Africans in England were particularly vulnerable. When, in 1772, Mansfield's Judgement had undermined the slave status of African servants in England by forbidding their forcible repatriation back

Figure 57 This detail of Nicholas Pocock's sketch of Wapping, Bristol, shows two Black workers working alongside White workers at a Bristol shipyard.

to the plantations, many were 'let go' and forced into destitution. Some resorted to criminality and so further increased their disadvantage in a White society already alarmed by the lawlessness of their own indigenous workers. Traditionally discouraged as slaves from becoming literate, illiterate free men could find tramping for work a risky business as they could be easily tricked or forced by unscrupulous merchants into 'signing' an indenture agreement nullifying their free status. Most spoke a variant of Caribbean patois rather than English, which, given the extent to which it was burlesqued in the local and national press, could not have enhanced their employability.

Black people in Bristol were far less likely than their White counterparts to have family or friends who might offer them support. The registers of Blacks baptised in Bristol also show that, unlike other parishioners, they more often than not did not even know the names of their mothers and fathers, which in those days implied the stigma of being illegitimate or 'base born'. Even more than the Irish, they lacked access to the cultural capital which would have better positioned them in a capitalist economy.[152]

The fellowship and acceptance offered by Bristol's Baptist, Moravian and Methodist chapels did prove attractive to Black people and began to offer a few a way of gaining literacy and organisational skills. But, generally speaking, religious difference was still a factor in distinguishing African-Caribbean labourers from their English and Irish counterparts. If Britain's urban poor were increasingly isolated from the Church and not universally attracted to the Chapel, at least they were not positively forbidden from entering either. By contrast there had long been a Caribbean tradition of forbidding slaves to be baptised with many planters preventing the more egalitarian Baptist missionaries from gaining access to their workforce right up until Emancipation. This meant that many enslaved people retained animistic beliefs (that natural objects, natural phenomena, and the universe itself possess souls) derived in part from Africa and in part from other enslaved people in the Caribbean. Their widespread belief in spirits and sorcery was not a million miles away from the beliefs of the less educated rural poor in parts of Britain, but it had been forged in the brutalising fires of enslavement and it disturbed and horrified even committed abolitionists.[153]

If, by 1830, pro-slavery figures in Bristol like Christopher Claxton trumpeted an increasingly racialist contempt for Black people, progressives in the anti-slavery camp patronisingly idealised them. They claimed that, once freed, 'people of colour' would be transformed into icons of proto-Victorian virtue, model workers in the Protestant mould. The long-term impact of exile and enslavement and the structural inequalities which followed Emancipation were simply not taken into account. As we shall see, the failure of freed slaves to live up to liberal expectations was to sour race relations in the succeeding century. As the Victorian era approached, those Africans remaining in Bristol, easily distinguishable from the host population, were seen not as individuals trying to survive in a difficult and discriminatory world, but as unmistakably and quintessentially 'other'. Africans were still perhaps the ultimate foreigners in a city which did not always take foreigners to its heart.

Figures 58a and b
Newspaper advertisements for runaway slaves in mid-18th-century Bristol.

RUN away the 7th Inftant, from Capt. Thos. Eaton, of the Prince William, a NEGRO MAN, named *Mingo*, of a good black Complexion, fmooth Face; wears a black Wig; had on two fhort blue Waiftcoats, and brown Breeches; about 5 Foot 5 Inches high, his Legs a little bent, his upper Teeth fcagg'd and broken, has a *Cut* on his *Right Wrift*, which ftands up in a Bunch. He fpeaks pretty good Englifh; has been in and out of this City about eight Years. Whoever will deliver the faid Black into the Poffeffion of his Mafter, Capt. Eaton aforefaid, fhall have a Guinea Reward.
N. B. All Perfons are hereby forbid entertaining the faid Black at their Peril: And if he will return to his Duty, he will be kindly received, and have his Offences pardoned.

CARMARTHEN, *March* 2, 1757.
RUN AWAY fome time fince JOHN VOWLES, an Apprentice to Lazarus Thomas, of the County-Borough of Carmarthen, Peruke-Maker: This is to give Notice to all Perfons not to harbour, entertain or employ the faid John Vowles, for they will be profecuted as the Law directs; and likewife for all Merchants or Captains of Ships to pay no Prize-Money or Wages to the faid John Vowles, for the Time paft or to come, as they will be fued for the fame hereafter, by me   LAZARUS THOMAS.

RUN away fome Time fince, A NEGRO LAD about 18 Years of Age, near five Feet two Inches high, anfwers to the Name of *Starling*, and blows the French Horn very well, (from his late MafterCapt. James Pollock, deceas'd, but) now the Property of Ralph Cook, at the Sign of the Rifing Sun in Princes-ftreet, Briftol. Whoever fhall harbour or conceal the faid BLACK, will be profecuted as the Law directs; but if any Perfons will fecure him and give Notice to his faid Mafter Ralph Cook, fhall receive One Guinea Reward.

Chapter 8

Jews in Georgian Bristol

The Jewish community in Georgian Bristol was the first to be officially tolerated for nearly 500 years yet its re-establishment coincided with a ferocious national anti-Jewish propaganda campaign. This chapter describes how this campaign influenced Bristol, charts the Jewish community's development and subsequent consolidation and assesses the symbolic importance of the Jewish presence in a city whose identity had been so strongly rooted in Christian traditions.

Banned from landownership and Christian craft guilds for much of their time in the European diaspora, Jews had traditionally turned their energies to trade. The privileged few became wealthy merchants, professional men or bankers, but most were petty traders, artisans and small shopkeepers. Religious requirements meant that a large proportion of the men at least were literate and multi-lingual. Jews learned to speak the language of their country of residence, but shared a common written language, Hebrew, and commonly spoke either Yiddish (if they were Ashkenazi Jews from Central or Eastern Europe) or Ladino (if they were Sephardic Jews who had been expelled from Spain and Portugal). Like the Huguenots and Dutch traders (a few of whom were themselves converted Sephardic Jews) and their Quaker allies, they formed a loose-knit mercantile and cultural network that transcended national boundaries and facilitated their integration into the various ports of the expanding Atlantic economy, although unlike their Quaker or Huguenot counterparts, few if any Jews in Bristol appear to have been involved directly in the Atlantic trade.[154]

On the other hand, there were wide internal variations in Anglo-Jewry's national backgrounds, religious traditions and economic circumstances. Most of Bristol's Jewish community in this period were poor Jews from Germany, Poland and Russia, although nationality is hard to ascribe as borders separating these nations kept changing. Most came at first not as refugees but as itinerant peddlers, some of whom would periodically return to take money back to their families in Poland. Political conditions on the Continent were volatile. Poland, for example, became increasingly less safe for Jews after the nation's partition in 1772, making the line between economic migrants and political asylum seekers harder to draw.[155]

Occasional references to Jews in Bristol occur before the 1740s (such as Aaron Fictor, baptised at St Philip and St James in 1729,

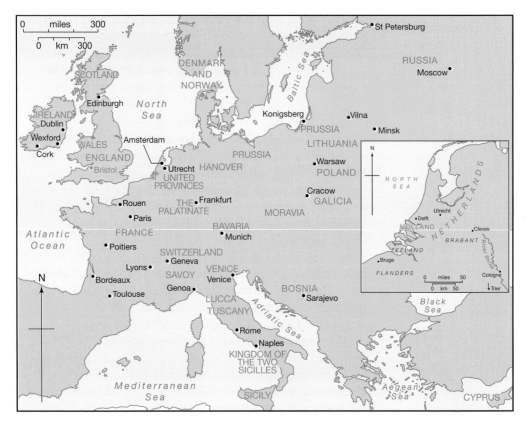

Figure 59 This map shows some of the places of origin of the Continental European migrants to Bristol in the 18th and 19th centuries.

or 'Colvin, a Jew', resident in 1732) but it was only in that decade that a Jewish 'community' could be said to have existed in the city. There was a synagogue of some sort and a burial ground by 1753, when the congregation, numbering some 40 people, took out an advertisement in *Felix Farley's Bristol Journal* offering a £20 reward leading to the conviction of the murderer of Jonas Levi, a fellow congregant who had been strangled and had 'his brains beaten out' when tramping with his peddler's pack in Abergavenny.[156]

THE CAMPAIGN AGAINST JEWISH NATURALISATION

Levi's death followed closely after a nation-wide campaign against the so-called 'Jew Bill'. This Bill offered naturalisation to foreign-born Jews, who as aliens and non-Christians were not allowed to hold shares in an English ship, hold office or own land.[157]

The Bill's passage into law in 1753 occasioned such ferocious opposition that it was repealed the following year. Restrictions on land ownership for Jews and their exclusion from political life on religious grounds were to continue until 1858.

The opposition was orchestrated on a national basis by Tory elements in London and their counterparts in Bristol, Oxford and elsewhere. The press campaign in *Felix Farley's Bristol Journal* and in various broadsides was intense. The rhetoric resurrected medieval characterisations of the Jews as cursed Christ-killers bent on crucifying or ritually abusing Christian victims, and fashioned new themes and catchwords which were to inform future anti-immigrant rhetoric for centuries to come. Bristol's Tory Steadfast Society pressed for the Act's repeal, as did some 1,600 of Bristol's 'gentlemen, clergy, Freeholders and Burgesses' (out of a total population of some 45,000), who met at the *Bush Tavern* to sign a petition expressing their 'great alarm' at the 'engrafting into our community [of] those avowed Enemies of our Saviour'. The hysteria bred by the campaign was short-lived but effective.[158]

Those who favoured Jewish naturalisation in Bristol included the Anglican dean, Josiah Tucker, an effigy of whom was burnt for his support, and the MP Robert Nugent. However, Nugent was subjected to scurrilous personal attacks on his religious integrity and eventually voted to repeal the Act. Bristol followed other communities in celebrating the Act's repeal with parades in which Jews or their supporters were burned in effigy. But once the repeal was obtained, the passions subsided and Jews in Bristol were generally allowed to get on with their lives. After such a propaganda onslaught it seems unlikely that these new migrants felt themselves to be Bristolian, but they were beginning to put down roots in the city.[159]

EARNING A LIVING

For much of the 18th century, Jews seem to have been concentrated in low status and disreputable trades south of the river and on the Quayside. Those who had the means set up 'stores for trading with the seafaring population', and supplied the wares for poorer Jews to become peddlers. In 1757 Moses Cohen was prosecuted by the Council for keeping a shop selling gold and silver 'without being a burgess'. Latimer adds that the fact that 'the Jew had placed glass windows in his shop was considered an aggravation of the offence'. Despite this inauspicious start, Moses Cohen seems to have re-invented himself by 1761 as a 'colour maker' and entered into a 14-year partnership, the first ever recorded between a Christian and Jew in the city, with one John Lowle, a Bristol Merchant Taylor. Together they set up a joint trade in Cohen's property in Redcliffe Street, each investing £163 into the venture. Documents in the town clerk's correspondence provide other evidence of Jewish economic activity. The correspondence for 1763-1765, for example, mentions

Bristol's 18th-century Jewish community

By a neat irony, the Jews' first public synagogue in the city since 1290 was located in Temple Street in the former residence of Sir John Knight the elder, an avowed enemy of Quakers and Catholics (and uncle to the anti-alien campaigner, Sir John Knight the younger). By 1766 Bishop Newton recorded a total of 42 Jews in the city, 40 of whom lived in Temple. Whilst the synagogue provided the focus for most of the community, there were others who must have assimilated into society at large. However, very few Jews seem to have formally converted to the Church of England, if the baptismal records are trustworthy. A young French Jew, the silver and goldsmith Abraham Barnard, seems to have been baptised at St Nicholas church in 1758, although he was still identified as a 'JEWeller' in a local row that began as a misunderstanding about Sunday observance.

Some Jewish men, such as Simon Vessels, a journeyman watchmaker, married non-Jewish women, which by Jewish law meant that their descendants would not be considered Jews. However, when the glassmaker Lazarus Jacobs married Mary Hiscocks from Temple Cloud in Somerset, their children were raised in the Hebrew congregation, suggesting that Mary had converted to Judaism.

Most Jews lived in the Temple, Redcliffe and St Thomas parishes until the end of the century. Because it is not always possible to distinguish Jews from Gentiles (non Jews) by their names, records such as rate books and directories are not an infallible source for tracing Bristol's Jews and their exclusion from apprenticeships and guilds also makes documenting their working lives more difficult.

House in Temple Street, Bristol, by Thomas L. Rowbotham or Hugh O'Neill (1821), used by the Jewish congregation in the mid-18th century.

References
Samuel, 64-65; BCRL, Braikenridge Collection, St James & St Paul's pt. 1, 81, St Philip's, 107; McGrath (1985), 47, 65-68; Anon. (1753), 10-11, 20; *FFBJ*, 01/12/53, 29/12/53. Barnard: BRO, 'Lists of Contents of Wooden Boxes of Town Clerk's Correspondence' file for 1768 bundle 1 (11); *FFBJ*, 13/01/70, 20/01/70; Cooper. *FFBJ*, 18/02/58, 25/02/58; TNA, PROB 11/1144. Isaac Jacob, Oxford DNB.

Figure 60 Bristol Blue glass was produced by the Jacobs family in the city.

Isaac Moses as 'a Jew shopkeeper' in the Quay and a silversmith, who worked with his wife, Mollie. Isaac probably did not write English as he was recorded as signing a legal document in Hebrew.[160]

Glass making was a trade with long-standing Jewish associations. Levi Pollock and Lazarus Jacobs were Bristol glass grinders by the 1760s. Lazarus Jacobs (1709?-1796), who came from Frankfurt-am-Main in around 1760, began as an itinerant glass cutter and seller of second-hand goods and cloth at Temple Fair. He seems to have commissioned the Bristol theatre designer and artist Michael Edkins to work for him early on in his career. In 1774 he set up his glass engraving business at 108 Temple Street with his son Isaac. Here began the manufacture of the famous 'Bristol Blue' glassware, designed and marketed with great flair by his son Isaac.[161]

Given their marginal status, it was unsurprising that some Jews turned to crime. The French-speaking Elias Castaigne or Castaing lodged in Bristol in 1744 before being sentenced to seven years' transportation for stealing jewels from Elizabeth Taylor's shops at Bristol's Hotwells spa. The following year, 'Jewish prizemongers' were denounced for buying sailors' shares in prize money for an unduly small consideration. In 1748 Lyon Lipman was implicated along with Mordecai Abraham and Elizabeth Willoughby in fencing stolen goods.

The selective coverage of the press reinforced this reputation for sharp practice. In 1790 *Felix Farley's Bristol Journal* printed 'Jewish Oeconomy', a sneering satirical poem which joked about the broken English and crass greed of a fictional Jewish old clothes dealer. Only occasionally would another image filter through, such as the brief mention in 1755 of Jeshwin, 'a Jew' who was described after his sudden death as 'a very sober man, and a Master of many languages'.[163]

Destitute Jews tended to be looked after within their own community, which was very fearful of alienating local authorities by becoming a charge on the poor rates or local charities. Evangelical charities were only too happy to assist Jews willing to convert, such as the 18-year-old Sarah Abrams, 'a Jewess' converted at the Magdalene, the home for 'fallen women' at Hooks Mills, Ashley Down, in 1791.[164]

ACCEPTANCE AND RELIGION?

By the time a new synagogue was opened in Weavers' Hall in 1786, the community was beginning to lose its pariah status. Lazarus Jacobs had prospered sufficiently in his glass business to help defray the costs of the synagogue. A letter from *Sarah Farley's Bristol Journal* recounts a Bristolian's visit to the synagogue's

Figure 61 This portrayal of Bristol's quayside dates from the mid- to late 18th century. By this time, archival evidence suggests that Jewish traders and shopkeepers did business here alongside more established Bristol residents.

opening ceremony in which he professes himself 'astonished and delighted' by the congregation's decorous atmosphere and their ritual prayers for the prosperity and well being of both the King and the city officials: 'The laudable spirit that so strikingly exists among them to worship the Supreme Creator with reverence and awful piety, makes me now esteem them very different from the usual prejudice I once harboured against them …'[165]

It was significant, too, that around the same time Samuel Liebman, a silversmith, and Harriet Hart, both of whom were involved in some financial transactions at Bristol's Old Market or Tolzey Court, were allowed to take oaths swearing on 'the Pentateuch' (the Old Testament) rather than on the St James's Bible.[166]

By this time, too, more established Jewish tradesmen were beginning to move across the river to Broadmead and Castle Street. These included pawnbrokers and jewellers such as James and Sarah Jacobs. Phineas Daniel, part of the well-known Daniel family of miniaturists, was based in Bristol in the 1770s. By 1810, although Temple was still seen as 'the Jew Quarter', Jews appear in the rate books for St Paul's with the more prosperous taking up residence in St James's and Brunswick Square, replacing those Quakers and other dissenting groups who were abandoning the area for the more genteel suburb of Clifton.[167]

Figure 62 Woodcut showing 'Highman' Palatine entertaining a Bristol audience. Palatine was a German Jewish magician living in Temple, whose rather gruesome acts, flamboyant dress and charming manner caught the public imagination in the 1770s.[162]

Evangelical Christians and the Bristol Jews

Bristol's non-conformist Protestants (especially the Moravians, Methodists and Quakers) had generally been more cordial to the Jews than Anglicans, although always with an eye to the Jews' eventual conversion. Older prejudices remained, however. Sarah Ryan, a Wesleyan convert in Bristol, admitted she had been kindly treated by the Jewish family who employed her as a servant, but in her spiritual account published by the *Arminian* magazine she still characterised Jews as people of the devil. The conversion of a doctor's wife, Hannah Nonmus, 'born at Frankfort Germany [and] ... brought up in Jewish prejudices' was celebrated in a Methodist pamphlet in 1798 which managed to convey both a sympathy for the convert and a contempt for her origins.

Shortly before her conversion, Hannah had been reduced by circumstances to peddling perfume at Bristol's St James's Fair. At the centre of Samuel Colman's 1824 painting of St James's Fair, which vividly attacks it as morally corrupt, stands a Jewish peddler. Bearded and wearing a caftan, his peddler's box of trinkets around his neck, he has sold a ring of dubious value to a young couple whose betrothal might, it is implied, not lead to a legal marriage. This 'wandering Jew' is one of many figures in the picture symbolising double-dealing and corruption, but his is a stereotype which combines both contemporary references and older and more sinister tropes.

'Marginally genteel': Social disgrace and upward mobility

In 1821 Isaac Jacobs, creator of Bristol Blue Glass, leader of the congregation and freeman of the city, was made bankrupt. His public disgrace must have affected the entire Jewish community. Isaac had embraced gentility, obtaining a coat of arms, membership of the Chamber of Commerce and a large house outside Bristol. He had ensured that his daughter made a good marriage, to Abraham Alexander, another prosperous local Jew. But when the demand for glass declined, he borrowed unwisely; his business was ruined and he was charged with fraud. Although these charges were eventually dismissed, he sank into ignominious obscurity as a dealer and chapman (peddler). He died in 1835, and was buried in the burial ground he had purchased for the Jewish community some twenty years before.[168]

Despite Isaac's failure, the Jewish community as a whole quietly prospered in the early 19th century; although not the only jewellers and pawnbrokers in Bristol, they continued as a visible presence in these trades. *Pigot's Directory* of 1830 lists Joseph and Levy of

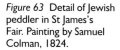

Figure 63 Detail of Jewish peddler in St James's Fair. Painting by Samuel Colman, 1824.

Union Street as silversmiths and jewellers and Isaac Solomon as 'a working jeweller'. But there was diversification, too, with Joel Solomon listed as a pen and quill manufacturer, while Joseph Cohen was a Bavarian-born straw hat maker in High Street. However well their industry and community organisation had served them, the Jewish community still suffered disadvantages. They were still unable to hold freehold or leasehold property in an age when property holding was so crucial to social and political status. Nor could they hold office unless they were willing to take a Christian oath, which would have effectively meant repudiating their Judaism.[169]

Attempts in 1830 and 1833 to remove 'Jewish disabilities' were broadly supported by the more Whiggish elements in Bristol. The *Bristol Mercury* revealed its ambivalence towards the Jews when it stated that the Bill should be passed on the grounds that 'a man's religion, no matter how mistaken, was between him and the Deity alone'. *Felix Farley's Bristol Journal* seemed to prefer Jews to Catholics, and favoured Jews becoming councillors while drawing the line at the judiciary: '... to suffer a Jew to be a judge would in a Christian court, be indeed a mockery of all religion. We may as well surrender at once *our natural religion* and let the SPIRIT OF LIBERALISM have its full play [emphasis added].'[170]

By the end of the long 18th century, the Jews had largely lost their pariah status, but had not yet been fully accepted by their adopted city. Later in the 19th century, this progress was to be threatened by a new wave of impoverished Jewish refugees.

Conclusion

From1688 up until the early 19th century, Bristol played host to an increasing number of visitors and immigrants from abroad as well as acting as a magnet to rural migrants from within England, Wales and Scotland.

The city had become more diverse and more prosperous as a result of engaging in the emerging global economy. In some respects trade acted as a solvent to intolerance and parochial ties, as it meant that people had to meet and do business with one another regardless of religious or national background. But the political and cultural apparatus of the city, as well as popular attitudes, was slower to keep pace with these changes. At the beginning of the period, prices of bread were still fixed by civic officials, 'strangers' could not lawfully open shops and the freedom of the individual to engage in foreign trade was limited by royal monopolies. Local power was still firmly vested in those propertied merchants in the city who were members of the Church of England. By the 1770s, the economic and social climate was beginning to change as the rising professional and manufacturing classes, many of them non-conformist Protestants, began to challenge the old merchant elite.

By the turn of the 19th century, Evangelical Christianity became increasingly respectable in the city, bringing with it a double-edged attitude towards Jews, Irish Catholics, Africans and the English poor: repudiating cruelty towards these groups but at the same

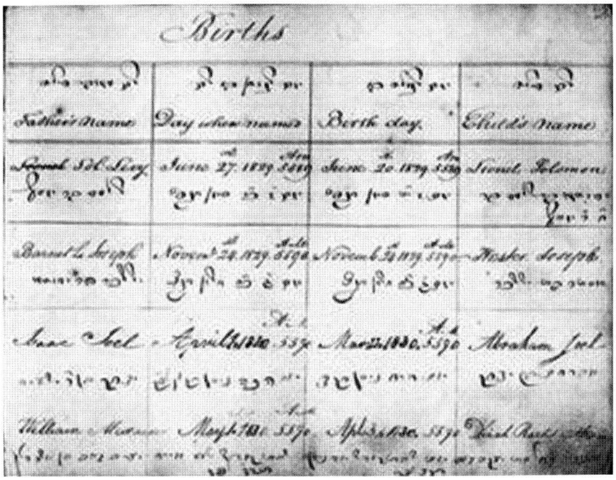
Births

Father's Name	Day when named	Birth day	Child's name

Figure 64 Extract from the register of births for the Temple Street synagogue for the year 1829 (years 5589 and 5590 in the Jewish calendar). The Jewish community kept records in Hebrew and English; among other things these related to circumcisions and gave details of Jews who were not members of the synagogue.

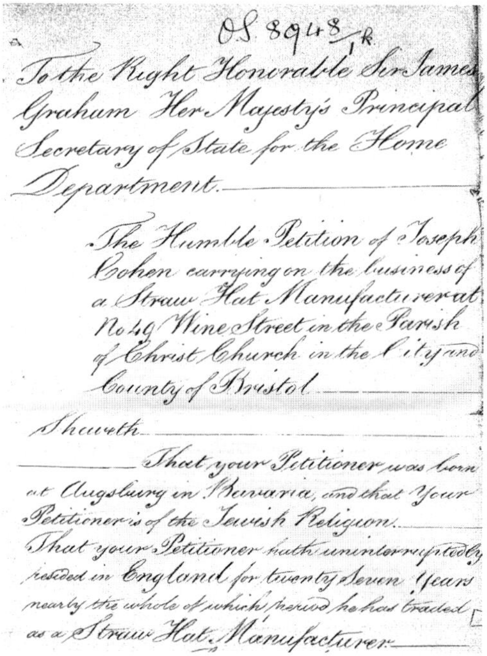

O.S. 8948/1R.

To the Right Honorable Sir James Graham Her Majesty's Principal Secretary of State for the Home Department.

The Humble Petition of Joseph Cohen carrying on the business of a Straw Hat Manufacturer at No 49 Wine Street in the Parish of Christ Church in the City and County of Bristol

Sheweth

That your Petitioner was born at Augsburg in Bavaria, and that your Petitioner is of the Jewish Religion.

That your Petitioner hath uninterruptedly resided in England for twenty seven Years nearly the whole of which period he has traded as a Straw Hat Manufacturer.

Figure 65 Petition of Moses Cohen for Naturalisation, 1844.

time seeking ultimately to convert and assimilate them to their own world view. The removal of restrictions on Protestant Dissenters and Catholics by 1829 left only the Jews and the property-less labouring classes (whatever their ethnic origins) outside the political fold. The early 1830s saw the push for change gather pace and the middling classes gain political power. Colonial slavery was abolished but at the same time economic dislocation at home and in the Caribbean, and a deepening sense of imperial destiny, resulted in a hardening of attitudes towards both the Irish and English poor at home and the 'aliens' from abroad. This will be explored in the next chapter.

Chapter 9 — Protestant Culture

Bristol was decisively reshaped in the Victorian era. The city's borders were extended and its population tripled in size from just over 120,000 in 1841 to over 339,000 in 1901. Political reform meant its elite included more and more members of the professional and manufacturing classes, many of whom had a more liberal outlook than the Anglican merchant princes of old. The progressive extension of the franchise gave, by the 1880s, political voice to a new constituency of male workers. Yet in some respects, Bristol became less dynamic than it had been a century before. No longer a premier port, it simply did not attract large numbers of immigrants from outside England. Mid-century Bristol owed nearly half its population to internal rural migration. By the 1870s, most of the city's growth was due to natural increase rather than to migration of any kind. Bristol's relative demographic stability and long-standing links with its rural hinterland gave the city the feel of a large village, and the reputation for being unfriendly to strangers.[171]

The panels which form the first part of this chapter offer an overview of mid-Victorian Bristol's migrants and immigrants, based on analysis of the 1851 Census. The chapter then moves on to examine the experience and reception of those immigrants who came from Germany, Scotland and Wales and who were, in the main, Protestants. Further consideration of non-Protestant immigrants is left to the next chapter. The Protestantism that so helped to forge the notion of British identity in the 18th century still held sway in the Victorian period. It was by then a less exclusively Anglican Protestantism, and one that more equally embraced non-conformist denominations. This shared religious culture profoundly shaped Bristol's civic self-image and, it will be argued, eased the integration of the German, Scottish and Welsh immigrants into Bristol society. The accommodation of those who did not fit so neatly into Bristol's Protestant fold will be dealt with in subsequent chapters.[172]

As we have seen for previous periods, class and religion appear to have been major factors in determining the pace of assimilation. The evidence indicates most 'respectable' Bristolians (that is, the skilled working and middle classes) still felt religion to be the only glue that could successfully bind together a city (and nation) otherwise divided by social class. Bristol was more religiously observant

The 1851 census

In 1851, nearly half of Bristol's 137,000 residents, some 45 per cent, are estimated to have come from outside the city boundaries. Nearly a third (30 per cent) of these newcomers were West Country people, from the bordering counties of Somerset (11.5 per cent), Gloucestershire (10 per cent), Devon (4.5 per cent) and the remaining 5 per cent from Wiltshire and Dorset. Unsurprisingly, the largest groups from outside England's borders were the Irish, Welsh and the Scots, in that order, as the diagram below shows. In sharp contrast to the more economically dynamic cities of Manchester, Glasgow or Liverpool, where Irish migrants made up between 13 to 22 per cent of the inhabitants, Bristol's Irish-born population comprised just 3.4 per cent, the Welsh just 3.2 per cent and the Scots a minuscule 0.5 per cent. Even allowing for under-reporting, the numbers of Irish, Welsh and Scots immigrants are surprisingly small, only about 9,000 people out of the total population. By 1891, the Irish, still Bristol's largest foreign-born group, had declined in both absolute and relative terms to a mere 1.1 per cent of the population.

But compared with that, the proportion of truly foreign-born immigrants was even smaller. Just over 700 seem to have been born outside the United Kingdom in 1851. The largest category of foreign-born residents was the Germans, who will be discussed below.

The 1851 census can help us to identify parishes inhabited by first-generation immigrants. It tells us their place of birth and enables us to see that, as in the late 20th century, Bristol immigrants were often more widely distributed throughout the city than popularly supposed. Some may have been noticeably clustered in certain streets or within certain parishes, but there was no large ghetto of foreign-born migrants. What the Census of 1851 cannot tell us is whether ethnically mixed households or second-generation immigrant families identified themselves as being part of an ethnically distinct neighbourhood. Take, for example, Lawford's Gate, an area in what had been the parish of Sts Philip and Jacob. According to the 1851 Census, there were few Irish-born there. Yet the priest of the adjacent new church of St Nicholas de Tolentino saw his 1,000 Catholic parishioners as largely Irish. This implies that he included second- and possibly third-generation Irish in his estimate and that Lawford's Gate had a bigger 'Irish neighbourhood' than the Census figures alone would indicate.

Temple parish still retained its reputation as a 'Jewish' area, but this was hardly warranted by the actual numbers of foreign-born and native Jews there in 1851, with just over one per cent of the parish's residents coming from Central or Eastern Europe, not all of whom would have been Jews. Its association with Jews derives from the fact that the

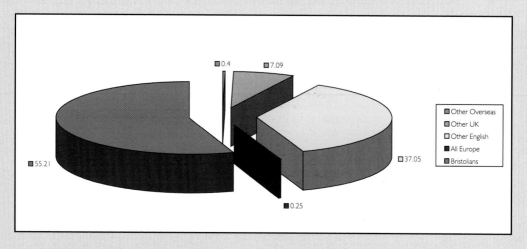

Bristol's population in 1851 (actual and factored).

city's synagogue at the Old Weavers' Hall was in that parish, joined briefly in 1825 by a short-lived rival synagogue. By 1842 the surviving synagogue had been moved from the Old Weavers' Hall to the larger Quakers' Meeting House in the same parish. Temple still remained an initial point of arrival for most of the city's new Jewish migrants. Only 260 Jews were formally affiliated to the synagogue, and the more affluent had already moved into St Paul's and a few even to Clifton. Not all Jews were synagogue members and some must have assimilated into the wider population through inter-marriage. Some, like the Huguenots before them, anglicised their names, thereby obscuring their ethnic origins.

Outside the 'old city' of Bristol, new suburbs like Bedminster were rapidly springing into existence. Still partly rural, the composition of its largely working-class population is noticeably less ethnically diverse than both Bristol as a whole and the quayside parishes of the old city. But even a parish-by-parish breakdown of immigrant populations can be misleading. Such findings for a parish can mask concentrations of ethnic groups in particular streets and courts. Thus we have some virtually all-Irish streets and courts in St Stephen's parish, yet very few Irish in other locations within that same parish. The 1851 census is therefore a valuable but limited tool. We cannot assume that everyone surveyed told the enumerators the truth or that its questions adequately probed the working lives of the population (for example, it under-reports female employment). Nevertheless, it affords us a valuable snapshot of where people were born, where in the city they settled, with whom they lived and, to some extent, what they did for a living.

References
Swift, 12; Meller, 19-33; Large (1985), 38. Samuel, 70-72; Adler, Schlesinger & Emanuel, 10-11. Pooley, 73; BRO, 38460 R 3(a).

Peter Newley

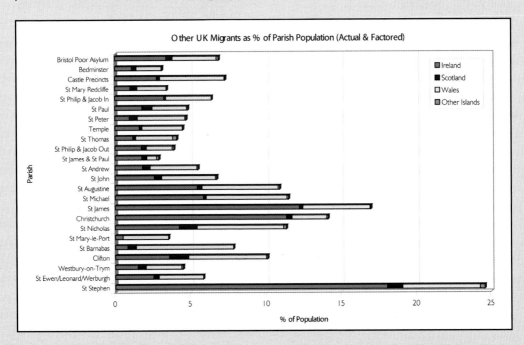

UK migrants in Bristol, 1851.

than most other large cities in the period. According to the three major religious surveys made in Bristol, around a third of the city's residents attended Sunday services between 1841 and 1881. This period saw the establishment in Bristol of 'a common religious subculture' uniting Anglican and non-conformist Protestants, which included not only the city's elite but also a relatively broad section of the middle and working classes. The influence of this subculture extended beyond those who attended church services, for it informed the values of schools and civic celebrations. Bristol's Anglican and non-conformist camps both had strong missionary traditions, which focused with increasing professionalism on the unconverted both at home and abroad. It is unsurprising then that, of all the minority groups described above, the small community of relatively well-educated, largely Protestant, Germans were perhaps the most easily absorbed.[173]

THE GERMANS

Figure 66 Portrait of George Müller (1805–1898). The son of a Prussian excise collector, Müller led a rather privileged and dissolute life before a religious experience in 1825 made him a strict evangelical devoted to a life of charitable works. He came to England in 1829 and moved to Bristol in 1831 where he lived for the rest of his life. He was naturalised as a British subject in 1861.

A small but unknown number of Germans came as refugees, in flight from Napoleon's advance into Prussia. Cultured and anti-revolutionary, they were welcomed to Britain. Johann Samuel Müller was one such individual. A passionate geologist, Johann had married into the well-established James family of Bedminster, Bristol, changed his name to John Miller and, aside from fathering one of Bristol's most famous artists (William James Müller, 1779–1830), he became curator and guiding light of the Bristol Institution which formed the basis of Bristol's present-day Museum.[174]

Another German refugee was Conrad Finzel. A farmer's son from a village near Frankfurt, he fled being drafted into Napoleon's army, reportedly escaping in an open boat. He eventually made his way to England and after learning the sugar business in London, arrived in Bristol, where he was first employed as a sugar boiler. By the 1830s, Conrad had founded Finzel's refinery, which was a major feature in the early Victorian townscape. In his lifetime it employed over 200 men and needed some 50-60 large ships to supply it with sugar. By 1873 it employed some 700 workmen.[175]

Conrad Finzel and his friend and contemporary George Frederick Müller, no relation to Johann, both made a profound mark on Victorian Bristol; the first as a self-made industrialist, the second as an Evangelical missionary and philanthropist. Politically Tory, Finzel was decidedly a liberal Dissenter in religion. He was elected as one of Bristol's alderman and urged to become mayor, but declined, styling himself as more of a businessman than a politician. He retained his German identity to the end of his life,

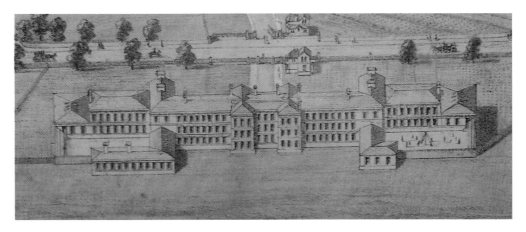

Figure 67 A late 19th-century depiction of Müller's Ashley Down orphanage. Building began in 1855, inspired by an 18th-century German orphanage which Müller had visited in Halle as a student. Charles Dickens, who visited the Bristol orphanage, expressed some concern about the regime there. By 1886 it had housed well over 7,000 orphans. After decades of use as a technical college, much of it has now been developed as private flats.[178]

when he returned to his native village. His much admired religious fervour intensified after a fire burned down his original factory on Bristol's Countership, the road between Temple Street and the Avon. Afterwards he was said to have decided to donate one third of his profits to charity, much of which was thought to have financed the orphanage started by George Frederick Müller. Müller (1805–1898) was a German evangelical from Kroppenstaedt. Originally involved in a mission to evangelise the Jews, he eventually came to Bristol via London and Exeter looking for a new outlet for his religious energies. Both men were lauded in the press and other publications. Muller, who had a major road named after him, was, we are told, especially 'loved and respected', 'by every citizen of his adopted city'.[176]

The reception of these two immigrants exemplifies the contradictory strand within the Protestant 'self-help' culture of mid-Victorian Bristol. Its doctrine of universal salvation under Christ logically welcomed all, regardless of race, colour or national origin. But such acceptance was, in practice, predicated on class, and in any case came at the price of religious and cultural conformity.

Finzel and Müller were part of a tiny population of just over a hundred or so Germans of Protestant or Catholic backgrounds listed in the 1851 census. Most of them were, given their apparently largely north German origins, probably Protestants, and some two thirds were men. Of those whose occupations we know, at least 14 worked in the sugar industry, where Conrad Finzel was to make his mark. Another 11 were musicians, including Bertram Mark, whom the Census described as director of the Bristol Conservatoire of Music. Most of the other musicians seem to have been young men in their twenties and may have comprised one or more of the German bands which were reportedly such a 'ubiquitous' feature of pre-war England. Others fit the familiar stereotypes of language

Figure 68 Müller's house (now demolished), Paul Street, Kingsdown, an early Georgian suburb of Bristol which continues to this day to have a reputation for attracting professional residents with an interest in social reform.

teachers, 'impoverished' governesses, and watch and clock makers, with a further sprinkling of servants and seamen.[177]

However, the grouping of between 137 and 156 Germans as listed in the 1851 census needs further refinement since analysis of their names and occupations suggests that perhaps as many as a third were actually Jews, who were regarded as ethnically as well as religiously distinct from the rest of the German population. Despite sharing a common language with their gentile compatriots, it is likely that most German Jews identified more closely with the small Jewish community already established in the city. By the same token, most of the 42 Poles and four Russians seem likely to have been Ashkenazi Jews, as were a few of those listed as London-born migrants.

THE SCOTS

A few Scots had made Bristol their home in the 18th century. While a small number were vagrants, arousing concerns that they would have to be repatriated at ratepayers' expense, others found prosperity and acceptance. Archibald and Alexander Robe, whose family had property in St Michael's parish, served as masters of Bristol slave ships. Also involved in the Atlantic trade were more prominent merchants such as Charles Bell, George Inglis, Robert Gordon and Evan Baillie of Dochfour, some of whom held political office in the city (Gordon was mayor of Bristol in 1775 and Evan Baillie MP in the early 1800s). Perhaps the city's most celebrated immigrant was John Loudon McAdam, a 'Scotch country gentleman' who arrived in the early 1800s to 'macadamise' the roads of Bristol, and the nation. Another innovator was John McArthur who arrived in 1839, and bought out a local iron-monger's business which he developed into a major national firm which still exists today.[179]

These prosperous Bristol Scots seem to have retained properties and family links with Scotland, and there is mention of a Bristol Scots Association established in 1835. Most, too, seem to have been members of the Episcopal Church, the Scottish counterpart to the Church of England. This follows the pattern we saw for Welsh and Irish migrants coming to Bristol in the previous century, whose elite also tended to belong to Episcopal denominations. By 1851 wealthy Scots were still in evidence in Bristol, along with their Scottish servants, especially in the suburb of Clifton. York Crescent, the Mall and the aptly named Caledonia Place were well stocked with genteel Scots, some of whom had retired from the East or West Indies. There were five Scottish households in the Mall alone, and nine in York Crescent. They ranged from landed proprietors like William Ritchie, his family and Scottish born servant Mary Aitchere, to Jemima Leith and her son George (a baronet) and George Buchan, their manservant.

In contrast to these elite families and their servants, there were Scottish sailors and labourers to be found down the hill in Hotwells along with their Irish and English co-workers. Horfield Barracks, built after the Bristol riots of 1831 just to the north of the city, hosted more than 250 Scottish soldiers and dependants by 1851. Most were single young soldiers, listed as labourers, textile workers and printers and the like. Some of their non-commissioned officers lived there with their families, and a number of their wives worked as servants or dressmakers. Of the 11 Scotsmen resident in Temple parish in 1851, no fewer than four were professional or skilled men, including a physician, a printer and two railway clerks.[180]

Figure 69 The pub sign of *The Scotchman and his Pack* pub in St Michael's Hill, Bristol.

Figure 70 Bristol's provincial press was much enriched by the activities of a Glaswegian-born businessman, Peter Stewart Macliver, who first issued Bristol's *Western Daily Press* in 1858 and added the *Bristol Evening News* in 1877. By the end of our period there was still a well-heeled Scots constituency within the city. The Bristol Caledonian Society had 99 members as late as 1905, who celebrated Burns' Night with toasts and speeches that affirmed both their distinctive identity and their loyalty to Bristol.[182]

A Bristol pub on St Michael's Hill, *The Scotchman and his Pack*, still testifies to the presence of another cohort of Scots, the Scottish drapers or 'Scots duffers' as they were colloquially called. A number of these drapers seem to have been from the south of Scotland, displaced by the intensive commercialisation of farming there. For example, James Borthwick (1815-1851), the son of a rural blacksmith, travelled from Kirkpatrick Juxta in Dumfriesshire around the 1840s to practise in Bristol as a draper. Also described as 'credit tailors', the drapers had 'extensive business out in the surrounding villages to which they travelled by pony and cart to collect … payments'. They would travel 'around their allotted or chosen area with a pack containing samples, and measured customers for suits in the selected material, which were then made up and delivered'. The 1851 census shows that 30 such drapers were concentrated largely in three streets (Newfoundland Road, Pritchard Street and Wilson Street) in what is now the St Paul's area of the city. It was possibly for this constituency that the city's first Scottish Presbyterian chapel was opened in 1859 in St James's Parade.[181]

THE WELSH

It is immediately apparent from the 1851 census that Welsh-born Bristolians were better represented amongst the middle class than were the Irish. Irish-born people could be found in virtually every parish of Bristol, but as the figure on page 105 shows, almost two thirds lived in less well off areas, namely the 18 parishes and one extra-parochial district called Castle Precinct (the site of present-day Castle Park) that made up the old city. The Irish were most densely settled in certain streets near the Quayside (in the parishes of St Stephen, St James, St Augustine and St Nicholas). Just over a thousand Irish-born people lived in the large parish of St James, constituting some 12 per cent of the total population there. The proportion of Irish-born people was even higher in the smaller quayside parish of St Stephen, where around 18 per cent came from Ireland.

The Welsh, by contrast, were more evenly spread throughout the city. More seem to have been concentrated in affluent Clifton than in any other parish, where most worked as servants and domestic staff. Though three Welsh-language chapels were located in or near the Castle precincts, a bustling district of small manufactories, the precinct as a whole did not have a large concentration of Welsh, just 4.2 per cent compared to the city average of 3.14 per cent. Even on Castle Green, a main street bordering one of the Welsh chapels, only around 5 per cent of its residents were Welsh.

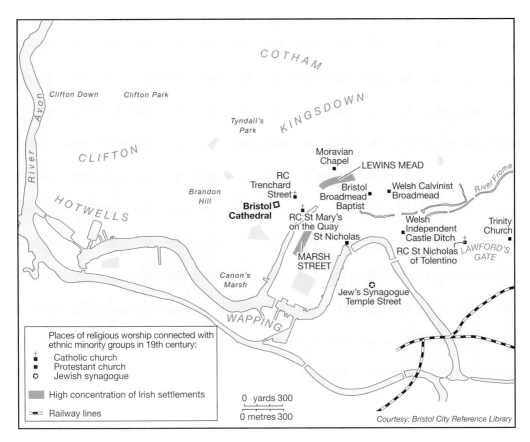

Figure 71 Places of
worship connected with
ethnic minority groups,
*c.*1850.

That is not to say there were no Welsh amongst the destitute
or unskilled; indeed, most Welsh worked as servants, mariners
or labourers of varying sorts and there are references to one
poor woman whose occupation was listed as an envelope folder.
Contrary to what one would expect, there are few Welsh coal miners listed in 1851 and, except for a visiting engine driver, no Welsh
railwaymen. On the other hand the Welsh appear as shipwrights,
cabinetmakers, engineers and plumbers to a greater extent than
do their Irish counterparts. A significant minority of Welsh men
in Bristol were skilled artisans, such as the Welsh coachmaker
resident in St Andrew's and a Welsh-born master carpenter,
Thomas Morris, whose three Welsh-born nephews also worked as
carpenters.

There is also a sprinkling of Welsh ministers and others whose
occupations denote some degree of education, if not prosperity,
such as Joseph Stock, a 'teacher of the Blind', Martha Brown, a
school teacher, and Robert Evans, a Glamorganshire accountant.
While a few Welsh figured among the usual array of hawkers
and labourers in Temple parish, hardly any Welsh hawkers were

Black Victorians

We do not know much about the presence of Black people in Victorian Bristol. The fragmentary evidence we do have is largely due to the increased availability of internet sources and to the efforts of family historians. It seems a small number of black people were residents in the city whilst others came as visiting entertainers or political campaigners. Most immigrants had direct or indirect links with slavery, although a few owed their presence to Bristol's palm oil trade with West Africa and the activities of Christian missionaries. While numerically insignificant, the existence of Black Bristolians is important to document, as they bridge the gap between what we know about the black presence in the city when it was a slaving port and when it was the destination of 20th-century migrants from the Caribbean and West Africa.

We know Manga Bell, son of 'native chief' King Bell (probably the King Bell of the Douala people) from what is now the Cameroon, was baptised at St Mary Redliffe in 1868 and may have been the same Prince Alexandre Manga Bell who was a student in Bristol in 1889.

Otherwise there seem to have been very few Black people in the city by the second half of the century. Although a number of visiting African-American anti-slavery campaigners such as Frederick Douglass and Ellen Crafts were lionised when they visited the city and Black entertainers were also accorded a genuinely warm, if patronising, welcome, those who lived permanently in Bristol seem generally to have been poor and of low status. George Barnard Freeman Elias was a young boy who lived in Granville Place in Clifton before his premature death in 1857. He was probably of African-American origin as he was listed as 'a redeemed Slave' in the burial records. There is a passing reference to Black West Indian workers in an Old Market sugar house in the city and better documented evidence of the presence of an elderly Black man who worked as a road sweeper on the Downs by the century's end.

One exception was Henry Parker, an escapee from American slavery, who made his way to Bristol some time in the 1850s, married a White Irish woman in Bristol and became a lay preacher at the Hook's Mill Church (now the Ivy Church),

A Black road sweeper in the late 19th century.

and father to a number of children whose descendants still live in the city.

By the time James Peters (1879-1954) came to live in Bristol in the late 1890s, colonialist attitudes about White supremacy were widespread. Born in Salford, Peters had worked in a circus as a bareback rider with his West Indian father, until the latter was mauled to death by a lion. After a spell in an orphanage, Peters moved to Bristol when he was 19 and played rugby, first for the Dings team (the Dings being near the area around Lawford's Gate where many Irish and other poor workers lived), and later for Knowle in South Bristol until 1902, at which point he moved to Plymouth. Although Peters went on to become the first person of African descent to play rugby for England, he faced a good deal of racism during his career and his time in Bristol was no exception. Some White members of the city's Knowle club reportedly resigned in protest at his inclusion in the team. It is telling that he was known in his day as James 'Darkie' Peters.

Manga Bell: BRO, FCP/St MR/R/2(d)4 frame 4, 24/11/68.
Elias: BRO, P/St A/R/5/c, 1857, 204, no 1629.

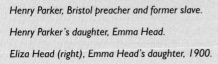

Henry Parker, Bristol preacher and former slave.

Henry Parker's daughter, Emma Head.

Eliza Head (right), Emma Head's daughter, 1900.

found elsewhere in the city. Old Market Street, which was over-whelmingly English with very few Irish, did have a slightly larger number of Welsh residents. These included not only the inmates of an almshouse (admission to which denoted their respectable character along with their decayed circumstances), and a married couple who both worked as tailors, but also Nathaniel Llewellin, an engineer from Dowlais.

Those Welsh women whose occupations were listed appeared largely as servants. A significant proportion of them appear to have worked in the wealthier areas such as Clifton, where a few are listed as cooks, ladies' maids and nurses. There seem to have been more Welsh female migrants than men, whereas the reverse seems to be true for the Irish. This preponderance of females, along with the sobering influence of Welsh non-conformity, arguably helped the Welsh prosper more in a modernising urban economy.

By 1849 Lavars's Map lists three specifically Welsh chapels: Methodist, Baptist and Independent. The Evangelical revivals that periodically swept over Victorian and Edwardian cities like Bristol saw the Welsh playing a prominent role. Non-conformity seems to have acted as a means of assimilating many Bristol Welsh into the mainstream, both through intermarriage with local non-conformists and through the sharing of a common religious culture. This trend intensified after 1870 when compul-sory education was split on sectarian lines between Anglican and non-conformist Protestants. By then the trade union and the co-operative movements attracted both Welsh and English members.[183]

Yet a distinctively Welsh presence in the city was also preserved throughout this period. In 1869 the Cambrian Society was estab-lished, replacing the by-then defunct Society of Ancient Britons. Claiming that some 20,000 of Bristol's 160,000 inhabitants were 'welchmen' [sic], its ostensible aims were to revive St David's Day and celebrate Welsh achievement in Bristol.[184]

Entrepreneurial and professional Welsh were active in the Victorian city. The Broad Plain Soap Works, a major mid-Victorian factory in Bristol (later to become part of Lever Brothers), had been founded in 1825 by the Unitarian Thomas Thomas of Carmarthenshire. After merging with the old Bristol firm of Fripp and Co. in the 1840s, it was eventually taken over in 1856 by Thomas Thomas's sons. If the Thomases exemplify business success and civic philanthropy, Dr David Davies, the city's energetic medical officer of health, personified professional achievement, as he did much to set the agenda for sanitary reform in the city.[185]

By the late 19th century, new steamship services and railway links made Bristol's Welsh Back less relevant to the city's expand-ing trade with South Wales. Even without a detailed analysis of

Figure 72 Thomas's Soap in Bristol was founded by a Camarthenshire-born entrepreneur in 1825. The company's claim that it was founded in the 1740s probably refers to the older Bristol firm Fripp and Co. with which it merged in the 1840s.

the 1901 census, it is clear that the expansion of mines and other industries in South Wales drew migrants from the Bristol area to work there. At the same time, the expansion of Bristol's service sector drew some Welsh to Bristol, as suggested by a cluster of drapers' assistants living in cramped lodgings in Portland Square and City Road in St Paul's parish.[186]

The developing image of the Welsh as Liberal in politics and Celtic by 'race' and culture was consolidated by the early 20th century. An extraordinary editorial in the *Western Daily Press* in 1903 shows just how the Welsh were then regarded, at least by the paper's editor. Seen in racialised terms as more loyal than the Irish,

We in Bristol have much to thank Wales for ... some of the most respected names in recent Bristol history are of Welsh origin. 'I hear they want more Welshmen' would not be a bad advertisement for Bristol to circulate.

and more 'emotional, excitable [and] impressionable' than the English, the editorial celebrates the Welsh for their 'Celtic' love of education, literature and art. The Welsh, in short, were represented as complementing the admirable but rather stolid virtues of a largely 'Anglo-Saxon' Bristol.[187]

Of course, so far as the middle classes were concerned, the most acceptable Welsh were the prosperous and anglicised ones. The strongly Methodist ethos of Bristol's labour movement probably helped to ease tensions between Bristol's English and Welsh workers, especially during times of unemployment.

CONCLUSION

Bristol's press, manufacturing industry and charitable institutions were enriched and enlivened by the contributions of those who, although they came from beyond England's borders, found they shared a common religious culture with that of their adopted city. Religion aside, the integration of immigrants and their families was also determined by their class and by individuals' survival strategies. However, when religious and ethnic or class differences combined, the process of mutual accommodation between the majority and minority populations could sometimes be more fraught, as we shall see in the next chapter.

Chapter 10

Catholics and Jews, 1837–1910

Any hostility shown towards immigrants in this period was not solely a product of Bristol's traditional insularity, but must also be understood in the context of more general worries about public health and poverty, crime and corruption, social injustice and modernisation. For although prosperity did increase in this period, its distribution was at best uneven. In these circumstances minority communities could serve as scapegoats for wider anxieties.

THE IRISH

There was a small minority of Bristol Irishmen and women of property, many of whom were resident in Clifton, but their English- and Scottish-sounding names suggest they were almost exclusively Protestant. Certainly, the few Irish-born officials or professionals listed in the 1851 census have Protestant names. One possible exception is John Lysaght (1832–c.1895) of Cork, who in 1857 founded a galvanised bucket manufactory in Temple Backs, which came to have an international market. But Robert Price Strachan, who co-founded the engineering firm of Strachan and

Figure 73 Lysaght's factory in Silverthorne Lane, St Philip's. Established in 1857, these specially designed offices were erected in 1891. Still known as St Vincent's Works, the building, noted for its beautiful interior tiles by Doulton and Co., has recently been renovated and is again in commercial use.

Henshaw in 1879, seems almost certainly to have been Protestant as was Joseph Leech who founded one of the city's major Victorian newspapers, the Conservative *Bristol Times*.[188]

The lives of these favoured few were far distant from those of the mass of their fellow countrymen and women living in Bristol. Few Bristol Irish 'tradesmen' were masters, and employment at the casual end of these trades was precarious at best. Shoemakers like Richard Flyn and Jeremiah Fitzgibbon, identifiable as Catholic by their names, lived in a crowded lane off Marsh Street and would have been typical of 'wretched' Irish cobblers in Bristol.[189]

In fact, the overwhelming majority of Irish migrants were unskilled, partly reflecting the fact that many Bristol Irish came from Cork, one of the poorest and least developed parts of Ireland. It would have been more difficult, too, for Catholics to get apprenticeships with established firms even if they had the aspirations to do so. Sampling of the 1881 census suggests this pattern continued for some time. Although many worked as labourers and street porters on the Quayside, it seems few Irish worked on the Bristol Docks and this may be related to tensions between Irish and English workers in the Bristol area reported in 1842. Others worked as labourers on various civil engineering and construction projects and the enumerators' reports attest to groups of 'agricultural labourers' in the city.[190]

The occupations of Irish women are harder to discern as part-time employment, which is what many women with children would have sought, is not recorded in the census. Nearly a third of those who did have an occupation listed in 1851 were servants. Another third were evenly divided between, on the one hand, laundry work and charring and on the other tailoresses and milliners. Some, like the poor widow Mary Dunn and her two young children living in the Castle Precinct, worked as Lucifer Match sellers, while Anne Palmer of Bedminster was a cobbler. Millinery jobs were so notoriously seasonal and ill-paid that they were popularly associated with occasional prostitution. Certainly, Lewin's Mead in St Stephens parish (Figure 71), which was seen as an Irish area, was characterised as a red-light district. Irish women continued to find employment as laundry workers, dressmakers and servants as the middle classes further expanded over the century. As the service sector expanded, so new opportunities arose for Irish women. The 1881 census shows Irish-born women employed as hospital nurses and shop assistants, two trends that would continue into the 20th century. By this time the expansion of Catholic schools had afforded a few jobs as schoolteachers, and there was a significant coterie of Irishwomen (most probably Anglo-Irish) of independent means living in Clifton.[191]

'Low Irish' in Bristol

The Irish had the reputation of being the roughest of Bristol's rough working class. How much that reputation was the product of anti-Irish stereotyping is a moot point. Certainly the Irish were under-represented in the crime figures, but it is equally true that there were areas where no policeman would dare arrest an Irishman. The 1851 census reveals an Irish 'micro-ghetto' on Marsh Street and neighbouring courts such as Little Tower Court, where Irish-born migrants constituted between 80 and 90 per cent of the inhabitants.

The Irish poor were under-represented in the workhouse and most of Bristol's charities, but that might be in part because the charities were geared to Protestant clients or because two of the workhouses were in areas of low Irish settlement. The magistrate who discharged two Irishmen arrested at the Horsefair, remarking, 'Irish again. They are never satisfied unless they are fighting', may have been prejudiced, but even sympathetic Irish priests in Bristol saw drink as a particular problem for the Irish.[192]

Although the Bristol public raised a generous sum for Irish famine relief in 1847, the prospect of an increased flow of largely poor, unskilled and Catholic Irish migrants into the city drew a less enthusiastic response. Mainly from Cork and Waterford, some used Bristol merely as a temporary staging post for America, but others stayed. Their arrival coincided with heightened anxiety about papal influence, public health and Chartism. However, Bristol did not experience anti-Irish riots as did Stockport in the immediate post-famine period.[193]

The famous Bristol reformer, Mary Carpenter, though she recognised the existence of the 'respectable Irish' poor, saw Bristol's low 'Anglo-Irish', which for her included the Bristol-born children of rural Irish migrants, as the 'most uncivilised' of the city's lower orders. She despaired at how the whole of Marsh and Host Streets would miss school to go hop-picking. She hated what she saw as the dirtiness, the illiteracy, 'the wild behaviour' of the young boys of 'low Anglo Irish' background whom she had welcomed into her ragged school before they were, she said, warned off by the Catholic priest. The 'low Anglo Irish', combined, she said, 'the vices of the English in a large commercial town with their natural … character in a very undesirable way', a comment which reveals the anxiety which middle-class commentators had about both the foreign and indigenous poor.[194]

But while the depth of poverty in Ireland had inured many Irish people to terrible conditions, squalor was not an Irish preserve. Bristol was then the nation's third most unhealthy city. Streets in Clifton as well as in the most deprived courts of the ancient

Figure 74 Extract from
report to the General
Board of Health on
the sewage, drainage,
supply of water and
sanitary conditions of
the inhabitants of Bristol,
1850.

151. In *Marsh-street*, in St. Stephens, is *Sugar-loaf-court*, narrow, badly paved, very close ; water very bad and not useable. This street has been lately much improved by the erection of ware-houses. It is to be regretted, in the improvements in some of the dwelling-houses, that better attention has not been paid to elevating the floors, and to drainage. Recently, during the cholera, 64 people were ejected out of one house by the Corporation of the Poor, and the house was closed. The people here are chiefly low Irish. The cholera was severe.

city fairly heaved with sewage and vermin. In 1845 the sanitary reformer William Budd stated: 'The lower classes of people in Bristol are … very dirty in their habits.'[195]

Such people might also be resentful of having to compete for jobs and dwellings with in-comers even more desperate than themselves. The Irish did not monopolise the most fetid courts and alleyways, but they were over-represented in them.

Reformers might characterise the filthy hovels where Irish families and lodgers lived as uniformly chaotic, but a closer look at census enumerators' reports indicates the existence of support networks of family, workmates or friends. As so many migrants were from Cork, it seems likely that many knew each other from their home village or town. Contrary to expectations perhaps, the Bristol Irish generally lived in relatively small family groups of husband, wife and two or three children. A relative, sometimes an elderly dependent, might share the dwelling along with paying lodgers, some of whom might well be English. By the same token, Irish lodgers often lived in English or Welsh households. One of the most striking findings of the 1851 census is the high propor-tion of marriages which occurred between Irish-born men and Bristol-born English and Welsh women, although to what extent this intermarriage occurred within the confines of the Catholic Church is not clear. The Bristol-born trade union leader Ben Tillett was himself the offspring of Irish and English parents. How many of their offspring retained a sense of their Irish identity remains to be seen, although it is clear that the children of Irish families in the inner city did do so.[196]

Irish and Catholic

The belief system that the Irish poor brought with them to Bristol was a particular blend of peasant folkways and orthodox Catholic theology. Mrs Linaker, who came to Bristol in the 1840s, was represented as typical of many Irish poor in retaining a lifelong belief in 'Banshees and Phookas and fairies'. Her claims to a Bristol journalist that she 'once heard the cry or coine of a Banshee' and that a leprechaun was 'a little ould man as cute [canny] as a fox and as hard to grasp hold of …' were reported in 1887, when a revival of interest in Gaelic traditions began to change English attitudes to Irish culture. Before then, such beliefs, along with the public processions and distinctive sacramental vestments popularly associated with Irish religious practice, were more likely to offend Protestant sensibilities in this most Protestant of cities. The habited order of the Sisters of Mercy, who regularly walked together through the streets of St Paul's to St Mary's on the Quay, fuelled rumours of sexual misconduct in the cloisters, a favourite Victorian theme.[197]

Irish communal life was also condemned on the grounds of intemperance. The Hibernian Benefit Society based at the *Moon Inn*, Broad Street, and operative from at least the 1830s, may have promoted self-help but it was notorious in the local press for its drunken processions. The St Patrick's Day parades were similarly characterised as an excuse for drunken affrays, as were Irish wakes, which had the added association of heathenism.[198]

But the view of the Irish as heathenish and lawless was the perspective of the unsympathetic outsider. When begrimed Irish workers finished their Saturday night shift at the Canon's Marsh Gasworks, they did not always go straight home to sleep. Instead, some put on their best suits brought to them by their children at 6 a.m. the following morning, so they could 'march along the quay-side to the special early Sunday morning mass at St Mary's'. Although Bristol's Catholic priests fretted constantly about erratic church attendance amongst the Irish poor, the mass was clearly a source of comfort for many and served as a way of affirming their identity.[199]

The establishment of the (Catholic) Clifton Diocese in 1850 alarmed many Bristol Protestants, occasioning the burning of 'a rude effigy of the cardinal archbishop of Westminster on [Bristol's] Brandon-hill'. The diocese provided an institutional framework for assisting the poorest Catholics, usually new Irish migrants and, in the sixty years that followed, its efforts to support the Irish poor earned grudging regard from the established authorities. The diocese's activities can also be seen as an effort to retain the religious loyalties of the Irish in the face of the competing diversions of Irish nationalism, secularism, and the aggressively proselytising efforts of Protestant groups.[200]

One such group began to set up Irish schools in the city at a time when it was estimated that only around 20 per cent of the thousand Irish children needing education were receiving any. In response, a Catholic Poor School Committee was established in 1843. In the absence of government funding, building schools depended on the pennies donated 'by the poor sons of Erin' and

The Bristol Italians

Italians had long visited Bristol as traders and sailors, and by the 18th century professional singers and musicians came to perform in the city. Sometime in the 1800s, a small number of largely impoverished Italians, some from the mountainous regions of Northern Italy (mainly around Tuscany), made their way to England on foot. A few seem to have come to Bristol earning a living as street musicians and street traders with an increasing number from Southern Italy by the century's end.

The Italians did not figure significantly in the 1851 census. Only two dozen or so were listed in Bristol, six of whom worked as 'figure makers', sculpting plaster-of-Paris models. Their distinctive traditional costumes made a vivid impression on the locals, as this illustration of Bristol's cathedral choirmaster dating from later in the century demonstrates.

The 1881 census specifies Neapolitans amongst those from Italy, such as the musician Cosimo Jack, his two daughters and four other musicians who were listed as dwelling in Silver Street, St James parish, in the Broadmead area, and other Italian and German musicians lived on that same street. Erico Diciccio of nearby Montague Street was one of those Italians who came as a marble mason, producing memorials for Bristol's cemeteries, a tradition that would last into the 21st century.

References
TNA, RG/11/274, 22-23, /12/1963, 2; Gilbert, 261; Medaglia, 74-75; Bottignolo, Winstone, 66.

Detail of organ grinder from St James's Fair painting by Samuel Colman (1824).

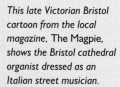

This late Victorian Bristol cartoon from the local magazine, The Magpie, shows the Bristol cathedral organist dressed as an Italian street musician.

Col. 1 No. of Schedule	2 ROAD, STREET, &c., and No. or NAME of HOUSE	3 4 5 HOUSES	6 NAME and Surname of each Person	7 RELATION to Head of Family	8 CON-DITION as to Marriage	9 10 AGE last Birthday of Males/Females	11 PROFESSION or OCCUPATION	12 Employer	13 Employed	14 Neither Employer nor Employed	15 WHERE BORN	16 (1) Deaf-and-Dumb (2) Blind (3) Lunatic, Imbecile or Idiot
9	4 Lr Montague St	1	Josepha Capallo	Head	M	30	Musician Street			X	Italy	
			Marianne J. do	Wife	M	28					do	
10	do	1	Louige Baulachilde	Head	S	14	Musician			X	do	
11		1	Antonia Vallendo	Head	M	40	do				do	
12		1	Acostino Resa	Head	M	24	do			X	do	
			Marie do	Wife	M						do	
			Carmello do	Daur		6					Bristol St James	
13		1	Angelo Q Funda	Head	M	40	Musician			X	Italy	
			Curello do	Wife	M	24					do	
			Theresa do	Daur							Bristol	
			Acostino Qualiola	Father-Law	M	64	Musician			X	Italy	
14		1	Francesco Funda	Head	M	31	do			X	do	
			Lena do	Wife	M	19					do	
			Elizabeth do	Daur		8					Derby	
			Felumina do	Daur		6					Bristol	
			Vincentia do	Daur		3					do	
			Antonietta do	Son		9mo					do	
15		1	Rosa Capallo	Head	M	24	Musician			X	Italy	
			Carlo do	Son		2					Bristol	
			Marianne do	Daur		9mo					do	
			Germane do	Serv	S	28	General Servant		X		Italy	
16	1 John's Court do	1 2	William Wood	Head	M	42	Hotel Porter		X		Somerset Taunton	
			Willie H do	Son	S	18	Green Grocers Assistant		X		do do	
			Sydney do	Son	S	15	Waiter		X		do do	
			Annie do	Daur	S	13	Scholar				Bristol St Pauls	
17	2 do do	1 2	Thomas Wright	Head	M	23	Printer Compositor				do St James	
			Ethel do	Wife	M	25					do St Augustines	

Total of Houses and of Tenements with less than Five Rooms	2	0	Total of Males and Females	14	13	1891 RG12 1963

Italian musicians registered as resident in a street in St James' parish (from the Enumerator's Report for the 1891 census).

Italian women street traders with donkey in Wellington Park, Bristol 1895. Probably from Southern Italy, their regional dress distinguished them from their English counterparts.

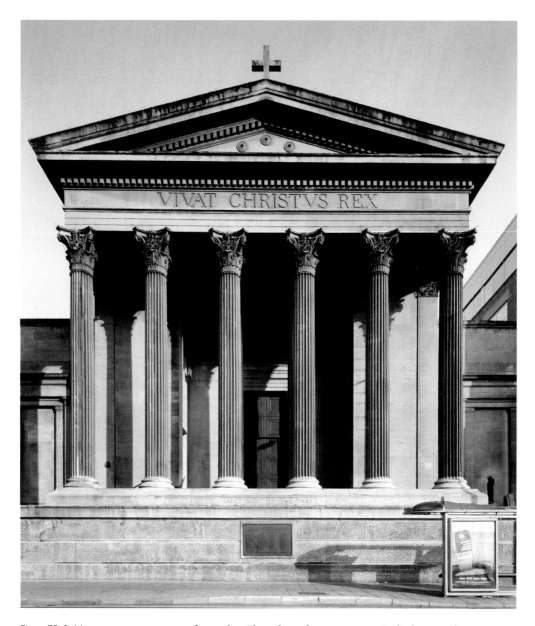

Figure 75 St Mary-on-the-Quay church (2007). Designed in 1839 by the staunchly anti-Catholic Irvingites, a short-lived Protestant sect, this building was purchased by the Roman Catholics in 1843.

support from the Church and aristocratic Catholics, such as the Earl and Countess of Shrewsbury. One of these schools was St Mary-on-the-Quay in St Stephen's parish. The teachers and student monitors were largely Irish, and English priests and Irish teachers and monitors organised treats for the children (temperance teas), and tried, with varying degrees of conviction, to lure their parishioners away from drink. The parish was relatively wealthy, and the school was supported by local Catholic charities and individuals.[201]

The relatively small numbers of Irish distinguish the city's experience from Liverpool, Stockport or Preston. But the accommodation of the Bristol Irish was destabilised by the volatile relationship between Ireland and England, as famine gave way to Fenianism (the revolutionary brand of Irish nationalism), and the issue of Home Rule split both Britain and Bristol.

BRISTOL'S JEWS

'Civic and religious Liberty' rather than 'Home Rule' was the rallying cry for Bristol's organised Jewish community, that is, Jews who were members of a synagogue. It was this community who pressed for an end to the formal exclusion of Jews from political life. To make the point, Joseph Frankel Alexander stood for office in the newly reformed Council in 1835 and was duly defeated, but support for ending Jewish disabilities was growing. The following year the *Bristol Mercury* warmly supported the prospect of Jewish councillors serving the city and by 1841 reported that most of Bristol's Town Council did so, too.[202]

Indeed Joseph Alexander's brother Abraham Alexander was elected as a Bristol councillor in 1844, the year before Parliament formally lifted restrictions on Jews holding municipal office. In 1850 their brother, William Wolfe, was elected alderman by the councillors. The Alexander brothers were the leading representatives of Bristol's Jewish community, but were not typical of it. Their family were wealthy shipping agents and commission brokers, and they served as consuls for various European states. Their politics were Conservative, their lifestyle genteel and cultured, and their addresses as fashionable as the yellow barouche that William Wolfe Alexander of Berkeley Square drove around Clifton. They endeavoured to be part of city affairs in a variety of ways. Abraham Alexander as a young man had joined the Bristol Volunteers (the local militia formed in response to the threat of French invasion). In his prime, he was a driving force behind the successful 'Free Port Association' which aimed to put the increasingly uncompetitive city docks under Corporation ownership. Both brothers donated to municipal as well as Jewish charities. Their wealth and civic conduct earned them respect, although their continued adherence to Judaism remained a marker of difference. The lavish Bristol wedding of W.W. Alexander's daughter to a London Jew was reported in the Bristol and Somerset press as 'an impressive and picturesque rite.'[203]

The third Jewish member of the Bristol Corporation in this period was Joseph Abraham, the son of an optician. Himself a wine

Figure 76 The Platnauer Brothers' clockmakers' shop, Victoria Street, Bristol (2007). The Platnauers came to England around 1838 from Wreschen, a Polish town then under Prussian rule. Variously described as clockmakers and jewellers, the family traded in Temple from the 1840s and occupied this shop from around 1870 to the 1940s.

merchant, he was elected to the Council in 1861 where he became active in pushing for public health reform. He briefly served as Bristol's first Jewish Mayor in 1865 but fell ill that same year. John Braham (d. 1865), a leading optician and freemason, whose patent 'pantoscopic' spectacles were exhibited at the Great Exhibition in 1851, was treasurer of Bristol's synagogue.[204]

By contrast Abraham Levy (1799-1855), who was also active in the congregation, was not quite so genteel. He lived not in Clifton, but in the altogether less fashionable area of Temple. He was a boot and shoe manufacturer of modest success who bequeathed a silver watch and the proceeds of his manufactory to his nephew, with equal shares to his nieces when they reached thirty or when they got married 'in the Jewish faith.' His intimates were people like the pawnbroker Joel Solomon, mainstays of their synagogue, but unlikely to be welcome in Bristol's politer circles.[205]

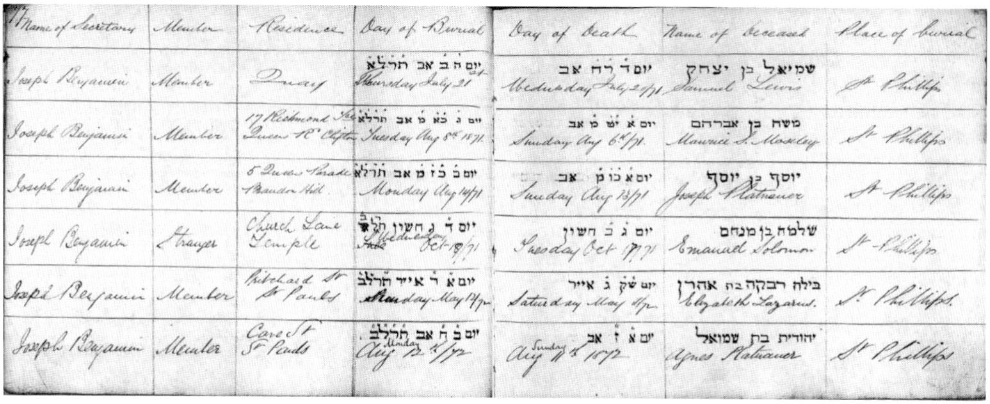

Name of Secretary	Member	Residence	Day of Burial	Day of Death	Name of Deceased	Place of burial
Joseph Benjamin	Member	Quay	יום ה׳ ב׳ אב תרל״א Thursday July 21	יום ד׳ ר״ח אב Wednesday July 20/71	שמיאל בן יצחק Samuel Lewis	St Phillips
Joseph Benjamin	Member	17 Richmond Ter Queens Rd Clifton	יום ג׳ כ״א מ״א תרל״א Tuesday Aug 8th 1871	יום א׳ י״ט מ״א Sunday Aug 6th/71	משה בן אברהם Maurice S. Moseley	St Phillips
Joseph Benjamin	Member	5 Queens Parade Brandon Hill	יום ב׳ כ״ז מ״א תרל״א Monday Aug 14/71	יום א׳ כ״ו מ״א Sunday Aug 13/71	יוסף בן יוסף Joseph Platnauer	St Phillips
Joseph Benjamin	Stranger	Church Lane Temple	יום ד׳ ג׳ חשון תרל״ב Wednesday Oct 18/71	יום ג׳ ב׳ חשון Tuesday Oct 17/71	שלמה בן מנחם Emanuel Solomon	St Phillips
Joseph Benjamin	Member	Pritchard St St Pauls	יום א׳ ד׳ אייר תרל״ב Monday May 14/72	יום ש״ק ג׳ אייר Saturday May [illegible]/72	בילה רבקה בת אהרן Elizabeth Lazarus.	St Phillips.
Joseph Benjamin	Member	Cave St St Pauls	יום ב׳ ח׳ אב תרל״ב Monday Aug 12th/72	יום א׳ ז׳ אב Sunday Aug 11th 1872	יהודית בת שמואל Agnes Platnauer	St Phillips

Figure 77 Platnauer burial register record, Bristol Hebrew Congregation.

Generally the community, which was a highly mobile one, became in the middle years of the 19th century more prosperous and increasingly accepted by the wider community. With the expansion of retailing in the city, more made the transition from peddlers and pawnbrokers to shopkeepers.

Politically, too, things were improving. The end to the exclusion of Jews from Parliament, supported by a majority of Bristol councillors since 1857, was effected in 1858. The 1867 Reform Act would have given a number of the community's poorer men the vote. The organised community was anxious to ensure that any poor Jews would not be a charge on the rates or a shame to Anglo-Jewry. In Bristol, local branches of The Board of Guardians of British Jews provided material relief, whilst the Bristol Hebrew Ladies Benevolent Society, first formed in 1845, increasingly aimed 'less [at] almsgiving than [at] an improvement by systematic superintendence' of the 'moral religious and social condition' of the resident Jewish Poor.[206]

By 1871, after the old synagogue made way for a road-widening scheme, the community was able to erect its first purpose-built synagogue, in the airier climes of Park Row. Synagogue presidents, like the Prussian-born Henry Simmons, were active within both the Jewish and the wider civic communities. A member of the Jewish Board of Guardians and a mason, Simmons worked closely with the vicar of St James's on charitable causes and instituted the synagogue's annual service to raise funds for Bristol's hospitals. The small Bristol congregation was dependent both on its Gentile neighbours and on a far-flung web of extended family and friends. Its members were highly mobile, enjoying close links with London and other centres of Jewish population, and were increasingly accepted by Bristol's Christian majority.[207]

Figure 78 The Park Row
synagogue of the Bristol
Hebrew congregation
was built in 1871 on
the site previously
occupied by a Catholic
religious order, the Little
Sisters of the Poor. The
London architect was
a descendant of Isaac
Collish (aka Zvi Hirsch
Kalisch), who had served
as the community's rabbi
(minister) from 1765
to 1785. Expenditure
on the building left the
congregation in debt for
over a decade.

Religious Tensions between Christians and Jews

Nevertheless, religious difference remained an impediment to
full acceptance. Throughout the century, conversionist societies
in the city still targeted Jews, such as the two brothers whose
conversion in 1845 was widely trumpeted. The tone of such stories
was usually triumphalist, scornfully noting the hostile response
of the Jewish community to such conversions. Such was the case
when in 1858 a Bristol Jewish girl eloped with her Gentile partner,
subsequently marrying him in a Christian ceremony. The Jewish
family, devastated by what they saw as the betrayal of trust and the
loss of family continuity, were seen as repressing both true love
and the true faith, not to mention their child's individual rights.
This theme of the vengeful Jewish family and their converted
child, favoured by Victorian novelists, went back to the Middle
Ages. The letters page in the *Bristol Mercury* contained a rejoinder
from a member of the congregation that Jews were happy to act
together with other Bristolians on common social and charitable
causes but, as they did not proselytise, neither did they wish others
to proselytise them.[208]

Joseph Leech, the Protestant Irish proprietor of the *Bristol
Times and Mirror,* wrote two sketches about Jews in Bristol. In the
first, entitled 'A Tooth for a Tooth', Leech revisits the tale of the
medieval Bristol Jew who had his teeth extracted to force him to
pay the extortionate medieval tax levied on Jews. Leech invents a
romance between a poor young Jewish suitor and the daughter of
the wealthy Jew who lost his teeth. Leech portrays the father as a
grasping miser who wants a richer son-in-law. The suitor becomes,
anachronistically, a dentist, who wins over the father by skilfully
replacing his teeth with artificial ones, and gains both a wife and
a father-in-law who becomes his business partner. The intended
joke is on the flamboyance of Jewish advertising techniques, the
then current debate over 'Jew quacks' (as they were known in the
medical press) and the rise of Jews into what was then a lower-
middle-class occupation, dentistry. The punning title itself alludes
to the contrast often made in Victorian Christian religious literature between Christian mercy and unyielding 'Jewish justice', using
a biblical reference.[209]

In his second piece, part of his 'Church Ramblings' series,
Leech describes his visit to St Werburgh's where Joseph Wolffe, a
converted Jew, preaches to a nearly empty church:

> Though he were a thousand times a doctor of divinity, Wolff is
> still a thorough Jew. He has a Jew's feelings, a Jew's aspirations,
> and a Jew's patriotism. Though only a handful came out through

the driving sleet of the night to hear him, he could not resist
the opportunity of vaunting his own nation and rebuking their
Gentile presumption.[210]

Leech racialises Wolff and calls into question the patriotism
of all British Jews; for Leech also refers to Wolff's criticism of
the Liberal peace party of the time. Wolff is thus identified with
Benjamin Disraeli (Prime Minister and converted Jew), who in the
1870s was attacked by Liberals for taking too soft a line on Turkish
massacres of Bulgarian Christians. Disraeli's stance caused a wave
of anti-Jewish feeling or 'Judeophobia' in which British Jewry as
a whole were characterised as essentially alien and unpatriotic.
In response, Anglo-Jewish Associations were formed throughout
Britain to defend Jewish interests and Bristol's branch was established in 1878, with Henry Simmons and Samuel Platnauer as its
President and Vice-President.[211]

New Jews in Old Bristol

As the political climate became more polarised, new waves of
immigration from the 1880s changed the profile of England's
Jewish community. Eastern European Jews were fleeing restrictive
economic policies and anti-Jewish riots or pogroms. Those few
who came to Bristol were typically poorer and less 'Westernised'
than the largely German community already established in the city.
      Aaron Harris Vyernick arrived in England from Russia in 1896
with his pregnant wife Rachel and their three young children. After
three years, the family made their way to Bristol where Aaron
became naturalised and changed his name to Harrisberg. They set
up a small bakery business in Newfoundland Street where his wife
baked challa bread for her Jewish customers and harvest loaves for
her Christian ones. Henry Festenstein, naturalised in his thirties,
had left Russia to work as a 'general house furnisher' in Redcliffe,
where he Anglicised his name to 'Henry Denton'.[212]
      Some East European Jews became Bristol pawnbrokers, others
boot and shoe manufacturers. Raphael and Harris Goldberg lived
at 4 City Road with their 10 children, nine of whom were born
in Bristol. This is where Harris had his boot factory, which was
little more than his family dwelling. The 1901 census reveals that,
despite their priestly pedigree which conferred on them a special
religious status, the various Bristol Cohens (more than half of
whom were born in Russia) were employed in ordinary occupations. One was a baker, another (a youth of 14) was a boot maker,
a third Cohen was a cabinet maker and another a travelling linen
goods salesman.[213]

Figure 79 The birth certificate of Isaac Rosenberg shows the Bristol origins of this famous war poet. His parents had arrived in England three years before his birth from Kovno in Lithuania, then part of Imperial Russia. His father, Barnett, listed in the certificate as a 'hawker', had fled to avoid conscription into the Czar's army where Jews were notoriously badly treated.

One of the more impoverished families to settle in Bristol were the Rosenbergs, one of whom was the war poet Isaac Rosenberg. Isaac was born in 1888 near St Mary Redcliffe Church. His father worked at a series of jobs, including peddling, his wife did charring and took in laundry. The family left for the East End of London around 1900, but Isaac continued to visit his friend, the son of the Bristol rabbi, right up until 1914.[214]

Many of the new immigrants rejected the Anglicised synagogue and established their own, with a Russian *chazan* (cantor) and more emphasis on Hebrew. This Bridge Street congregation lasted for only three years and was united with Park Row after the latter provided more Hebrew education. The new arrivals

Figure 80 Sketch by Samuel Loxton of the Working Jewish Girls' Club, Portland Square, in the *Bristol Observer*, 1906.

Figure 81 Sketch of Cohen and Ballin's 'Fur Manufactory and Straw Hat Establishment' in Wine Street, taken from an undated plan of central Bristol. By the late 19th century a number of Bristol Jews were shopkeepers. Ballin and Cohen are common Jewish names and by then a disproportionate number of Jews worked as furriers in Germany, Poland and Russia after centuries of exclusion from this trade. The 'I. Cohen' identified here with the hat-making side of the business may well have been related to the Bavarian hat-maker Joseph Cohen, mentioned in chapter 8, who had settled in Bristol earlier in the century.

FUR MANUFACTORY & STRAW HAT ESTABLISHMENT,
49. WINE STREET, BRISTOL;

Fur Department Conducted by J. Ballin.
Straw & Tuscan Department by I. Cohen.

were also supported by a Jewish working men's club and a Jewish girls' club, organised by the ladies of the synagogue to teach 'hygiene, drill, cookery and dressmaking as well as Hebrew and the fundamentals of Jewish religion'. While Bristol Jews were increasingly accepted, there remained an undercurrent of resentment and distrust. Although some of this was religious in origin and had medieval roots, much of it was precipitated by very modern fears, namely about unemployment, mass immigration and 'racial deterioration'.[215]

Towards immigration restriction

Figure 82 This anti-alien cartoon in *The Bristol Magpie* of 1906 characterises all 'aliens' including the caricatured Jew as picking the pockets of a local ratepayer. This echoes the arguments of those favouring the 1905 Aliens Act that many aliens had criminal tendencies and would in any case be an economic burden on the nation.

By the 1880s concerns were growing nationally about the increased numbers of Jewish immigrants, and even the Anglo-Jewish elite was ambivalent, wanting to support them but worried that they would precipitate a backlash against Anglo-Jewry in general. Their fears of anti-Semitism were well-founded. The resurfacing of the blood libel accusation from an anonymous correspondent in the *Manchester Guardian* was noted with particular concern by the *Jewish Chronicle*. The East European Jews arrived just as the Great Depression (1873-1896) was causing high rates of unemployment, especially among unskilled manual workers. These impoverished Jews, often from depressed and under-developed villages, were blamed for de-skilling traditional trades, depressing wages, bringing in disease and increasing crime. Jewish intellectuals amongst them, many of them political refugees, were suspected of importing terrorism and subversive political doctrines such as socialism and anarchism. Disquiet was exacerbated by the growth of Social Darwinist theories, prompting worries about the 'dilution of the race' and notions that policies of 'racial purity' were the best way to effect social improvement.[216]

Bristol's small congregation was sensitive to the changing climate. Around this time members founded the Bristol branch of the Anglo-Jewish Association, established to counter anti-Semitism, and the Bristol Hebrew Literary and Debating Society. The latter involved both women and men (including newly arrived immigrants), and raised funds for the Jewish Guardians of the Poor. Among its founders was John G. Levy, who was also involved in founding the Bristol Parliamentary Debating Society, which had a number of Jewish members.[217]

Within Bristol, Levy tried in 1881 to persuade Bristol's mayor to call a public meeting to promote awareness about the plight of Russian Jews and to raise funds on their behalf. The mayor was politic enough to donate £2 2s. to the Anglo Jewish Society, but no public meeting seems to have been called. The Bristol Labour movement was ambivalent about Jewish migrants. There were protests in 1894 when H.H. Gore, a Christian Socialist, trade union activist and member of Bristol's School Board, refused to employ a young female teacher on the grounds that she was Jewish. Workers feared competition from non-unionised Jewish workers. Momentum gathered throughout the 1880s and 1890s for limiting alien immigration as the persecution of Jews by Czarist Russia intensified the flow of poor refugees westward.[218]

At a Bristol meeting in May 1905, Walter Long, the MP for Bristol South, spoke in favour of the new Aliens Bill that was to empower the Home Secretary to exclude 'undesirable and destitute aliens'. Soon after, Bristol's Jewish community expressed alarm about the Bill to the Conservative MP for Bristol West, Michael Hicks-Beech. In December that year the lord mayor was again approached by synagogue members to call a public meeting about the persecution of Jews in Russia: although he donated 10 guineas to the cause, he declined the request for a meeting.[219]

The congregation's renewed efforts must be seen in the light of national developments. In August 1905 a national movement, spearheaded by the Conservatives and largely opposed by the Liberals, secured the passing of the Aliens' Act, the country's first legislation to control immigration. Of all four Bristol MPs, only Charles Hobhouse, the Liberal member for Bristol East, spoke against the Act. More work is needed to gauge local reaction, but it seems to have been muted. Perhaps the small size and relative prosperity of the city's Jewish community meant 'alien' immigration was not perceived as directly threatening to Bristol.[220]

Chapter 11

Ethnic Diversity in the 20th Century

How can we bring to light the experiences of the main ethnic minority groups in 20th-century Bristol, and reveal the attitudes expressed towards them? Family histories, which are only just beginning to be traced and made public, are one way forward, but generally speaking the historian must explore the archives and undertake interviews. The sources ethnic minorities produce in this context are often rare and fragmentary and not always representative. Like the official accounts by statutory and voluntary agencies, such sources need to be read with caution. By the same token, chronicling the prevailing racial attitudes of the day is especially difficult given the political sensitivity and complexity of the subject. What follows, in the face of such challenges, is a preliminary survey intended to encourage more work on Bristol in this era.

At the beginning of the 20th century, few Bristol residents came from beyond the British Isles. Bristol did not experience the wave of violence against Black workers that swept through nine other British ports in 1919. In 1934, although a small fascist element, including the vicar of Hillfields Park, was on hand to welcome Sir Oswald Mosley, head of the British Union of Fascists and 500 of his 'blackshirts' to Bristol, and some 3,500 people came to hear him speak at the city's Colston Hall, nearly twice that number waited outside to protest against his presence.[221]

Class, not colour, was the social marker that mattered most to inter-war Bristolians. This remained true in the immediate post-war period as displaced Poles and other Continentals were accommodated in the city. But by the century's middle decades, as immigration from the New Commonwealth began to make a visible impact on the city, 'race' began to enter the national and civic vocabulary as an indicator of difference. From the 1960s successive laws were passed, which on the one hand sought to limit immigration on implicitly racial lines and on the other to outlaw racial discrimination in public life.

Throughout the 1980s and 1990s, the demographic landscape of the city, as of the nation at large, changed at an accelerated pace. The children and grandchildren of Caribbean and South Asian migrants were born Bristolian. There was also a growing constituency of people of 'mixed race' or 'dual heritage'. The continuing influx of newcomers meant that Bristol was becoming

Figure 83 Reuben St Clair, the son of Joseph St Clair, is pictured here with the rest of the St Barnabas rugby team which was located in the St Paul's district of Bristol in the 1930s.

more cosmopolitan. Newly arrived Kosovan, Kurdish, Iranian and Somali refugees made African-Caribbeans and South Asians seem like old hands in the city and generated new, more complex tensions which could not be reduced to those between Black and White. If 'immigrant' and 'race' had been the catchwords of the 1960s, 'asylum seeker' and 'ethnicity' came to prominence by the century's end.

Yet compared with London or other industrial cities, Bristol's ethnic minorities still constituted a small proportion of the city's total population. The 2001 census provides a statistical overview of people's 'ethnic background' — as opposed to their place of birth. According to these official figures, about eight per cent of Bristol residents (some 30,400 people out of a total population of 380,000) described themselves as from 'non-White ethnic minorities', including nearly 8,000 people of mixed backgrounds; this is in contrast with the 27 per cent of residents of Greater London and 29 per cent of Birmingham. Bristol's ethnic minority population rises to 12 per cent, or 45,600 individuals, if those claiming Irish or 'White other' descent are also included, compared with 40 per cent in Greater London and 34 per cent in Birmingham.[222]

Figure 84 Invitation for Bristol Cambrian Society's annual dinner.

BEFORE 1945

Our picture of ethnic diversity for the inter-war period is particularly sketchy and anecdotal, leaving plenty of scope for local and family historians to make a real contribution to the subject.

The Welsh and Irish communities were the largest and longest established of all non-English groups in Bristol, yet very little is known about their development in this period. The collapse of the Welsh coalfields in the 1920s caused an influx of Welsh poor, both female and male, whose welfare was in part attended to by well-heeled members of the city's Cambrian Society.[223]

The continuing Irish presence in the Lawford's Gate and Redfield areas of Bristol is indicated by the founding of St Patrick's Church, Redfield, in 1923, and by occasional references in the local press, but awaits further research. Some Irish families from central Bristol may have been relocated through 1930s slum clearance schemes to outlying council estates such as Knowle West.[224]

Figure 85 St Patrick's church, built in 1923, was established by Father William Dillon, who was also the priest at St Nicholas in Lawford's Gate. Now used as the parish hall, it was replaced by a new church building in the 1990s. The congregation is ethnically diverse, serving Poles and people from South East Asia, as well as English and Irish Catholics.

Figure 86 This racialist caricature of an anonymous Black 'bell boy' supposedly employed at a Bristol department store in the 1920s was typical of a certain strand of popular humour at the time.

Figure 87 Photograph of Joseph St Clair, an unlicensed dentist in Bristol in the 1920s.

Figure 88 Dixie Brown, a boxer in Bristol in the 1930s.

The estimated 120 or so Jewish families in the city were divided between the working-class Jews living mainly in St Paul's (then seen as a 'Jewish area'), who were largely engaged in shoemaking, tailoring and cabinet making, and wealthier business and professional people in Redland and Clifton. The Park Row synagogue still served as a focal point for a lively cultural life, with increasing attention given to raising funds for refugees from Nazi Germany.[225]

The small Italian community is less well-documented, but notably included the migrant Eugenio Verrecchia, who in 1925 founded Bristol's first ice cream parlour, the *Modern Café* in Coronation Road in Bedminster, which formed the basis of a prosperous ice-cream company in the post-war period.[226]

There were a few people of African-Caribbean, Chinese and South Asian descent who settled in Bristol before 1939, in addition to a small number of foreign students at Bristol University. Their rarity value alone seems to have afforded them some acceptance, but such acceptance was still suffused with racialist assumptions about people of colour.

Joseph St Clair, 'the Black Dentist' from Barbados, married a Bristol girl, Mabel Stallard, and made a relatively good living in inter-war Bristol. His daughter-in-law remembers as a child being told by her father to 'touch the black man for luck' when she first saw St Clair, who was plying his trade pulling teeth at a street market. St Clair did this work at county fairs and on the Bristol Bridge, and sold his own brand of toothpowder along with other herbal remedies based on Caribbean ingredients sent to him by his parents back home. Eventually banned from practising dentistry without a licence, he continued to prosper as a herbalist and he and his wife raised a family in the city.[227]

The St Lucian-born boxer, Antoine George Charles, aka 'Dixie' Brown, was a popular Bristol figure in the 1930s. Specifically banned on account of his colour from fighting for a British title, he 'failed to receive the official acclaim and recognition that his neat ring style warranted'. He married a Welsh girl and founded a close-knit family living first in Philadelphia Street and then in the slum clearance estate of Knowle West; 'When he went blind from a boxing accident, fellow Catholics and others clubbed together to send him to Lourdes for a cure just before the war'.[228]

At least five Chinese families were reportedly established in Bristol by around 1914, when Hong Pang (*c.*1890-1958) first arrived in Bristol. A ship's laundry worker, he came from Canton via America and Liverpool. Pang was befriended by a former Christian missionary in the Horfield district of the city, where he soon set up his own laundry business that supported succeeding generations of Bristol-born Pangs. His acceptance was eased by his

joining local Christian organisations, there being no place where he could practise his Buddhism.[229]

Aside from an unknown number of Indian seamen in Avonmouth, we only know of a handful of Indians resident in Bristol by the 1920s. Two were physicians, the better known of whom was Dr Sukhsagar Datta (1890-1967), a Bengali who graduated from the University of Bristol medical school in 1920 and went on to play a distinguished role in inter-war Bristol as a medical man and as an active member of the Bristol Labour party. Two others, known only as the Suri brothers, had a business of some sort at Kashmir House in fashionable Queen's Road.[230]

As a significant proportion of European migrants in this period were displaced by war, they will be discussed in more detail in Chapter 14, which deals with displaced people, asylum seekers and refugees.

RACE AND WAR

During the Second World War the presence of American GIs in Bristol elicited a raft of contradictory responses as far as race was concerned. Racial segregation still operated in the US armed forces, so with the cooperation of local Bristol authorities, White soldiers were billeted at Bristol's only public school, Clifton College, whilst 'negro' soldiers found themselves in Muller's orphanage in Ashley Down and, according to one source, in a tented camp in Patchway, north of the city. Kept under restrictive conditions aimed to minimise any fraternisation with local White women, Black soldiers were surprised and delighted to find that many Bristol women did not share the Jim Crow sentiments (favouring racial segregation) still prevalent back home. Bristol police reports complained pointedly about the impropriety of Black soldiers 'kissing and fondling' local girls in public houses.[231]

White GIs were enraged by these inter-racial romances and in July 1943 a race riot broke out in the city between hundreds of American GIs, leaving one Black GI dead and an undetermined number wounded. There was widespread sympathy for the Black troops but locals proved less supportive when Bristol girls gave birth to illegitimate 'brown babies'. Some of these doubly stigma-tised children reportedly went into care and their stories have yet to be told.[232]

POST 1945

Bristol had been extensively bombed during the war and awaited redevelopment, but city authorities had first to deal with incomers from war-torn Europe. By the 1950s, the collective experience of the Second World War and the institution of the Welfare State combined to erode the extremes of class difference within both the nation and Bristol itself. At the same time, the arrival of New Commonwealth migrants into Britain's cities began to draw public attention away from class and onto notions of 'colour' and race.[233]

From 1952 until the mid-1960s the main preoccupation was with the increasing number of New Commonwealth migrants coming from the British Caribbean. Their numbers were tiny, fewer than 150 in 1952, rising to 700 in 1957 and 2,000 in 1960, far fewer as a proportion of the population than in London or Birmingham. But the unease this caused was considerable.[234]

From the outset, the Home Office viewed this wave of immigration as a law and order issue. It was the police who were mainly and most publicly involved in monitoring the progress of these new arrivals. The worry all round was that young West Indian men without means, 'finding it increasingly difficult … to obtain employment' might 'well drift into committing some offence'. We can now gain a fuller appreciation of the difficulties these men encountered once in the city. Not only were most dogged by a lack of industrial and professional training, but they faced rejection from many in the majority community as well.[235]

Throughout the 1960s 'West Indians' of African descent out-numbered 'Asians' both nationally and in Bristol. Police surveys undertaken in the 1950s and the racial hostility evidenced in the violence at Notting Hill and Nottingham in 1958 and at Avonmouth in 1961 suggests that it was immigration from the Caribbean rather than the Indian sub-continent that was initially seen as a cause for concern.

The Police and Caribbean migrants

The reception given to Caribbean migrants by Bristol's various civic authorities during the 1950s and 1960s would set the scene for subsequent 'race relations' in the decades to come. Given their particularly high public profile in this regard, we shall focus here on the police service. The newly released records of the Bristol Constabulary allow us to document police attitudes towards the new migrants more extensively than is yet possible for other statutory service providers. The records include reports of various officers to their chief constable and to the Home Office and their relatively unguarded frankness affords new insights into why relations between the police and Caribbean migrants evolved in the way that they did. The language employed in these records on occasion recalls that of the 'colonialist' towards 'the native'. There are repeated complaints about the suspicion and hostility with which some West Indians regarded the police. One police sergeant, based at the Trinity Road division in Bristol, explained this hostility on the basis of his own war-time experience supervising 'native labour' in the Caribbean:

> Prior to his arrival in this country the coloured man has only known the white man as the boss in the sugar and banana plantation, and the factories. To them he is the ... symbol of tyrannical rule and exploitation ... Inevitably the coloured man has brought his personal feelings concerning the white man to this country ... [and]the policeman ... [is] the man who to them represents the symbol of white power rather than the law or the person to approach for help and advice. The consequence is that far from respecting the policeman, the coloured man tends to fear and distrust him.[236]

At first sight this seems a fair enough assessment, although the author later expresses his view that old colonial injustices (such as slavery and its aftermath) were being unduly exploited by anti-colonialist agitators. The report then distinguishes between the better-educated Jamaicans in Kingston and those from the more impoverished parishes of Westmoreland and St Thomas (who, as it turned out, made up the majority of the city's Caribbean population). These rural poor are branded by the sergeant as morally inferior and described in a generally contemptuous tone.

Most strikingly, his report also asserts that most Whites despised 'the coloured man' because of his 'association with prostitution and drugs ... the white man has come to look upon the coloured with a similar distrust and contempt owing to the immoral code of life which exists amongst the native population in which prostitution and drug trafficking is rife.'

There is no doubt that a small minority of West Indian men were profiting from prostitution. However the terms in which the police expressed their concern about it, and the practices they followed to combat it, indicate deeper prejudices at play. For a start, they assert that prostitution was 'practically unknown in Bristol' before their arrival, which was hardly the case.[237]

Police attitudes here need to be understood in historical context. Inter-racial liaisons, long a fraught topic in Britain, were particularly so in Bristol, given its long connection with the slave plantations of

Figure 91 This cartoon from the *Bristol Evening Post*, in 1956, links 'Rock and Roll' music to the experience of enslaved Africans. But the accompanying text betrayed an anxiety about what it saw as the 'primitive' rhythms of the New Rock and Roll: 'Today, we are faced with a type of music that reaches deep down into the ancient savagery of the African forests, and its rhythmic and insistent throb recalls the primaeval urges of ju-ju and devil worship'. The implication was to link the notion of dangerously violent and sexualised behaviour with Black music and thus to Black people more generally.

the Caribbean. Surviving prejudices about vengeful and sexually rapacious black men can be traced right back to local press coverage of slave revolts in the 18th century and to the Morant Bay and other colonial uprisings in the 19th and early 20th centuries. A wider acceptance of co-habitation in the Caribbean at a time when it was not considered respectable in Britain also contributed to the way West Indian family relationships in Britain were misunderstood.[238]

Just as striking is the inconsistency these police reports demonstrate when 'analysing' the 'coloured' population. Repeatedly acknowledging the majority of West Indian migrants to be law-abiding, these same reports increasingly conflate the whole of that community with a 'hustler' minority whose exploits were luridly featured in the local press. One superintendent stated that 'the coloured population [was] more prone to commit offences of this nature than the white', as if this were a natural inclination. Another generalised about the children of these immigrants, 'many of whom are born out of wedlock' as 'lack[ing] the parental control normally associated with English homes'. Such children, he continued, are therefore 'suspected of associating with prostitutes and pimps', a suspicion justified in his eyes, given the actions of their parents who 'usually provide the accommodation so vitally necessary for prostitutes', and who have 'in some cases been convicted for living on … the immoral earnings of such women'. Such families did exist, but they were hardly, as his language seems to imply, typical of the community as a whole.[239]

This stereotyping was perhaps rooted in negative assumptions about West Indian masculinity, and a definite failure by the police in this period to acknowledge the racial discrimination migrants suffered in Bristol. Bristol's constabulary was then completely united in its opposition to a law banning racial discrimination in public places, such as dance halls, reasoning that it would increase disorder if the White man felt the 'coloured man was foisted upon him'. When 'coloured parties' in the St Paul's area did cause noise late in the night, police zeal for raiding them was seen by some of the immigrants, who had very few places where they could safely congregate, as misplaced or even malicious.[240]

Their concerns were not taken seriously. A senior officer characterised the 'West Indians' in Bristol as 'gregarious by nature and prone to a very strong insistence for the smallest right to which they think they are entitled … many of them, who are obdurate and unintelligent, press [and] … their demands to the utmost limits'.[241]

In 1961 the Bristol police came under increasing pressure from the Home Office after complaints about their own 'colour prejudice' and discriminatory behaviour. A Bristol conference was called at the Home Office's behest, attended by a British West Indian commission and '60 coloured men and women' from Bristol, Gloucester and Swindon. A statement from the chief constable (who did not attend) instructed the audience on their duty to be law abiding 'whatever colour they may be' and curtly dismissed the very idea that colour prejudice existed in Bristol's Police Service as a 'figment of imagination': 'I want you to know it is a myth … and I hope that we shall hear no more of it.'[242]

In the 1950s and 1960s the police were not free from racial prejudice and the discrimination they consequently practised affected Black people at a variety of levels. As one liberal police officer later recalled:

> … my Sergeant used to tell me years ago, you see a Black man in a car, you know, you stop him because he won't have any insurance and you could guarantee that he didn't, but when you look at it the man would say, well I tried and insurance companies won't insure us. They won't take bookings for holiday, they won't take deposits unless we pay cash and things like that, you know, all sorts of little things that you or I take for granted …[243]

Their own records suggest that Bristol police in this period appeared to be uncritical of their own approach and doggedly resistant to reforming the complaints procedures or prioritising community liaison. They were at best insensitive to the impact which racial discrimination had on the lives of immigrants and were generally hostile to the idea of outlawing it. Some change in the 1960s seems to have come after Home Office pressure, but it was largely superficial. Like their colleagues in the Metropolitan Police, the Bristol constabulary in this period failed to provide the good governance that might have reassured the law-abiding majority and avoided alienating the young.[244]

1962–1980

Other groups also came in to Bristol in this period besides the 'West Indians'. Increased numbers of Irish men arrived to work on the M32 motorway and other construction projects, and Irish women continued to come to the city to work as nursing assistants, teachers, cleaners and midwives. By the mid-1960s, the shortage of manual labour also saw South Italians/Sicilians joining the small coterie of former prisoners of war and pre-war immigrants.[245]

There was also a growing contingent of the Hong Kong and the Malaysian Chinese and people from the New Territories. By 1966 there were 10 Chinese restaurants in the city. As we shall see, the 2,000 or so Indian and Pakistani residents kept a relatively low profile in the city, at least until 1972, when the small but much publicised influx of Ugandan Asians drew public attention to the increasing South Asian population. Foreign students were a growing and continuous presence, and an African Students' Circle at Bristol University Union was established in this period.

The 'Voluntary Liaison Committee' was established in 1967 to promote good relations between ethnic minority groups and the wider community under the guidance of the National Committee for Commonwealth Immigrants. Variously known as The Community Relations Council (1971), the Bristol Council for Racial Equality (1978) and the Bristol Racial Equality Council (1991), it served the city for nearly forty years until its demise in 2005. It was the only civic forum in the city open to both Bristol Council, local trade union, business and church members and to representatives from all ethnic minority group organisations. It evolved from a largely paternalistic and White-dominated organisation under the control of the city council to one which, by the 1970s included on its books representatives from a wide range of grass-roots minority organisations. How truly representative it was of these groups remains a matter of some debate. The attendance of some of the representatives was at times patchy, and the existence of salaried officers laid the organisation open to criticism for being part of a self-serving 'race relations industry', which was variously

Figure 92 Mary Perkins née Williams. She came to Bristol in 1948 from a small farm in Tipperary and worked as a nursing assistant in Manor Park and later Glenside Hospital in Bristol.

Fig 93 Roy Wan Loi Wong, born in 1935 in a village in the New Territories of Hong Kong, reportedly employed a number of his former fellow villagers in the restaurant trade in Bristol and provided communal leadership within that community.

condemned for being either too complacent or too critical of the political status quo.[246]

Nevertheless, throughout its life the Bristol Racial Equality Council demonstrated a consistent interest in the problems encountered by the city's ethnic minority groups and an enduring interest in their achievements. As such its records are an invaluable source of evidence for the concerns of the various minority communities, and for their changing status within the city.[247]

The 1960s had seen 'race' increasingly figure in public debate. In 1963, the nation's first black-led boycott against a company openly practising a colour bar was organised in Bristol, and this will be discussed in the next chapter. By 1967, a branch of the far-right National Front was established in the city and the following year the extensive coverage given to Enoch Powell's notorious 'Rivers of Blood' speech reportedly caused much anxiety amongst local minority groups. The Community Relations Council, as it was then known, tried to implement the Race Relations Act passed that same year, which outlawed racial discrimination in employment. To this end it reported on its casework regarding instances of alleged racial discrimination in the city's hospitals, hotels and other institutions, but lamented the very limited success it had in addressing them. It expressed consternation, too, about the Commonwealth Immigrants Act of that same year which restricted immigration to the UK in favour of those with 'patrial ties' with the United Kingdom (that is, mainly White New Commonwealth residents from Canada and Australia).[248]

Figure 94 Children of 16 different nationalities at St Nicholas of Tolentino School, Lawfords Gate, Bristol, *c.*1960s.

THE 1970s

The decade opened with increasing layoffs in Rolls Royce and
British Aerospace and mounting opposition to immigration.
The feeling of 'depression and apathy' reported amongst the
immigrant community in Bristol was no doubt deepened by the
Conservatives' Immigration Act of 1971. This Act, which came
into effect in 1973, consolidated the priority established in 1968
given to those who had a parent or grandparent born in the UK
and required a work permit from those without patrial status,
most of whom came from such New Commonwealth countries as
Jamaica, India and Pakistan.[249]

By the mid-1970s the warden of a community centre near
St Paul's offered his own assessment of relationships between
Blacks (by which he meant mainly Caribbeans of African descent)
and Whites in a racially mixed area:

> … [T]here is a great deal of half conscious 'twilight' racialism,
> which stands firmly in the way of solid links being forged
> between the various communities. The whites of St Werburgh's
> make up a host community which has seen a gradual influx of
> immigrants into its ranks over the years. Many local whites feel
> threatened by this. They feel 'swamped' by outsiders. They may
> also feel hostility to strange life styles and envy too, though this
> latter is usually based on ludicrous fantasies such as: 'they get all
> their money from Social Security', or 'they all live off prostitutes'
> etc. etc. Such attitudes often co-exist with superficially good face
> to face relationships with immigrants. Many of the local West
> Indians sense the unease of the whites and are rather 'touchy' in
> the sense that any conflict with whites is very quickly interpreted
> as racialism.[250]

Figure 95 Bristol school
children visit Concorde,
the iconic symbol of
Bristolian achievement.

By this time, Asian immigrants were beginning to attract public attention. Widespread consternation was expressed in Totterdown at the prospect of some 50 to 100 Ugandan Asian families being relocated there (there were fewer than 600 East African Asians in Bristol throughout the decade). Like St Paul's to the north, which was being gutted by the construction of the M32 motorway, this once picturesque Victorian neighbourhood had been severely blighted by road development, but its decline was popularly blamed on 'the coloureds', a term then commonly applied to people of both African-Caribbean and South Asian origin.[251]

Irish workers on Bristol's motorways, along with more permanent Irish residents in the city, also encountered more hostility during this period, especially when an IRA bomb exploded in Park Street in 1974. In other ways, too, 1974 did not bode well for community relations: the oil crisis further undermined economic confidence and unemployment rose. In that year, local television coverage of the St Paul's area gave an open platform for the expression of racist views, and two of the 90 candidates the National Front put up in the General Elections of October 1974 were in Bristol. Between them they received fewer than 2,000 votes, but this figure belies their wider influence. By 1977, the macho skinhead culture, which had earlier admired Jamaican reggae and rude-boys but indulged in 'Paki and queer bashing', had been successfuly targeted by the extreme right. As one former skinhead and National Front member in Bristol recalled, a section of the Bristol Rovers football fans: '... had become a bastion of right-wing politics. Rigid arm salutes were a common sight and NF, British Movement and Column 88 badges were de rigeur. The black [African-Caribbean] kids who had followed Rovers in the early seventies had, understandably, disappeared from the terraces ...'[252]

That same year church leaders in Bristol were expressing concern at the large number of National Front candidates then standing for election in the Avon county elections, denouncing them for whipping up hysteria against immigrant communities at local meetings. Organised resistance to racism did occur in the city, mainly through a collaboration of left-wing campaigning groups such as the Anti-Nazi League and Rock Against Racism. The latter was spearheaded by the Socialist Workers' Party, the left-leaning Bristol Trades Council, and by some local churches and charities as well as through the work of the Community Relations Council. Left-wing anti-racism was a largely White affair, although most left-wing anti-racist activists felt uncomfortable with the traditionalism and religiosity of many African-Caribbeans and Asians.[253]

The role of local government

Local government, which could have taken a leadership role in assuaging these tensions, had been split by the creation of Avon County Council in 1974. This took over some of the functions of the Bristol City Council. In particular, Avon (which unlike Bristol was under Conservative control) took over responsibility for local schools. If the records of the Community Relations Council are any indication, Avon initially displayed a marked lack of interest in the educational concerns of minority parents and pupils. Certainly Avon did not seem particularly proactive in its first few years, despite the continuing representations about the growing alienation of young African-Caribbean people made to them by activists such as Vera Pitt and Owen Henry. But more research is needed to see if the Labour-held Bristol City Council had been any more responsive to the needs of this constituency in the preceding period.[254]

The passing of the Race Relations Act in 1976 appeared to provide a more robust legislative framework for bringing charges of racial discrimination, although remarkably few cases seem to have been successfully prosecuted under Avon's stewardship. Home Office money (known as 'Section 11 money') was made available for helping New Commonwealth pupils with language skills, but it was alleged that some Section 11 money had been siphoned off into general school budgets by a number of head teachers. After a good deal of lobbying, a multi-cultural education unit was established in 1977, but there was little immediate increase in the small number from ethnic minorities employed as teachers. Avon continued to be charged with failing to provide an effective education for its ethnic minority (mainly Caribbean) children. In fact, White working-class children were also under-achieving in Bristol's schools, but ethnic minority children faced additional difficulties, which will be detailed in the following chapter.[255]

'BRISTOL YESTERDAY, BRIXTON TODAY': BRISTOL'S ETHNIC RELATIONS IN THE 1980s

The distribution of immigrant groups had begun to change by the end of the decade. Although the Caribbean community was still the largest after the Welsh and the Irish, some 5,000 people of South Asian origin now lived in the city (overwhelmingly Indians and Pakistanis), mainly concentrated in South and East Bristol (Lawrence Hill, Totterdown, Eastville, St George and Ashley wards), but also resident to the north, in middle-class Bishopston and working-class Southmead.

Immigration was a key issue in the 1979 General Election, with both parties taking the line that good race relations were dependent on limiting the numbers of immigrants coming into the country. Margaret Thatcher's harder stance helped to ensure her victory. The popularity of the new government made many in the city's ethnic minority population, especially those from the Caribbean and from the Indian sub-continent, feel very much under siege. Talk of a new Immigration Bill set the tone and instances of harassment of Black, Asian and mixed race people on Bristol's estates, although as yet officially unrecognised by the Housing Department, were on the increase. At the same time, mental health problems among alienated African-Caribbean youth and children of mixed race were beginning to come to light.

Despite their many differences, the sense of being beleaguered in a hostile political environment did foster some sense of solidarity between representatives of the Caribbean and South Asian groups on the Community Relations Council, although the Council seems to have been careful to distance itself from the more militant pronouncements made by some African-Caribbean activists on law and order issues.

In April 1980, a police raid on the *Black and White Café* in St Paul's for illegal drinking unexpectedly escalated into a major violent incident involving Black and White youths and the burning of a bank, a post office and widespread looting. The so-called St Paul's riot, or uprising as some in St Paul's preferred to call it, came as a profound shock to the city and the nation at large. Copycat violence also occurred in the deprived but mainly White housing estate of Southmead soon afterwards.[256]

The growing mood of militancy amongst the city's Black groups did impact on central government's consciousness. The Commons Home Affairs Select Committee came to Bristol for its first sitting and the Home Secretary of the day (William Whitelaw) sat down with both local authorities (Bristol and Avon) and with local Black people to discuss matters. The group became a focus for further policy developments that ensured a number of training schemes, and community facilities were subsequently provided or upgraded in the city.[258]

Local authorities, too, began slowly to respond. At last racial discrimination was formally recognised as a serious matter by the Education Authority. There was an initial honeymoon period between the police and St Paul's residents after 1980, during which more constables were put on the beat in the area, some of whom, like Derek Lane, forged good relations with the community. But it is not clear if such police were marginalised within the force, as they had been in 1980 when neither the community-liaison officer nor

Figure 96 A group self-
portrait of some St Paul's
'rioters', 1980. Although
it was not strictly a race
riot, local community
groups in St Paul's
were clear that racial
discrimination, especially
in education, employment
and housing, was at the
root of the violence.[257]

the home-beat officer for the area seemed to have been informed
about the impending raid on the *Black and White Café*. Significantly
perhaps, Lord Scarman's recommendation to dismiss police found
to have acted in a racist manner seems to have been ignored.[259]

Race relations in early 1980s Bristol, described as a 'slumbering
volcano', became increasingly politicised. This politicisation was
reflected in the language used. 'Multi-culturalism', earlier celebrated
as an alternative to 'assimilationism', was now criticised as a diver-
sion from explicitly anti-racist approaches. Equal opportunities
policies were now called for and 'ethnic monitoring' had begun to
be promoted as a means by which these more strategic goals could
be achieved.[260]

Relations between the police and the Caribbean community,
particularly young men, continued to sour. Most of those arrested
during the St Paul's disturbances of 1980 had been acquitted the
following year. In 1982, a fight between youths from Barton Hill
and St Paul's had ended in a violent attack by Black youths on a
popular community policeman, PC Ian Bennett. In 1985, riots
in Broadwater Estate in Tottenham, London and Handsworth in
Birmingham, led to the formulation of a tougher national police
strategy to impose law and order on the inner cities. [261]

In 1986 that new strategy saw 600 of Avon and Somerset's
police carry out another raid on the *Black and White Café* as part
of 'Operation Delivery'. Police estimated that there were some
200 hard-core criminals out of a population of some 15,000 in
the St Paul's area, and cited concern that the café was used by
these criminals for dealing in hard drugs. Some locals, including

the vicar of St Paul's, saw the intrusion of a heavily equipped unit into the area as provocative and heavy-handed, whilst others characterised it as a revenge attack for the 1980 riot and the attack on PC Bennett. The response was what one eye witness described as 'organised guerrilla warfare', with armed police being 'regularly bricked' by angry youths. William Waldegrave, then MP for Bristol West and influential in Thatcher's government, eventually persuaded Avon's police to pull back from their hard-line policy of containment, but Operation Delivery marked the nadir of police relations with St Paul's.[262]

By contrast, Bristol City Council had recently formally committed itself to an Equal Opportunities strategy. The Labour Party had just gained control of Avon County Council and it, too, declared itself committed to Equal Opportunities. In practice, Avon was slower to deliver. Policy pronouncements were one thing, actual implementation, quite another. Bristol's Housing Department did pioneer some anti-racist initiatives in the late 1980s in response to increased instances of racial harassment of council tenants, but it would be some time before other local authority departments in either Bristol or Avon followed suit, let alone those in the private sector. A multi-racial team of investigative reporters went undercover in Bristol for a BBC documentary in 1988. Their experiences graphically revealed to the nation at large the persistence of widespread discrimination in housing and employment in the city.[263]

Figure 97 Bristol councillor Ray Sefia (left) next to William Waldegrave, Conservative MP for Bristol West (1979-1997), appearing at a community radio event in St Paul's in the mid-1980s.

THE 1990s

The following decade saw the term 'ethnic minority' beginning to replace that of 'immigrant' as a second generation of people born in Britain to parents from the New Commonwealth came of age, and in 1991 Jim Williams, a Jamaican bus driver, trade unionist and publican, became Bristol's first Black lord mayor. In 1992, Councillor David John became the first Black chair of Avon County Council. Although the power they held was more symbolic than real, these appointments did signal that a sea change was occurring.[264]

Nevertheless, parochialism and a White resentment of 'immigrants' still remained. Racial harassment became increasingly recognised as a national problem. Black and Asian people in central Bristol, as well as those isolated on the outer housing estates like Hartcliffe and Withywood, single mothers with mixed-race children, and refugees of various backgrounds, could find life made intolerable by instances, even campaigns, of abuse and intimidation. Local authority bodies were slow to adopt anti-harassment policies and, even when they did, it was reportedly 'all too easy for staff to continue working as if these policies did not exist'.[265]

As ever, far-right groups were quick to exploit racial tensions for racialist ends. A significant proportion of the 157 incidents of racial harassment formally reported to the police in 1994 occurred in the Bristol suburb of Fishponds, where the British National Party had been active. A particularly vicious attack that year, which left a young Black man, Marlon Thomas, permanently paralysed, did shock the police into taking such attacks more seriously. A year after Labour's sweeping victory in the General Election of 1997, a new offence of racially aggravated harassment in the Crime and Disorder Act came into effect. One of the first people prosecuted under the Act was a Bristol teenager who had subjected a Chinese owner of a fish and chip shop to a four-month campaign of intimidation. In 1999 Avon and Somerset Constabulary recorded some 545 'racial incidents' in the Bristol area but by 2001 Bristol City Council still did not seem to have a corporate strategy for dealing with racial harassment and violence across all its services.[266]

Generally speaking, violence against ethnic minorities seems to have been less a matter of popular concern than crimes committed by Black people. The drug culture was popularly seen as a product of the Black presence. Some 70 per cent of all the city's reported street robberies in 1986 were said to have occurred in the Trinity Road Police division, which included St Paul's at its centre. Sometime in the late eighties crack dealers from outside Bristol first ensnared young Black people who were already casually smoking cannabis into selling crack cocaine, and there is no doubt that by the 1990s crack use was destabilising the Black community in St Paul's. There was a widespread perception that crack use was a Black crime, and that the *Black and White Café* was a centre for its distribution.[267]

The resulting increase in Black on Black crime alarmed White Bristolians and strengthened the association of Blackness with criminality. The injustice of stereotyping was epitomised by the death of a Jamaican-born school caretaker, Evon 'Bangy' Barry, in January 1996. He was murdered by members of a Black drugs gang from Birmingham when he tried to intervene in a violent drug-related incident in St Paul's. Barry's death caused widespread revulsion within Bristol's African-Caribbean community. In an unlikely partnership, a Black-run pirate radio station, Unity FM, helped police to gather information from the Black community about the perpetrators.[268]

In truth, hard drug use knew no racial boundaries and had helped to undermine social order in the outlying and mainly White estates in Knowle West, Hartcliffe, Withywood and Southmead, but it was St Paul's which, to the increasing despair of the families living there, had become a magnet for drug users of all colours and a haunt of prostitutes and kerb crawlers.[269]

TOWARDS 2001

Throughout the 1980s and 1990s, the cultural landscape of the city had been changing at an accelerating pace. The continuing influx of newcomers meant that Bristol was becoming more cosmopolitan, its arts and music scene more vibrant, its eating culture more varied. Although it is perhaps telling that Bristol's suburbs and commuter villages had come by 2001 to form a very 'White doughnut' around the city's multi-ethnic centre, African-Caribbean and Asian youth culture was beginning to have a wider influence on young Bristolians wherever they lived.

The increase in migration and the spread of higher education also began to reshape the city's sense of itself and, in some respects, its attitude to ethnic minorities. The still vigorous institutions of Bristol's elite, such as the Society of Merchant Venturers, became subject to more critical scrutiny about their historical involvement with the slave trade and as a result it became more aware of the sensibilities of the city's contemporary Black residents. Legislation, although subject to changing political imperatives, was beginning to promote more opportunities for those from minority backgrounds, and Bristol's local authority increasingly took a more effective stand against discriminatory practices.

Reflections

Oral Interviews as an historical source

Although oral testimony cannot always be depended upon for factual accuracy, it is a good way of getting some insights into the way people view the world, how they structure their lives and how they regard others. Oral testimony is also a means of identifying issues or events that might otherwise go undocumented.

What are the risks?

Testimony from individuals may not be representative of a wider constituency. In small-scale research such as our own, it is often impossible to interview more than a small proportion of people from a particular group. In the case of outside researchers investigating disadvantaged or marginalised minorities, it is easier and thus more tempting to make contact with the head of a community organisation rather than to seek out the rank and file members of that community, especially when poverty, caste, gender and/or language differences make some people less accessible than others.

This is where the depth and quality of one's community contacts, the knowledge one has about the internal divisions within a particular group and the time one takes to cultivate relationships with individual interviewees can make all the difference to the quality of the knowledge obtained.

Rais Hyder as a young man, c.1960. Hyder fled from India shortly after Partition and later came to Britain, where he eventually settled in Bristol.

Asking the right questions

Those who come to this country to seek a new life bring with them their existing values and experiences. How much the interviewer needs to ask them about their life in their home country is a matter of judgement, but we have only lately come to realise that such questions show respect for the complexity and richness of an individual's experience and so elicit a more informative response.

Confidentiality

Gathering oral testimony brings with it ethical obligations. In particular, the issue of confidentiality has raised its head in various ways during this project. Many people asked for anonymity for a wide range of reasons: the wife subjected to physical violence by her husband, the illegitimate child of mixed race, the immigration worker who did not want to compromise her professional position, the asylum seeker who did not want to jeopardise his application, the social worker who feared violent reprisal. By contrast, a few people opened up during the semi-structured interviews in ways that made them more vulnerable and thus more needful of anonymity than they realised. One person spoke so frankly of his deprived and brutalised childhood and subsequent involvement in criminal activity, that his identity would have been instantly evident had the transcribed interview been made public.

Mukhtyar Singh Bhakerd (second from left) with elders and a friend of the Ramargharia Gurdwara in Chelsea Road, Bristol (2007). The second oldest of Bristol's four Sikh Temples, it was founded in 1977 in an old factory which began life in 1901 as the Small Free Brethren Gospel Hall (Bristol 2007).

How valid are the results?

Another dilemma which oral history poses has to do with the way testimony is gathered and the status of the knowledge it yields. During the course of this project, some people would speak only when the tape recorder was turned off; others would be willing to speak informally but not in a structured interview. Was the knowledge gathered by taking notes after an encounter as legitimate as that transcribed directly from a tape recorder? To put it another way, when does the oral historian become an ethnographer garnering information by way of participant observation in the field? What is the dividing line between contemporary historical research and investigative journalism? There are no easy answers here, but careful documentation and a willingness to wrestle with contradictory and complex evidence are the ways to begin to find out. In the case of this project, oral interviews have proved invaluable for opening up aspects of Bristol's 20th-century history, but there is clearly scope for much more work to be done.

Nevertheless, even in the late 1990s, traditional prejudices might still surface in the city. The local press was hostile to gypsies and six pubs were forced to take down 'No travellers' signs in their doors in 1997. The following year saw the emerging controversy over the statue of Edward Colston, the 17th-century merchant. Colston, so long uncritically honoured as the city's most generous benefactor, was condemned by a city councillor of partial Nigerian descent for his slave-trading activities, and his statue was subsequently daubed with an obscene slogan expressing a similar sentiment. These events elicited a vigorous correspondence in the local press, which laid bare the resentment many White Bristolians felt towards anyone who challenged Bristol's traditional sense of itself, and the statue became a lightning rod for the city's racial tensions. Evident in this controversy was an implicit nostalgia for an idealised 'bygone Bristol', a Bristol before mass immigration had made the question of being Bristolian such a vibrant, contended and complicated affair.[270]

Chapter 12

African-Caribbeans, 1948–1990

Few migrant communities have had such an ambivalent and transformative relationship with Bristol as has the African-Caribbean community. This chapter offers a brief overview of key developments and trends in the history of that community and will begin to explore the continuities and differences in the experiences of the first generation and second generation of Black Bristolians.

PUSH AND PULL: WHY MIGRANTS CAME

You see them gathered:
Passports stamped
Their travel papers wrapped
In old disused news –
Papers: lining their patient queues.
Where to?
They do not know …[271]

Previous chapters have discussed the intermittent presence of people of African descent in Bristol. The contemporary African-Caribbean presence is the legacy of post-war migration. The overwhelming majority of these migrants came from the many Caribbean islands that were until the 1960s part of the British Empire. Centuries of British rule had led the people of the Caribbean to regard Britain as the Mother Country. The reality was more complex. Caribbean culture was actually a unique fusion of African and European elements and the 'Mother Country' had left her Caribbean colonies woefully underdeveloped.

Caribbean migrants came to Britain to explore opportunities that were inconceivable in the sending societies. Migration was made possible by legislative changes on both sides of the Atlantic. The British Nationality Act of 1948 had granted West Indians right of entry to Britain, whilst restrictive legislation passed in the USA in 1952 made Britain the destination by default for West Indian emigrants. Yet most came not to settle but to work for five years and then return to the Caribbean. Even in later life many continued to entertain the hope of one day returning home. Bristol's first Caribbean settlers were ex-servicemen who had either remained in the city after demobilisation or come back after a temporary return to

Figure 98 Fred Walcott, originally from Barbados, in RAF uniform. Walcott joined the RAF Bomber Command in 1944 before settling in Bristol to work as an engineer.

the Caribbean. Like many West Indian servicemen in other parts of Britain they had served primarily in the Royal Air Force.[272]

The Colonial Association, which emerged between 1948 and 1949, included 'about half a dozen' such servicemen, such as Bill Smith and Fred Walcott, and their wives. Supported by the Bristol Co-operative Education Department and by the British Council's Bristol office in King Street, it acted as a bridge between the Caribbean community and British society. These early settlers were integrated into local society, some marrying local White women and living in predominately White neighbourhoods. It is likely that Bristol's attractions were made known by word of mouth by this vanguard group.[273]

Avonmouth was known as a destination for Caribbean produce – primarily bananas – and police reports refer to some 159 stowaways apprehended there between 1950 and 1955 on board banana boats from Port Antonio and other Caribbean ports. A key attraction of Bristol, which drew migrants from Britain's other urban centres, was that it was regarded 'as a city of diverse industries and thus good chances of employment' and, more controversially, that it had 'a reputation of little or no feeling of racial intolerance'. Bristol followed the classic pattern of chain migration in which migrants who had previously settled in the city received family and friends arriving from the sending societies.[274]

Chain migration may explain why Bristol's Caribbean population is overwhelmingly Jamaican. Of 76 elderly West Indians interviewed by University of Bristol researchers in 1983, 61 were from the island of Jamaica, 25 of whom were from the four parishes of St Andrew's, St Thomas, Clarendon and St Catherine's. Migrants from Barbados, Dominica, Antigua and Guyana formed smaller Caribbean contingents in the city (see figure 100).[275]

Some 500 African-Caribbeans were estimated to be resident in Bristol in 1957 (as opposed to 4,400 in Birmingham). The rate of Caribbean migration to Bristol reflected the national trend. Many of those who arrived between 1958 and 1962 were dependents coming in anticipation of immigration restrictions. As Table 3 below indicates, Caribbean migration peaked between 1958 and 1965. [276]

Table 3: African-Caribbean Migrants in Bristol 1953-1965 (based on police estimates)

Year	Number of Migrants
1953	200
1958	2000
1960	2500
1965	7000

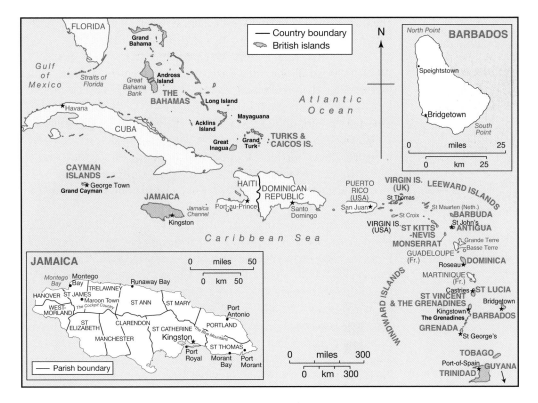

Figure 99 The Caribbean, showing highlighted in red the islands formerly of the British West Indies. Most post-war Caribbean migrants to Bristol came from Jamaica which became independent from Britain in 1962.

St Paul's Prior to Caribbean Settlement

Ashley ward served as the main reception area for Caribbean migrants to Bristol, although a few early settlers could be found in South Bristol's Knowle West area. Ashley ward is often popularly referred to as 'St Paul's'. Such a conflation masks the differences between the various districts (St Paul's, St Agnes, St Werburgh's, St Judes and Montpelier) that make up the ward. Montpelier for example, retains the greatest number of owner-occupiers. Previous writers have found that for White residents outside the inner city, 'St Paul's' was a euphemism for a supposedly 'Black' area of 'vice and shame'.[278]

Yet, according to official statistics, the Black presence in St Paul's has been consistently overestimated. Even as late as 1991, the census reveals that the Black population of the sub ward of St Paul's comprised less than 31 per cent of its total population and only 18 per cent of the Ashley ward as a whole. Even allowing for inaccuracies in the census collection, St Paul's is far more diverse than is popularly supposed.[279]

Central Bristol, including St Paul's, had suffered heavily from the wartime bombing. By the late 1950s, the area had become a reception area for Polish, Hungarian, Cypriot and Irish families, and a

Figure 100 Black
Settlement in Bristol
(2001 Census). 'Black'
denotes those of African-
Caribbean or African
origin.

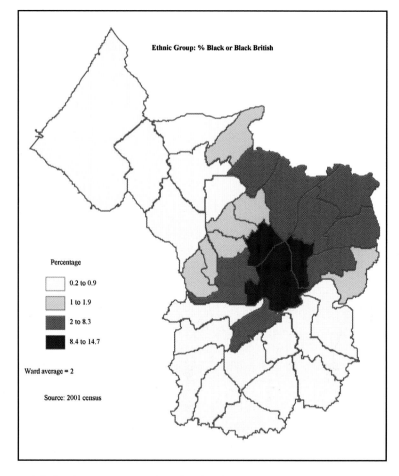

red-light district. Earmarked for development, 'St Paul's was the last
great reservoir of rented accommodation in the city.' By the early
1960s, many established families of English ethnicity in the ward
had relocated to new estates such as Oldbury Court, and European
migrants had also begun to leave. Around the same time, English
migrants from other parts of the country, among whom were
'socially inadequate and deprived families' began to come in.[280]

Settling In?

A 1953 police report compared the 'coloured' settler with the Irish
migrants in that: 'despite good wages [they] are often content to
live in conditions of squalor'. The written and oral evidence collected for this book contradicts the report. Few British landlords
outside the inner city were prepared to rent accommodation to
Caribbean migrants. Discrimination in private sector housing was
often compounded by local authority policy. Migrants had to be

Figure 101 George
Molyneux, Bristol
resident at Southmead
Estate, a post-war council
estate, in the 1950s.

resident in the city for at least one year in order even to qualify for
a five-year waiting list for council housing.[281]

Faced with few alternatives, the Caribbean settlers had little
option but to live in Ashley ward. Caribbean migrants rented
accommodation from a narrow range of English, Polish and Asian
migrants. Others became tenant landlords and sublet property
to fellow Caribbean migrants. One Jamaican migrant described
his shock at the overcrowding and conditions he encountered on
arriving in Bristol in December 1961. He was guided to a basement
room on Alfred Street, St Paul's:

Figure 102 Sculpture of Alfred Fagon (1937-1986), playwright in St Paul's, Bristol. Born in Jamaica, and resident in Bristol for many years until his death, Fagon's plays included 'Death of a Blackman' (1975), 'Four Hundred Pounds' (1983) and 'Shakespeare Country' which was produced by the BBC.

Dis lady dat was dere. She was de landmissus. De stones on the floor. No carpet. No lino. Nothing at all just de stone. Just damp. An it was three in a bed an' me come now to mek four. Luckily three work nights and me worked days. I say oh Gawd.[282]

The increase in the number of settlers, and the limited housing options open to them caused acute overcrowding in St Paul's during the first decades of settlement. Rat infestation and fly tipping in Brighton Street was so bad in 1967 that local residents petitioned the City for action and expressed their despair at being 'shackled' in such bad conditions.[283]

Overcrowding in Ashley ward began to ease as some migrants bought property outside the area and as others qualified for the public sector housing built as part of the slum clearance schemes of the 1960s. Migrants moved out of St Paul's to neighbouring St Werburgh's, Easton, Eastville, St George, St Anne's and Lockleaze. From the early 1960s Easton became the second home to migrant settlers, a trend which intensified over the following decades.[284]

Just as for White working class communities elsewhere, slum clearance was a doubled-edged sword for Bristol's Black community. The proximity of the St Paul's, St Werburgh's, Easton and St Jude's districts encouraged a sense of unity among the burgeoning migrant community, linked by Ashley Road stretching from St Paul's into Easton, but the building of the M32 fragmented the community in 1960s and 1970s. Similarly in Easton the dual carriageway separated lower and upper Stapleton Road. From the 1990s, more affluent Black Bristolians moved further afield to areas such as Fishponds, Lockleaze and Keynsham, although many continued to work within and identify with the community centred on St Paul's and Easton.[285]

Employment

Bristol did not suffer from acute labour shortages in any one industry. Migrant settlers found employment in construction, in the factories located in Avonmouth – in particular the chemical companies – at Brook Laundry in Montpelier, at the Wills' tobacco factory in Bedminster, at Fry's the chocolate manufacturer, Dirkson and Knight the sugar firm in St Paul's, and at Rolls Royce. As well as the aforementioned, Black women found employment in the food industries, in tailoring firms and in the National Health Service. Some migrants worked as carpenters and engineers, attesting to the survival of trade skills learnt in the Caribbean.[286]

Most of the Caribbean workers were employed as semi or unskilled labour. Social scientists have debated the extent to which this predominance of Caribbean workers in low-skill, low-paid employment was due to discrimination or to the lower level of skills training then available in the Caribbean. The sociologist Anthony Richmond suggested that there was no easy equivalence between qualifications in the Caribbean and in Britain:

> In the West Indies a man tends to be a 'jack of all trades' … the result is that his skill at any particular trade is only sufficient to warrant his employment at semi-skilled rates, rather as a skilled workman which by West Indian standards he is.[287]

In Bristol members of the Colonial Association attempted to create an understanding between British employers and Caribbean employees. One of its members, the Barbadian Derek Sealy, described how they would speak to the personnel officer at a factory and explain that:

> … we wanted them to employ West Indians coming from the Caribbean and we would say now they are not used to working on production lines so you would have to take them on a small line to show them exactly how they were expected to work and how fast they were expected to work.[288]

A combination of irrational prejudices, untested stereotypes of Caribbean workers, and fears of upsetting White workers lay behind the refusal by many White employers to take on Black workers or to promote those they did.[289]

Unlike men, Caribbean women were concentrated in the National Health Service. Of Fenton's sample of 35 women, 21 worked in hospitals at Frenchay, Glenside, Ham Green, Hortham and the Bristol Royal Infirmary. Out of this sample only two women were nurses. The rest described themselves as ancillary, auxiliaries, nursing assistants and domestic staff. For some, their concentration on the lower rungs of the NHS ladder was due to racial discrimination. Nursing was one of the few occupations in the Caribbean that conferred social prestige and decent pay. Many Caribbean women came to Britain in order to train to become nurses in the anticipation that they would be able to return home and continue to practise. To do so they had to obtain the State Registered Nurse (SRN) as opposed to the State Enrolled Nurse (SEN) certificate. The latter was a lower qualification, and oral testimonies suggest that many Caribbean nurses were deliberately misinformed, not entered or steered away from obtaining the SRN certificate. They were in effect kept in the position of a subordinate workforce.[290]

The following extract from the testimony given by Bristol resident Mrs Princess Campbell sheds light upon the experience of many Caribbean nurses:

> We worked 48 hours a week. Some days the duty commenced at 8 am and finished at 8 pm. Most of the heavy and unpleasant work was allocated to the Black workers. The White students would be sitting drinking tea while we would be asked to go and clean out the bed pans and vomit … We were made to clean up their trolleys as well as cleaning ours. At times we were demoralised and we were not valued and your self esteem was low.[291]

Figure 103 Princess Campbell as a young nurse in the 1960s. She became Bristol's first Black nursing sister in mental health.

Racial tensions in employment were also exacerbated by the economic and political context. Britain experienced an economic recession in 1961-62 and 1966-77. White workers feared they would be undercut by, and lose their jobs to, cheap foreign labour. The increasingly racial nature of parliamentary discussions heightened anti-immigrant feeling at the grassroots.[292]

By the early 1960s tension between White and Black workers turned into open conflict. Such was the case when on 9 July 1962 a fight between a Jamaican casual labourer and a White docker from Shirehampton on the SS *Tilapa* turned into a major race relations incident when all Black workers were dismissed after White dockers objected to working with them. The following year a cadre of Caribbean migrants, including the West Indian Association and Black and White Christians led by Paul Stephenson, organised a boycott of the Bristol Omnibus Company along the lines of the civil rights campaign in the USA. The company had been operating a colour bar. The story of the bus boycott has been documented elsewhere. Suffice to say that the Omnibus Company eventually

Figure 104 Tony Benn (Labour MP for Bristol South East, 1950-1961 and 1963-1983) and Paul Stephenson on board an old Bristol bus to mark the 40th anniversary of the Bristol bus boycott (2003).

capitulated under pressure from a coalition of Black protesters, their local White allies and political figures such as Tony Benn.[293]

The Bristol bus boycott and similar episodes helped to persuade the 1964 Labour Government to introduce the first raft of anti-discrimination legislation in Britain. Anti-discrimination legislation reduced incidents of overt racism, although discriminatory practices continued, as in Bristol's hotels and hospitals. As well as direct discrimination Black workers also encountered a glass ceiling in employment. One respondent recalled the moment when her father, a skilled worker at a chemical firm in Bristol, came home and lamented: 'They've done it again. They've promoted one of the young men I trained over me'. Bristol Racial Equality Council records show that these patterns of discrimination confronted Black youths as they began to enter the labour market in the 1970s.[294]

For some Black Bristolians success was not to be found in mainstream employment. Black businesses emerged to service the distinct needs of the community. Oral testimonies suggest that a small number of White proprietors began to sell West Indian goods in the 1960s along Grosvenor Road. They were joined and later replaced in the mid-'60s by Caribbean shop owners such as Mr Forbes, the Dawes family and the fondly remembered Dick Taylor. St Paul's, in particular Grosvenor Road, remained the main shopping area for migrants even when they began to disperse to other parts of the city.[295]

THE BIRTH OF BLACK COMMUNITY

It's fantastic in St Pauls. One of the best places in Bristol and there's music coming from windows and bluebeat everywhere; it's great.[297]

Leisure Evening leisure opportunities for the first generation in the 1950s were restricted. Those who ventured out of St Paul's risked being denied service, assaulted by 'the teddy boys or beatniks', or even arrested. People patronised the few pubs in Ashley ward and Easton that were prepared to receive Caribbean clientèle, and the dances put on by the Colonial Association. Migrants would otherwise hold house parties or, as they became known, 'blues'. Migrants could listen to the latest music trends imported from the Caribbean such as calypso, ska, bluebeat and, by the late 1960s, reggae. DJs such as Trojan, his playing partner Tarzan and High Priest were the first sound systems to emerge in Bristol. These parties were not held for profit. As one migrant recalled, 'It wasn't like something you pay – you go from house to house play music, dance, eat'.[296]

Similarly Mr and Mrs Hibbert recall how the unofficial barbershop run by duo Beddoe and Smith acted as a social centre. Migrants would gather at their Brighton Street basement premises to relax, listen to music, and exchange news. These gatherings sometimes evolved into impromptu parties. By the 1970s blues parties such as Valentines on St Nicholas Road, St Paul's, and Ajax on Ashley Road gained a semi-permanent status, becoming in the process Bristol institutions. For Black and White Bristolians the blues offered a raw, undiluted inroad into Black Bristol.[298]

Given the lack of licensed venues open to the community, club ownership became a viable investment for local business-men. Paul Stephenson liaised with Tony Bullimore, a descendant of Portuguese Jewish immigrants, to open the *Bamboo* club in St Paul's in 1964. The club gained iconic status as one of the first venues to cater for the Caribbean community. In keeping with later trends people of all colours from within and outside Bristol descended upon the club to sample its unique vibe and hear live artists such as Bob Marley and Desmond Dekker. Other venues soon followed. Caribbean entrepreneurs such as Cleon Green and Johnny St Clair ran nightclubs in the 1970s, and inner-city pubs such as the *Inkerman*, *St Nicholas*, the *Criterion*, and the *Plough* came under Caribbean management.

Sport provided an additional avenue for migrants to relax. The Empire Sports Club on Newfoundland Road was a haven for budding weightlifters, including the South-African born Olympic contender, Precious Mackenzie, and Newton Burrowes. Cricket was a popular pastime among the new settlers. Caribbean players initially played in mixed teams but eventually formed the Bristol West Indian Club. Caribbean migrants also came together to play dominoes, first meeting in a shop on Sussex Road owned by the aforementioned Dick Taylor. These players formed the Western Star Domino Club which proved to be a popular social centre.[299]

Figure 105 Bristol's West Indian Cricket Club (2007).

Figure 106 Worshippers at Bristol's Church of the God of Prophecy in Easton, a Black-led church, *c.* 1985.

Church life Discrimination in Bristol's churches combined with their general austerity of worship led many migrants to organise their own churches. The majority of Bristol's Black-led churches derive from the Pentecostal stream of Protestant Christianity with its distinctive belief in salvation through possession by the Holy Spirit. Not all the Black-led churches are Pentecostal, although nearly all share a literal interpretation of scripture. Evangelist Reverend Sawyer, for example, took over the existing Wesleyan Holiness church in 1963. The congregation first rented space from the Co-operative Society in Broadmead before moving to their current address on Brigstocke Road, St Paul's, in 1968. Such churches have acted as a hub of community life within the African-Caribbean community, providing a bridge between the older and younger generations. Not all settlers joined the Black-led churches. Those who remained in the older denominations revived declining inner city congregations such as St Agnes and City Road Baptist.[300]

Political organisation Bristol's voluntary sector emerged in order to meet the needs of the community that were not being met by the statutory agencies. In 1957 the West Indian Association subsumed the older Colonial Association with Bill Smith as its chair, but Smith and his Association was in turn replaced by Paul Stephenson's West Indian Development Association in 1964. The WIDA marked a more assertive phase in the community's liaison with the statutory authorities. The English-born Stephenson, who was of West African descent, was a community worker who led the Association with considerable political acumen.[301]

Figure 107 Carmen Beckford, MBE, appointed in 1967 as Bristol's first community relations officer.

St Paul's Carnival

The St Paul's Carnival is a barometer of the social and ideological changes within Bristol's race relations. The first festival was held in July 1968 when the St Paul's and Environs Consultative Committee appointed a sub-committee consisting of members of the West Indian Development Association. The vicar of St Agnes's Church, Roy Blake, also helped to steer the festival, as did Carmen Beckford, whose help was indispensable. The festival was conceived as a multicultural event that would bring together the European, African-Caribbean and Asian communities in St Paul's. Carmen Beckford described the sentiments that lay behind the first St Paul's Festival: 'We wanted the people in St Paul's to develop a certain amount of national pride.' In addition, the festival was a colourful riposte to the negative depictions of St Paul's in the media. The records of the Bristol Voluntary Liaison Committee suggest that it was organised on a shoestring budget owing to a lack of funds.

Researcher Thomas Fielding described the first festival as characterised by an 'extravagant multiculturalism which juxtaposed steel bands, Scottish dancers and a weight lifting competition.' The West Indian Dance team formed by Carmen Beckford and Angela Rodaway in 1968 articulated the Caribbean element of the festival. At this point in its history the carnival was more akin to a traditional British festival than to a Caribbean carnival.

However the identity of the carnival began to take on a more Caribbean flavour when Trinidadian Francis Salandy became the carnival organiser in 1975. Salandy brought with him a personal knowledge of carnival traditions and contacts with carnival artists in London. This marked a turning point in the carnival's identity. The 1980 riots and the subsequent focus upon African-Caribbean concerns consolidated that shift.

The vibrancy of the Black arts scene in music and dance driven by a resurgent Black consciousness had also begun to take centre stage. By 1986 the cultural events that comprised the festival and the acts on the carnival main stage were almost entirely African-Caribbean. Some of Bristol's best-known musical exports, such as Ronny Size and *Massive Attack*, learnt their craft performing to the crowds on carnival day.

By 1991 the St Paul's Festival was renamed the St Paul's African-Caribbean Carnival. The transition from multicultural festival to carnival in 1991 consolidated the shift away from multiculturalism to a greater emphasis upon the concerns of the Black community. Nonetheless, Bristol's carnival retained an inclusive ethos and still attracts a wide range of Bristolian celebrants.

Street scene at St Paul's carnival, c.1990.

Internal Differences

Aside from internal political differences, sharply divergent lifestyles have also divided Black Bristol's identity. Colonialism had fostered an intense inter-island rivalry that carried over into the early years of migrant settlement. But hostility between Jamaicans and Barbadians, for example, was increasingly undermined by the shared experiences of marginalisation. Over the successive decades the settlers forged a Pan-Caribbean identity, albeit one in which the Jamaican culture was and still is pre-eminent.[302]

St Paul's and Easton were home to what the Trinidadian sociologist Ken Pryce defined as hustlers, mainliners (skilled and professional workers) and the working class 'respectables' (which included the religiously observant 'saints'). Our research suggests that these lifestyle categories are too rigid and do little to reflect the fluidity of Caribbean lifestyles and activities. In reality, social events such as the blues and the St Paul's Festival, along with family and friendship ties, created allegiances that spanned these categories.[303]

Young, Black, Bristol

My parents stayed here and became part of the attire
They had become quite British, they helped set the culture on
    fire
But their children were born in this unequal, confusing, place
They had a different Agenda, a different identity, but they were
    the same race.[304]

Bristol, as elsewhere, was ill-prepared for the presence of British and Caribbean-born Black children in its schools. A former member of staff at a school in Ashley ward recalled that the size of the school doubled between 1961 and 1965 when it received 200 mostly Jamaican children. Staff in these schools received little official guidance on how best to accommodate the new intake. Many young people, like their parents, possessed a Creole identity expressed in particular through language. Until recently, Creole speech was regarded simply as corrupted or rather 'broken' English.[305]

Nor were many teachers aware of the profound adjustment that the education system demanded of their Black pupils. The first cohort of Caribbean youth in British schools was largely composed of young people who had joined parents who had settled in England years previously. Separation from their former guardians – family members, grandparents or close family friends – to join parents 'that [had] become like a dream' must have been stressful.[306]

While most Caribbean parents valued educational attainment, many were unable to create home environments conducive to

Figure 108 Simba Tongogara, shown here in 1969 when he was 13 years old, two years after his arrival from Jamaica. A Rastafarian and local activist, he was defended by Paul Boateng after his arrest during the 1980 disturbances in St Paul's. He has subsequently worked to promote opportunities for young Black people in the city.

learning. In addition to their overcrowded accommodation, parents had to work long hours in order to compensate for low pay. Home life stresses were sometimes translated into conflict in the classroom. African-Caribbean youth gained a reputation for openly challenging school authority.[307]

Young people raised and schooled outside the inner city also encountered low teacher expectations. Some had to struggle against racist bullying. One mixed race respondent brought up in predominantly White Clifton Wood recalled that his school life was characterised by, 'a lot of fighting, always getting into fights – always because of race'. Such problems led to many Caribbean children being classified as educationally subnormal.[308]

Conscious and unconscious racism also coloured the attitudes of some teaching staff. Oral testimonies by second generation Black Bristolians echo a common feeling that they were prized for their sporting rather than their academic prowess. One interviewee vividly recalled being dissuaded from pursuing O levels as a teenager: 'Oh don't worry about that concentrate on your sports because you're good at sports … and if you don't come back till the next lesson I'll understand.'[309]

Anecdotal evidence also suggests that many Black youths struggled hard to convince their parents of their experiences at school. In the highly stratified islands of the Caribbean, the teacher's word was sacrosanct. Parents who carried this attitude with them were slow to come to terms with teacher fallibility.

However, the underachievement of Black British youth became increasingly evident to parents and grassroots organisations. Successive reports by Bristol's Community Relations Council drew attention to the matter. By the 1970s this was done with increasing urgency as Black youngsters were entering employment without relevant qualifications. Alarmingly, a survey of West Indian school leavers in Easton, St Werburgh's, St Paul's and Montpelier conducted in 1977 revealed that 'whilst 141 had CSE grades 1-4 over 100 had no qualifications at all' and noted that: 'We are very concerned about the under-achievement of Black children, attitudes of some teachers to them, the lack of support given to some parents, as well as the lack of support given by some parents to their children and the schools.'[310]

Concern over the education of the second generation led the West Indian Development Association to concentrate its energies on raising the achievement levels of Black youth. Between 1974 and 1976 the WIDA, relaunched as the West Indian Parents and Friends Association, aimed to 'deepen the sense of mutual respect between parents and schools and to assist the relationship between parents and children'.[311]

Identity and Cultural Politics

> I have crossed an ocean
> I have lost my tongue
> From the root of the old one
> A new one has sprung[312]

Although young Black Bristolians joined the Boys Brigade, the
Salvation Army, the Girl Guides and local sports teams, many
adolescents began to question the logic of assimilating into a society
from which they felt ostracised. Black adults organised activities
for the youths, such as the West Indian Dance Team, as a way of
educating young people in Caribbean culture.[313]

For some, adolescence marked a departure from the survival
strategies of the first generation. Their sense of alienation may
have been heightened by Bristol's slaving past, but, in any case,
many turned to alternative expressions of identity, in particular
Rastafarianism.

Rastafarianism was a product of Jamaica and preached the
divinity of the former Emperor of Ethiopia Haile Selassie; it
stressed Black pride and identified Africa as the spiritual home
of all peoples of African descent. The response of one Bristol
interviewee typified the experience of many Black youths in
Britain. He became a Rastafarian after a process of reflection and
self-education:

> The [Christians] they know God they believes in God but the
> God of the Churches is not a God I can identify with … Rasta
> was simple and it was the simplicity of Rasta that's what made it
> interesting in terms of we belong somewhere and the words of
> Marcus Garvey talking about having self dignity about having
> pride which you don't hear from the churches … and y'know …
> look towards Africa because a King will be crowned [and] that
> was the only thing we had that could take us forward.[314]

The development of Rastafarianism in Bristol owes much to
the efforts of early pioneers such as Ras Kwetgena Sokoni and Ras
Bandele in the late 1960s and 1970s. The fact that Rastafarians
had to hold their early meetings in a hut on a bombsite in a still
blighted St Paul's tells us something about their sense of exclusion.
Rastafarianism was the dominant but not the only strand of Black
consciousness during the 1970s. An often contradictory mixture of
Marxist and Black Nationalist ideologies appealed to others.[315]

The Black consciousness movement of the 1970s inspired a
number of reggae bands in Bristol. Arguably Bristol's first success-

ful reggae band were the Black Roots formed in 1979, and albums with such evocative titles as *Black Roots*, *The Frontline* and *On The Frontline*, gained them an international reputation. Sound systems, based on those popular in Jamaica, were another way Black youth used music to articulate their sense of identity, with different sound systems reflecting the different permutations of Black consciousness in Bristol.

> Studio 17 was more of a culture … thing. Rasta people playing that sound rootical entertaining sound Basi (Sebastian) was more of a Rasta [sound] still but from a younger vibe playing a different form of music.[316]

In its early years, the Inkworks (later the Kuumba Centre) in St Paul's became widely associated with Rastafarianism and the Black consciousness movement more generally. It offered a distinct space in which Black Bristolians, particularly the second generation, explored themes of identity through creativity. Among its many successes Inkworks fostered the creative talents of the African dance and drumming group Ekome, established in 1977. During the 1980s Ekome was the premier African dance group in the country.[317]

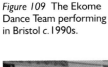

Figure 109 The Ekome Dance Team performing in Bristol *c.* 1990s.

For White and Black Bristolians raised outside the inner city, the music scene was an entry into Black Bristol. A former member of

multiracial circle 'the Half-breeds' recalled that after socialising in Clifton and in the Centre they would make their way to the blues parties in St Paul's and Easton. Situated in the centre of Bristol the *Dug Out* club was a multi-racial space in which White and Black musicians, DJs and promoters shared musical influences. The *Dug Out* spawned the critically acclaimed group *Massive Attack* and the music producer Nellie Hooper. Yet the vibrancy of Black youth culture in Bristol was not matched by wider employment opportunities.[318]

Hard Times

> Mama more police man come dung
> An beat me to de grung;
> Dem charge Jim fi sus
> Dem charge mi fa murda[319]

Between 1970 and 1980 the employment fortunes of Bristol's Black community witnessed two contradictory trends. Legislation restrained the overt discrimination against Black youths leading, in theory, to more employment opportunities. But this period also saw the savage effects of deindustrialisation.

The collapse of Bristol's manufacturing base from the 1970s onwards – a reflection of the national trend – exacerbated the discrepancy between White and Black unemployment rates. Since the mid-1980s, Black unemployment in Bristol has consistently stood at around 30 per cent. Most commentators consider this to be a serious underestimate because of significant under-registration of Black employment. In Bristol de-industrialisation was to some extent offset by the growth in the service sector. However, the concentration of Black workers in semi and unskilled employment was at odds with the demands in the service sector for skilled employees.[320]

No doubt high rates of unemployment, combined with other social stresses, contributed to an increase in criminality among Black Bristolians. However, policing methods employed in the inner city, such as stop and search, or 'sus', tended to criminalise the Caribbean community in general and Black men in particular. The CRC records show a negative shift in the way the police perceived the Caribbean community occurring by the mid-1970s and its report for 1975 noted that in

> recent months, we have noticed a change in the attitude of some members of the Police Force which has led to harassment of youngsters in the inner City area …With the help of chief

Inspector Dennis Reed and other responsible officers, every effort will be made to stop this trend.[321]

In view of what was to occur in the years following it seems that 'this trend' continued.

Varying social stresses and injudicious policing methods proved a volatile mix which finally ignited when police raided the *Black and White Café* on Grosvenor Road on 2 April 1980. The disturbance that followed was the first of many that swept through Britain's inner city communities during the 1980s.

After the Riot

The shock of the disturbances led to concerted efforts by Black and White statutory and non-statutory bodies to confront the problems of St Paul's. Funding was poured into the area to stimulate the local economy. The Association of Black Businesses, established in 1986, and Bristol Task Force, established in 1987, provided business advice and funds to local Black businesses. The Newfoundland Employment Agency, established in 1986, successfully provided skills training and office placements for Black Bristolians, surviving to date as the Centre for Enterprise and Development (CED).[322]

The post-riot period also invigorated new and pre-existing voluntary sector groups. In 1981 Black activists, including educationalist Cathy Waithe, established the first supplementary school in Bristol and also organised the first adult education centre, in St Paul's. The Bristol Community Growth and Support Association, led by Olive Osborne, secured funding for a multi-purpose community venue on Brighton Street, which opened in 1984. Neighbourhood House provided a meeting room for the elderly, a nursery, a mother and toddlers' group and a crafts centre. The Inkworks also received funding from the Manpower Services Commission to run vocational and creative workshops targeting the long-term unemployed.[323]

A New Day?

By the end of the period under consideration, Black Bristol was once more at a cross roads. Progress had been made but was challenged at every turn by larger socio-economic forces. A lack of business expertise hampered some Black businesses. A particular case in point is the Black-led commercial radio station FTP founded in 1989 and eventually sold by its controllers to Galaxy Radio in 1991. FTP's rise and fall also illustrates the dilemma of marketing

Figure 110 The Malcolm X Centre, City Road, St Paul's, Bristol was built in the aftermath of the 1980 Bristol disturbances.

Black cultural products while preserving sufficient integrity to maintain a Black audience. Many voluntary organisations also struggled with the realities of constantly searching for funds or satisfying the ever more exacting demands of funding bodies. Many worthwhile initiatives such as Neighbourhood House perished.[324]

Some community leaders were unhappy with the post-riot efforts arguing that the council imposed solutions upon the community without adequate consultation. A case in point was the furore over a new community centre based on the site of the former St Barnabas School on Ashley Road. Members of the St Paul's Community Association initially boycotted the Centre, although it eventually came into use some years later, pointedly renamed as the Malcolm X Centre.[325]

Black youth underachievement remained a salient issue throughout the period. Furthermore, according to the 1991 census, unemployment in Ashley ward was more than three times and in Easton twice that of the Bristol average. Local critics decried the post-riot initiatives as little more than 'window dressing which failed to tackle the real issues of unemployment'. By 1994, St Paul's still qualified as the most impoverished area in Bristol.[326]

Paradoxically, Black Bristol was never more visible. In 1991 Jim Williams, the Black Labour councillor for Ashley ward and publican, became the lord mayor of Bristol. The career of Bristol's first Black television presenter and broadcaster Sherrie Eugene was well underway by the beginning of the decade and Bristolian triple jumper Vernon Samuels competed for England in 1991. These successes came in the face of the many challenges confronting Bristol's Black community. How these challenges were faced by a third generation of Black Bristolians is a subject for future investigation.[327]

Chapter 13

South Asians, 1947–2001

By 2001, some sixty years of 'Asian migration' had had a discernible impact on Bristol's cityscape. The 'city of churches', as Bristol was once known, was, by then, home to at least five mosques, four Sikh gurdwaras (temples) and a Hindu temple, most of which were situated in buildings once used for Christian worship. By then, Indian restaurants and Asian corner shops were firmly established as an integral part of the commercial scene. But who precisely constitutes Bristol's 'Asian community'?[328]

The term itself (which actually refers to 'South Asian' or people from the Indian sub-continent) is shorthand for a wide array of peoples, themselves divided by religious allegiance, ethnic origins, language, kinship groups, caste and class. One objective of this chapter is to begin to set out the historical and social context within which 'Asian' migration to Bristol might best be understood. Given its almost exclusive focus on the first generation of migrants, it cannot claim to offer a definitive history of the Bristol Asian community, but hopes to stimulate more work in this area.[329]

Figure 111 St Mark's Road, Bristol. An ethnically diverse area with a particularly high concentration of South Asian residents, it is one of Bristol's most vibrant shopping areas. The area is further enhanced by the high quality of its street furniture, particularly its distinctive shop signs.

Figure 112 British
Council party in Bristol
celebrating Hindu Festival
of Colours (Holi) 1959.

COLONIAL AND POSTCOLONIAL DIMENSIONS

The migration of people from South Asia, which has to be understood in the context of British decolonisation, seems at first sight to fall into three discernible stages: The first wave, occurring from the late 1940s through to the early 1970s, came from what is now India and Pakistan and, with the exception of a small coterie of Pakistani Christian refugees, consisted of economic migrants. The second stage, which occurred roughly from the late 1960s and peaked in the early 1970s, was largely made up of refugees from East Africa (mainly Uganda and Kenya), most of whom were UK British passport holders. The latest group came mainly in the late 1970s and 1980s after a bloody civil war with what is now Pakistan resulted in the establishment of an independent Bangladesh (formerly East Pakistan) in 1971. However, such a periodisation is misleading, for it ignores the persistent interflow of marriage partners and, to a lesser extent, dependent relatives, between Britain and the Indian sub-continent up to the end of our period

Since its independence from formal British rule in 1947, the Indian sub-continent itself has been the site of shifting national identities each forged by war and population displacement. The India that won independence in 1947 was soon transformed by the establishment of (East and West) Pakistan in that year, and in 1971, after a bloody civil war, East Pakistan became the independent nation Bangladesh.[330]

The British government's decision in the early 20th century to disengage from India, and its manner of doing so, also affected migration patterns. One result of the independence settlement of 1947 was to split the Punjab between the newly created and

Figure 113 Indian
Independence Day
celebration in Bristol,
1959.

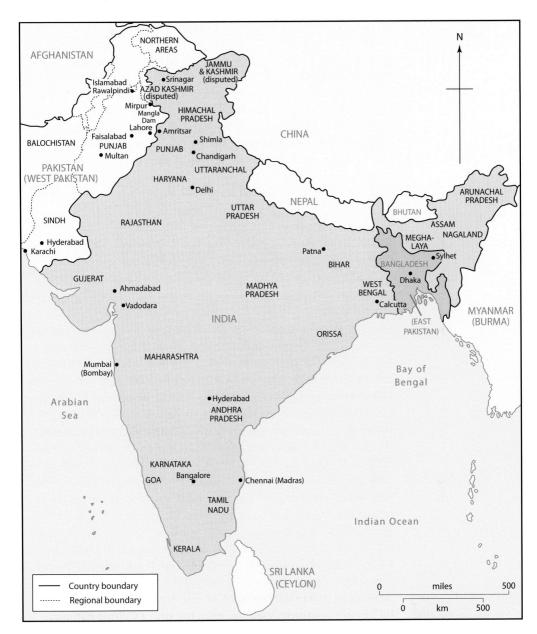

Figure 114 This map of India, Pakistan and Bangladesh illustrates how Partition in 1947 cut across historic regional boundaries, such as the Punjab. West and East Pakistan, created in 1947, became Pakistan and Bangladesh in 1971.

explicitly Muslim nation of Pakistan and an India which would increasingly identify itself (despite the secular nature of its leading Congress party) as Hindu. The communal violence between Hindus, Muslims and Sikhs which ensued in 1947 precipitated thousands to flee across the borders in both directions. Bristol resident Jernail Singh Sandhu, a Hindu, was 10 years old when his family fled from Pakistan into India leaving properties and Muslim friends and family behind:

The very first day while walking I got separated from my family.
People were riding on cars, on horses and walking on foot … in
a long Kafla [queue]. They were afraid … walking anxiously and
with no apparent destination.

Several times during our journey, we heard gunshot in the
surrounding areas. I remember, vividly, seeing a dead man on
the side of the canal. People were passing by in a very sombre
mood. It was a frightening and horrific time. Migration was
the single worst time of my life and I will always be haunted by
those memories.[331]

Another Bristol resident, Rais Hyder, a Muslim, also has vivid
childhood memories of the partition, although he and his family
fled in the other direction, hiding under a train seat for part of the
journey, and then walking through the borderland past bodies to
a makeshift refugee camp in Pakistan. '… you had to walk on foot,
you had no transport or nothing and while we were walking, and
I'm not exaggerating [there was killing all around]. Everywhere, to
the both sides, it was just horrible, it was.'[332]

The British boundary commission which determined the
borders between India and Pakistan also contributed to the region's
subsequent volatility in other ways. East Pakistan was created out
of parts of Bengal, some of which remained Indian. Although
predominantly Muslim, East Pakistan was profoundly different in
language and culture from West Pakistan. The drawing up of the
India-Pakistan border also left western regions of West Pakistan
short of water for irrigation. Such unfinished business would, as we
shall see, directly affect migration patterns not only to Britain but
to Bristol itself.

Bristol's South Asians in 2001

Compared with their counterparts in Bradford, Birmingham,
Manchester or London, Bristol's South Asian population constitutes
a relatively small proportion of the total population, estimated to
include some 10,000 residents (most certainly an underestimate) in
addition to more than 1,600 people of 'White and Asian' origin.[333]

Taken as a whole, Asians appear to be most densely settled in
central and east Bristol, that is, Lawrence Hill, Easton and Eastville.

But even in these 'Asian' areas their numbers are probably lower
than popularly supposed, being no higher than 10.5 per cent.
Pakistanis made up only 5 per cent of the residents of the Easton
ward with Indians and Bangladeshis accounting for a further
2.7 and 1.49 per cent. But Stapleton and St Mark's Roads in that
ward, with their rich array of Asian shops and nearby mosques

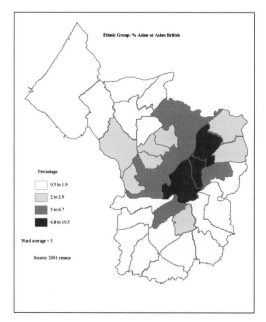

Figure 115 Asians in Bristol by ward (2001 census).

Figure 116 Indians in Bristol by ward (2001 census).

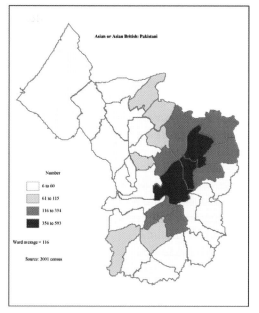

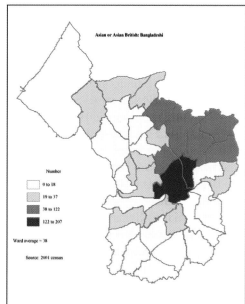

Figure 117 Pakistanis in Bristol by ward (2001 census).

Figure 118 Bangladeshis in Bristol by ward (2001 census).

and gurdwara, give the impression of a more concentrated South Asian presence and these general ward statistics undoubtedly mask higher density along certain streets.[334]

Settlement patterns differ between Indian, East African Asian, Pakistani and Bangladeshi residents in the city. Indians and East African Asians are spread more widely than are Pakistanis or Bangladeshis and feature more strongly in the wealthier neighbourhoods of Clifton, Redland and Cotham, indicating the relatively greater affluence of these sub-groups. Pakistanis are mainly concentrated in East and Central Bristol with a smaller subset in the South Bristol ward of Windmill Hill, particularly the area of Totterdown, where the city's second oldest mosque is located. The Bangladeshis, the poorest and most recent group to arrive from the sub-continent, are the most densely concentrated in the inner city.

Contrary to some popularly held misconceptions, Bristol's South Asian migrants were not drawn from the poorest people in the Indian sub-continent. One had, after all, to have the means to travel to the UK in the first place. Nor, as an opposite prejudice has assumed, were they all shopkeepers or successfully self-employed. Finally, contrary to common wisdom, although there were more extended Asian families living together than English ones, especially amongst the poorer Pakistani and Bangladeshi families, South Asians in Bristol did not, generally speaking, live in extended family units. In the following section we shall see how these contemporary settlement patterns evolved.[335]

SOUTH ASIAN MIGRATION 1947–1972

When Dr Sukhsagar Datta helped to found Bristol's Indian Association in 1947, the city's Indian population appears to have been largely comprised of a dozen or so well-educated professionals along with 'a fair sprinkling of Indian students' from Bristol University.[336]

Early Sikh Migrants

Among the first South Asian migrants who appear to have come in any numbers to Bristol were Sikhs from the Punjab. Anthropologists speak of the Bhatra (or Bhats), the Ramgarhias and Jat Sikhs as the main caste groups of ethnic Sikhs in Bristol by the 1970s, although others of lower traditional status also came. The point here is that the majority of Sikhs in Bristol and the first to come in any numbers to the city were Bhatras or Bhat Sikhs.

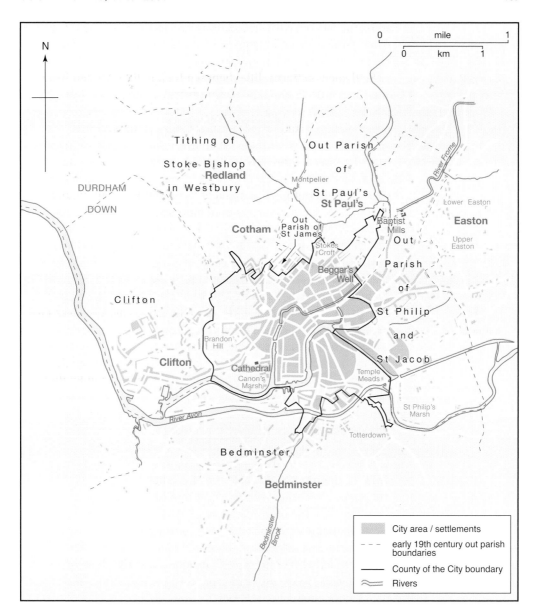

Figure 119 Bristol beyond the historic centre: 19th-century out parishes and selected modern suburbs.

They came from a very localised and close-knit network of 10 rural villages in what is now the district of Sialkot, Pakistan. They claimed a common pedigree as peripatetic poets and preachers, although one late Victorian ethnographer described them as traditional 'hawkers and fortune tellers', and they have been described in a recent Sikh website as of low 'gypsy' status. Whichever characterisation one adopts, the Bhats had a history of geographical mobility and a reputation for fluency and networking which served them well when they first arrived in Britain in the 1920s.[337]

Figure 120 Nagina Singh in Bristol. Born in 1926 in Sialkot in what is now Pakistan, Nagina Singh's family fled to India on foot in 1947. He arrived in England in 1948 and worked as a market trader and peddler in London, Glasgow and Cambridge, settling in Bristol, where he bought his first house in 1952.

By the 1940s a few Bhat men who passed through Bristol settled there, initially using the town as a base for regional peddling and remitting much of their earnings back to India. Like the Jews and Scots before them, they catered first to working-class clients and offered credit and a persuasive patter. Clothes, perfumes, jewellery, black market stockings and lucky charms were reportedly their stock in trade, along with the occasional offer of palm reading and astrological advice. In the immediate post-war years, they also began to ply their wares in holiday, prisoner of war and army camps and the new housing estates around Bristol and Gloucestershire. At first living together for both safety and fellowship in rented accommodation in Bedminster (South Bristol), Nagina Singh and his compatriots later rented a couple of rooms from another Asian in St Michael's Hill in the city. These early South Asian migrants to Bristol appear to have put caste and religious divisions aside, and assisted each other. After Partition some decided to settle permanently in Britain and purchased houses here in the cheaper areas of the city (Kingsdown, Easton, St Paul's, Eastville, Montpelier and Bedminster).[338]

Home ownership enabled Nagina Singh and others to rent out rooms to other castes at rents which were not strictly determined by the market, but varied with the closeness of the relationship they had with the tenant. Being a landlord conferred status within one's peer group and the income received from these often sub-standard houses helped them to pay off their mortgages and possibly invest in another house for the exclusive use of their own families. Some rented out houses to African-Caribbeans. The small Bhat community consisted, according to one source, of 10-14 households by the mid-fifties. Their modest means, depleted by remittances back home, meant that it would take them a decade to establish their own small temple or Gurdwara in a terraced house in St Mark's Road in Easton, Bristol.[339]

The other main group of Sikh men to come to Bristol before 1970 were Jat Sikhs, who came mainly from the Jullundur Doab, one of the Punjab's most densely populated districts. Although traditionally peasant farmers, many young Jat males had served as soldiers under the British Raj or taken advantage of job opportunities outside their immediate district and indeed throughout the British Empire. Their caste position and martial reputation afforded them higher social status than the Bhats enjoyed. Along with the Jats came Punjabi Sikhs from other caste backgrounds, most notably the Ramgarhias, who were traditionally associated with carpentry. The Jats in particular seem to have been less conservative with regard to education and the position of women. Yet, in an interesting instance of how changing circumstances help to redraw traditional hierarchies, the Bhats' early entry into the property market as landlords enabled some by the 1970s to prosper more than some Jats.[340]

Whatever their background, Sikh men faced real difficulties in getting jobs. For not only did they have to contend with language difficulties and open and legalised colour prejudice but their turbans and beards seemed to mark them out for particular discrimination.

> I don't think [I encountered racism] although when I came here I had a turban and a beard and I went for a few interviews [and was] rejected everywhere ... soon my friends asked me to shave my hair I did so and got a job.

... when [landlords] saw me with a turban, they used to say 'not for you'. This happened about five times.[341]

Economic necessity thus forced Sikh men of various caste backgrounds to seek similar employment. Those who kept their turbans obtained work by dint of working unpopular shifts at low wages. Bhats began to move out of peddling and found, alongside Jats, Ramgarhias and others, employment on building sites as labourers, as manual workers in bakeries, foundries, factories and private hire drivers. After 1963 and the formal ending of the colour bar on Bristol buses, Sikhs and other South Asians found employment as drivers and conductors, but discrimination against those wearing turbans persisted well into the late 1980s.[342]

The early settlement of Pakistanis

The other main group of South Asians to come to Bristol before the 1970s were Pakistanis. Their early days in the city are largely undocumented, but it seems that the first groups of migrants were male Punjabis who came at the end of the 1950s, although a few individuals may well have preceded them. A few of these were Christian refugees who probably came after Pakistan officially declared itself an Islamic state in 1956, but most were Muslims seeking to earn money to help their families back home. What evidence there is suggests that they came from the vicinity of great cities like Lahore and Faisalabad (formerly Lyallpur), and from small towns and villages near the urban centres of Jhelum and Gujerat. Like the West Indians and Sikhs before them, they initially saw themselves as temporary sojourners rather than permanent settlers.[343]

By the early 1960s, immigration from Pakistan gathered pace, with travel agencies in Lahore and Rawalpindi offering specialist help for would-be emigrants. The men came first to find their fortunes and help their families, but life in Britain was much more expensive than most anticipated, discrimination widespread and English difficult for many to master. They increasingly found they could not afford to go back and forth to see their families as often as they desired, much less retire back home in affluence. The wives of those married migrants were often left in Pakistan with their in-laws. Bhangan Bibi, for example, stayed for six years in the small village of Dhokawan whilst her husband Abdul Aziz emigrated first to Keighley (Yorkshire) in 1962, then to Bristol as a factory worker with Pardoes. She was separated from her son Mazhar for five years when he left at 14 to join his father.

Some Punjabi women recall being left with unsympathetic in-laws at this time, but one in particular, 'Fatima', describes being used as a household servant when her husband was away. Her memory is very vivid: 'When I was staying with my in-laws in Pakistan while my husband was in England, they only let me [have] two sets of clothes a year and a bath only once a month. They said, "Why are you bathing? Why are you wearing new clothes?"'[344]

Others reportedly worried at the strain long separations would have on their marriage and on the upbringing of their children.[345]

Punjabi migrants were soon joined by their neighbours from the Kashmiri district of Mirpur in Azad Kashmir. Azad Kashmir, literally 'Free Kashmir', was contested territory. In 1948 India had absorbed the whole of the princely state of Kashmir, despite the fact that most of the population was Muslim, and Azad Kashmir was a breakaway region claimed by Pakistan. Of the Pakistanis who came from Azad Kashmir to Bristol, most were born in the district of Mirpur and this fact, too, is a direct result of the repercussions of the 1947/8 settlement, for the Mangla Dam in Mirpur, financed in part by the World Bank, was part of a plan to redress the water shortages Pakistan suffered as a result of the 1947 settlement. The dam, completed in 1960, displaced many thousands of people. To avert widespread unrest, some of those displaced were offered financial compensation as well as passports, which before then had been difficult for rural people to obtain, and thus began a large-scale exodus to many parts of the world, including Britain. Mirpuris already established in the UK felt bound to afford traditional hospitality to those displaced. According to one source, Mirpuris constitute the largest group amongst Bristol's first generation of 'Pakistanis'.[346]

Although chain migration meant that friends and kin helped newly arrived compatriots get jobs and find shelter, post-war housing conditions for these isolated early migrants were grim. There were no mosques, hallal butchers or 'Asian' food shops before the mid-sixties in Bristol. One early migrant, Haji Muhammad Yaqub, resorted to buying 'Jewish Kosher' meat from a shop in the Old

Market district of Bristol (a practice permitted under Muslim law). Yaqub recalled four men to a room in rented houses with no hot water. As a respite from these dreary conditions he remembered how he and his friends would meet up to play cards or talk, or sometimes recite verses from the Sayfu Mulūk, the 19th-century epic by the Punjabi poet Mian Muhammad Baqsh. Baqsh's poetry would, said Yaqub, remind 'us of all the wonderful memories of Pakistan'. Yaqub and some of his friends found construction work in the city on such projects as the M32 motorway and the maintenance of the Clifton Suspension Bridge.[347]

Most rural Pakistanis had had only a few years of schooling and were further hampered by an uncertain command of English. Mohammed Yunis's father was originally from Mirpur, worked in Bradford and, fetching his son from Pakistan, returned to Britain in 1966, settling in Bristol three years later when a friend found him a job at Jackson's Engineering in nearby Yate. Jackson's employed quite a few Punjabis and Mirpuris in semi-skilled work, painting panels and assembling gas water heaters and cookers.[348]

Whether Indian or Pakistani, more educated South Asians faced another difficulty: often their qualifications were not recognised in Britain. Jernail Singh Sandhu began work in England as a machine operator on the night shift in a rubber factory, despite his BA in economics and accounting from the University of the Punjab. Raghbir Singh, Bristol's first Asian bus conductor, was a qualified engineer with a degree from the same university. Another degree holder who had hoped to teach in this country ended up working as a postman.

South Asian families in the 1960s

By the mid-sixties, wives and families began to follow from Pakistan, although immigration restrictions caused great anxiety and at times prevented families from being re-united. Less than a third of the 865 Pakistanis listed in the 1971 census were female, and of these only 180 were listed as married. The wives who had come over more often than not had little or no schooling and did not speak English. Mrs 'B' remembers being married at 15 and following her 30-year-old husband to Bristol in 1967, where she was horrified to find he was still living in lodgings:

> When I came over my husband was living as a lodger in an Indian house. He had two rooms and I thought it was our house because we never lived in lodgings. The owner was there and I thought he was the lodger. I asked my husband, 'Who is he?', and he said, 'he's the owner'. I was shocked and he said 'quiet,

quiet because I can't afford to buy a house'. I said, 'No way I'm
living with somebody else' … My husband had three weeks
holiday to take us out and I said, 'No, I'm not going out until
you buy our own house.' And on the 17th day I was in my own
house! I was that stubborn …[349]

By the end of the sixties more of Bristol's South Asians had a
mortgage on a house than their White working-class counterparts.
Home ownership was traditionally highly valued amongst Bristol's
Pakistanis and Sikhs but the homes so purchased were often in
the roughest and most rundown areas of central Bristol. Contrary
to popular belief, most Pakistanis lived in nuclear family units,
although households with a sibling or elderly relative living with
them were more common amongst them, so few terrace houses
were large enough to accommodate extended families.[350]

Because rural families in Pakistan would have traditionally
lived together or in close proximity, those in Bristol tried wherever possible to live near and visit members of their extended
kinship group (*biraderi*). Failing that, they 'adopted' other
Urdu speakers in their immediate vicinity as substitute kin.
Relationships with those outside their kinship network tended to
be more transient and superficial. Although a number of women
interviewed fondly remember kindness from some of their
English neighbours, and one recalled proudly giving her non-
Asian neighbours home-cooked food after her daughter's wedding
feast, another explained: '… we *are* different from the White
English. That is why we live in areas where there are more of us so
that we do not feel alone.'[351]

Language was a barrier, especially for those women who had
little or no schooling. Many rural women were illiterate in their
own language, could not speak English, and did not have the
confidence or support to attend existing language classes. There
was a large unmet need for home tuition in English, and the few
successful schemes for English classes for women were those which
were sensitive to the women's own priorities and values.

One of the MEC [Multi-cultural Education Centre] staff 'got
some funding and we drew in one or two people from the community who had worked with other cultures and started English
classes for the women'. The husbands were persuaded that this was
a totally women's group and that it was safe. 'We had a wonderful
group of women for three or four years.'[352]

Language and lack of literacy were not the only barriers to a
fuller engagement with Bristol's wider population. Fearfulness for
their personal safety in the inner city areas was another inhibiting
factor. But so, too, amongst the lesser educated village women

especially, was a suspicion of Western values which were widely seen as inimical to their own notions of proper moral conduct.

Since the reputation and marriage prospects of their children depended on the strict maintenance of their own respectability, a respectability governed by notions of purity, modesty and family duty, the Pakistani women new to Bristol tended to keep themselves to themselves, often in their own distinctive way. Those lesser educated women who lived near female relatives and fellow villagers could socialise and even keep abreast with developments 'back home', not by way of foreign papers as many of their menfolk did, but by word of mouth: 'I'm illiterate so newspapers are out but I keep in touch with the latest gossip.'[353]

They began, too, to explore Bristol, but in a way consistent with their own priorities. Thus one woman, in search of Halal meat, was delighted to discover one of Bristol's City Farms:

> We [her husband and her] found the place by chance. I used to enjoy just walking around and looking. It was one of these occasions: we heard chickens, we asked the lady if she would sell them to us, and so every two or three weeks we went to the farm to buy one. We would get the chicken ourselves and slaughter them in the house.[354]

So, many women were able to forge a social life for themselves and engage to varying degrees with life in Bristol. But others found themselves isolated, particularly as they got older and children left home: '… this loneliness I did not expect but there are other

Figure 121 Two Bristol residents, Nirmal Kaur from Pakistan and Gafoora Begum from India, *c.*1980s.

compensations for living in this country … I hope my husband will
not die before me for I would not be able to manage without him.'[355]

East African Asians

When Zy Siddiqi's mother fled with her nine children from Uganda
in 1971, eventually settling in Knowle in Bristol, she had only
her family's safety in mind. Her family were the descendants of
indentured Asian railway workers imported into East Africa by
the British in the preceding century. By the mid-20th century they
had come to form a buffer class of highly urbanised shopkeepers,
professionals and skilled workers, resented by indigenous Africans
but useful to their British colonial masters.

Political tensions in former British East Africa had begun to
encourage the migration of Asians from Kenya, even before Idi
Amin proclaimed his 'economic war on Asians', precipitating their
sudden and wholesale exodus from Uganda. Although those who
came to Britain had been relatively well off in Africa, many lost
everything in the exodus. As Zy Siddiqi recalls: 'We had two gold
bangles each [on our arms]. The [Ugandan] soldiers put guns
towards us and took our bangles and we got on the airplane …'[356]

Khursheed Thajdin remembers a nightmare journey to Kampala
airport with her ill son:

> We were stopped several times by armed troops; they ordered
> us out of the taxis, dragged off our luggage, searched and took
> whatever they wanted. We had only £50 a family and a few
> clothes. We had to leave everything behind. The armed men
> pointed their rifles at us; a shot was fired but missed. They shot
> other people in the legs. They tortured others.[357]

In the winter of 1972, perhaps a thousand Ugandan Asians
found themselves in the snowy grounds of a disused Doniform
army camp in Somerset. Others were placed in Honiton and then
Watchet. Although they gratefully received a warm welcome in
England (Zy Siddiqi fondly remembers camp managers trying to
make the refugees feel at home by putting curry powder in their
baked beans), the reality soon sunk in that most were suddenly
proletarianised. After some months at the relocation camps they
began the task of finding employment. As with the Huguenots
nearly 300 years before, Bristol Quakers were prominent in the
efforts at helping them to settle in the city, and, like the Huguenots,
East African Asians effectively utilised the wide-ranging network
of friends and families in the diaspora for the arrangement of
marriages and business contacts.[358]

Although Bristol's refugees included (mainly Ramgarhia) Sikhs and Muslims, most of the 600 or so East African Asians eventually relocated into the city were Hindu, with origins in the Gujerat region of India. Their intense devotional religious life began in a way analogous to the Christian house movement, where worshipers would invite others to devotional meetings in private homes. Yashu Amlani remembers inviting other Gujeratis over for a regular gathering: 'Everyone would bring a dish … we would sing *Bhajans*, talk, tell jokes, and we decided to meet every fortnight and take it in turns to host it. I had set up a shrine and a library in my house which people made use of …'[359]

Generally better educated and more urbanised than the migrants who came directly from the Indian sub-continent, the East African Asians injected new energy and expertise into the Bristol South Asian scene. Some individuals came to act as mediators both within the South Asian communities and between these communities and the wider one. For example, Mulk Raj came to Britain in 1960 from Kenya, where he had been a primary school head, and he and his wife Satya both acted as interpreters for non-English speakers in schools, hospitals and clinics, and also ran training classes for the local police. Hariprasad Joshi from Uganda, elected in 1973 to be Vice-President of the Bristol Indian Association, was a member of the Community Relations Council as well as a convenor of religious worship for several hundred local Hindu residents of varying caste and regional backgrounds. Bhupi Bowri would go on from his voluntary post in the Community Relations Council and various Asian organisations to become the founder of Bristol's Asian Council in 1974. Kassam Ismail Majothi (1924-2002), who was reputed to have arrived penniless in Bristol, went on to found, with his family, the *Bristol Sweet Mart*, a large and much loved emporium of Asian foods. Rohit Barot became a well-known sociologist at Bristol University, and Lalit Kumar helped to pioneer multi-cultural education at Bristol Polytechnic.[360]

Of course, not everyone was equally enamoured with this new injection of talent. As noted in Chapter 11, some White Bristolians expressed their concern about the prospect of some 50-100 Ugandan Asian families being resettled in Totterdown. Some White people were welcoming, some initially scared but won over by the efforts of their new neighbours, but racial harassment became an increasing problem for all Asians. As community organiser Zehra Haq recalls:[361]

> … in Barton Hill in the high rise flats … you know you never have contact with people, I don't know, because people keep to

themselves and also they [Asian women] didn't feel comfortable because racism was very very rife at that time [late 1970s]. Even my Mother in Law had been attacked a few times … yeah, she go to the park, she got hit, they pulled her scarf, the young kids, and they threw stones at her, so it was very frightening …[362]

GETTING ORGANISED

Male communal organisation in the 1970s

The period 1968-1983 saw the rise of organised communal institutions catering for South Asians, largely according to their national or religious affiliations and generally dominated by the men of these various communities. The Bristol Indian Association was joined by, among others, the Pakistan Welfare Association, the Hindu Association, the Muslim Society, the Bristol Sikh Society, and the small Bangladeshi Welfare Society, which last reflected the growing inflow of people from the economically devastated but newly independent state of Bangladesh (formerly East Pakistan). Although their genesis owed much to the economic and cultural stresses South Asians encountered, these groups were mainly organised along religious lines and recall that proliferation of non-conformist chapels and friendly societies that had been so typical of Victorian Bristol.

A Bristol Muslim Association had been established as early as 1968; at first members borrowed St Katherine's church hall in Totterdown for functions, but then purchased the church that same year. This first mosque in Bristol was Sunni and was followed in 1969 by the conversion of a small terraced house in the St Paul's area into a Muslim community centre and later a mosque run by the Ahmadis, whose relation to mainstream Sunni Islam is a matter of some contention.[363]

By 1976, a small grocer's shop in Roman Road in Easton was converted to the Easton Islami Darsgah mosque. By 1982, a breakaway group from this mosque established the Easton Masjid mosque in what had been the parish hall of St Mark's Church. Although they differed on doctrinal matters, both attracted a mainly Pakistani congregation from the Easton area. Pakistan's bloody civil war with Bangladesh caused bad feeling within the Muslim community in the late 1970s, but relations between the two communities were reportedly mediated by male leaders from both groups. The existence of the Bristol Community Relations Council ensured that at least community representatives from all the different faith and national groups knew each other and were in frequent contact.[364]

The Sikhs were also beginning to branch out. In 1970 a Gurdwara was established in St George on the site of a disused girls' church school that apparently attracted Sikhs who were not Bhats. The Chelsea Road Ramgarhia Gurdwara (its name indicating its caste association) was established in 1977 after members tirelessly raised funds from fellow Sikhs around the country for the purchase of the property. Two years later, Bristol's first gurdwara, in St Mark's Road, was relocated to a disused post office in nearby Fishponds Road at considerable cost, the event celebrated with a public procession attended by Bristol's Lord Mayor and local MP Arthur Palmer in attendance.[365]

Also in 1979, the Bristol Hindu Association, which had been using the rooms of Friends House in Gloucester Road, Horfield, where many of their members lived, began to lobby local officials for help in finding a nearby hall. They were eventually able to establish their Temple in Redfield, East Bristol, in a late Victorian gothic building (which had originally been a Methodist Chapel), with the assistance of the Methodist Superintendent of the Kingswood Area, the Rev. R. Stevenson and Bristol MP Tony Benn. The two-day celebration following the Temple's opening in 1981 included the Lord Mayor, MPs and eight Brahmin priests from London and Leicester, and was a matter of great pride, a public demonstration of 'what it was that penniless refugees were able to achieve'.[366]

Figure 122 Devotions at the Sanatan Deevya Mandal (Bristol's Hindu temple), founded in 1979 largely by Ugandan Asian refugees (2007).

Despite these public celebrations, the rise of non-Christian places of worship did cause ill-feeling in some quarters, as did the cultural self-containment of many South Asian families. The influx of East African Asians helped to promote White panic about an Asian invasion. In 1980 the Totterdown mosque was transformed by the addition of a green onion dome roof and non-functional minaret financed in part by Saudi Arabian money. These alterations seemed to some like an aggressive challenge to the city's traditional churchscape and such fears, clumsily fanned by the far-right National Front, caused controversy. Planning permission had been approved on the grounds that the minaret should be 'a decorative feature only and … not be used in any way as a "wailing tower" for the purpose of calling the faithful to prayer'.[367]

If such religious buildings proved a source of anxiety to some, they were literally a 'god send' to many first generation South Asian men. The recession of 1974 and the downturn in traditional manufacturing industries hit many semi- and unskilled workers hard, and Black and Asians hardest of all, causing a number of older Asian workers to retire 'back home'. In 1982, 20 per cent of Asian men and women were unemployed in the UK, compared with 13 per cent of White men, but in Central Bristol the figures rose to 25 per cent for Asian men. The disproportionate number of the Asian men interviewed in the Fenton study who had either been made redundant or left work through ill health or industrial accidents can in part be explained by another recession which hit Bristol in the early 1980s. The following remark is typical:[368] 'I do not see any bright future. I have been already made redundant at the age of 56. I have not been keeping good health for the last 12 to 15 months.'[369]

There does seem to have been an extraordinarily high number of this cohort suffering from heart problems, diabetes and high blood pressure. If cultural or genetic factors in part account for this, many in the sample attested to the toll hard work had also taken on their health and general well being. Twelve-hour shifts were not uncommon, and night work frequent. As one skilled machinist at Rolls Royce in the early 1980s put it: '… the worst thing is that I work seven days a week and long hours … very hard. I didn't know I had to work this hard.'[370]

But equally, unemployment was seen by the men interviewed as shameful and isolating, a loss of face not only within their immediate families, but to the wider network both in Britain and back home.

For these men in particular, their mosques and gurdwaras offered vital support. Not all surveyed were observant but a disciplined and supportive fellowship had its attractions when

Figure 123 Bristol Jamia mosque in Green Street, Totterdown, Bristol (2007). Originally an Anglican mission room, this building has been used as a mosque since 1968. Its redesign with a dome and minaret caused controversy in 1979.

redundancy and ill health struck. Mukhtyar Singh Bhakerd, who had cut his hair and gone through a 'wild' adolescence, recalled the deep satisfaction afforded him on his return to a more observant life in the early 1970s after losing a kidney and then being laid off during the recession. Local leaders like Lakhinder Singh, who also played an important role in Bristol's Community Relations Council, stressed the need for passing Sikh cultural and religious values to those Sikhs, especially young men, who had 'gone astray'.[371]

For many Muslim men, daily visits to the mosque staved off the loneliness and isolation they increasingly felt as children moved to found their own families, while other kin remained thousands of miles away. The Sikh Gurdwara served, too, as a community centre, with its Sunday communal dinner, its Punjabi newspapers and its Holy Books. Punjabi and religious schools there also acted as forums for discussing issues such as crash helmet legislation, the turban, the wearing of the kirpan (sword), and immigration legislation.

The Gurdwaras and mosques offered respite from poor living conditions as well. One man, who had left India midway through

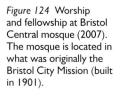

Figure 124 Worship and fellowship at Bristol Central mosque (2007). The mosque is located in what was originally the Bristol City Mission (built in 1901).

a degree in literature, ended his days in a damp house in the inner city where he and his wife fell ill. He had hoped to rekindle his early ambitions in retirement: he had 'wanted to write books but am too ill these days'. Yet he could point with pride to having worked as a volunteer community worker for the Sikh community in earlier times. The sense of achievement and respect men gained by serving on management committees in the mosques and gurdwaras, raising funds, refurbishing the premises, organising religious festivals and outings and doing an array of welfare work helped in some part to compensate for the discrimination and lack of status they experienced in the wider world.

The Rise of Women's Organisations

High male unemployment made traditional forms of purdah or female seclusion increasingly untenable and an unknown proportion of Sikh and Muslim women began to enter the workforce to make ends meet. Those we have interviewed allude to the initial opposition of their husbands to their going out to work on the grounds of the shame it would cast upon the head of the household. It took some determination to circumvent these prohibitions, but the women justified their defiance on the grounds of their children's needs.

After a lifetime spent cooking, sewing and visiting relatives, factory life came as a shock. One woman spoke of the harsh discipline at Brook laundry where toilet breaks were timed, but she and others also attested to enjoying the camaraderie of fellow workers, most of whom were Black or Asian ('White ladies wouldn't do that sort of work') working under White foremen. Another, working at a chocolate factory where White women were employed in considerable numbers, spoke of the kindness and understanding of her forewoman and workmates when her husband fell ill. Those interviewed enjoyed the camaraderie of fellow workers but the pay was low and there was a lack of opportunity for advancement. The work was often heavy and unhealthy, but it gave them a sense of individual achievement. Others found homework a more accessible and acceptable way of earning money, but here, too, the pay was very low.[372]

Changes in employment patterns had begun to challenge traditional patriarchal divisions of labour. This probably contributed to the rise of Asian women's organisations in Bristol by the late 1970s and 1980s. The intervention of more educated Asian women migrants who were able to obtain new streams of government funding made these organisations possible. The first

Figure 125 Asian Women's groups in Bristol provided social support and welfare advice from the 1980s.

Bristol Asian Group appears to have been set up in 1978. The Women's Committee set up by the City Council in the late 1980s was instrumental in encouraging local Asian women to apply for funding for local initiatives. Zehra Haq set up the Barton Hill Asian Women's Group (later Dhek Bhal), which would later grow to claim some 800 members. Since then other groups organised by local Asian women, financed by a range of funders, have appeared, including Humdard (1986), Awaz Utoa (1994) and the Bangladeshi Women's Association.

The Bangladeshis

There were very few Bangladeshis in Bristol in the mid-1970s. Dr Mohammed Aziz-Ur-Rahman, who had worked as a doctor in the city from the late 1960s, and Pabitra Kumar Ghosh, a teacher, were rare exceptions. Most Bangladeshis who came to the city in the late 1970s and 1980s were smallholders from Sunamganj, a tea and rice growing district in the Sylhet region of Bangladesh. A high proportion were men who worked in the city's 'Indian' restaurants owned by more established fellow Sylhetis such as Mohammed Abdu Wahab and Mohammed Akmal Khan. According to one study, it was customary for wealthier men to pay for the passage of less well-off compatriots to come to work in Bristol, with a portion of their wages sometimes being paid directly to their parents in Bangladesh.[373]

In the late 1970s, Mocklis Miah, his parents having returned to Bangladesh, moved from Burnley to Bristol to attend Monk's Park School before putting in eight hours each day working in his uncle's restaurant in Cheltenham Road, St Paul's. Typically, he and his brother and the rest of the male staff lived above the restaurant. Those with some capital combined to form business ventures: 'Our community is like, very close to each other … you know, they help each other … so they like, you know, four or five people get together – relation or friends and, you know, put some money into a restaurant …'.[374] By the age of 19, Mocklis, with his uncle as partner, had a restaurant of his own to manage and at 25 he went to Bangladesh for an arranged marriage with a local woman, returning with her to Bristol.

By 2006, the mainly Muslim Bangladeshi community had established a Bangladeshi centre and raised funds for two mosques. The distinctive lines of the most recent mosque can be seen by those driving into the city on the M32.

Figure 126 The Shal Jalal Jame mosque in Eastville (2007). Construction began in 2000 under the aegis of Bristol's Bangladeshi community.

CONCLUSION

An impressive number of the first generation of South Asians, both women and men, have participated increasingly in Bristol's civic life. Tom Mehra (d. 1995) was the city's first Asian Justice of the Peace and others have followed including Zahida Sadiq, who came as a young refugee from Uganda. Several Bristol Asians have been awarded MBEs, including Shiv Ranjan Singh (1993), Yashu Amlani (1998), Abdul Wahab (1999), and Batook Pandya, founder of SARI (2000). Others, less well known, did voluntary work in the wider community, ranging from helping heart patients at Bristol's Royal Infirmary, organising away days for Barton Hill's elderly residents and staging performances of Bengali poetry. But probably more South Asians were empowered by the deregulation of Bristol's Hackney taxis in 1997. Deeply unpopular with Bristol's White drivers who saw, with some justice, increased competition as a threat to their livelihood, deregulation enabled many Asians an alternative to lower paid private hire work while addressing the shortage in the city's supply of taxis.

The growing social mobility of some sections of the community, a trend most pronounced amongst those of Indian and East African origin, is perhaps most dramatically evidenced by the rise in Asian retail emporiums such as the much celebrated *Bristol Sweet Mart*. The influx of the higher caste Gujeratis, namely the Patels (from the Charottar district of Gujerat) and the Lohanas from London and Leicester, has also contributed to a larger mercantile and professional presence in the city. Although a number of affluent Pakistani families reportedly moved from Newport to Bristol at the end of our period to form a noticeable presence, social mobility is less marked within the Pakistani and Bangladeshi communities, whose future prospects in this regard have become a matter for debate. Despite worries about the way higher education might undermine traditional values, a number of elders are adamant that their children utilise education as a way out of low-waged employment, and the high priority the first generation placed on home ownership should also prove advantageous to them in the longer term.[375]

By the end of our period, two thirds of Bristol's Pakistanis and Indians were British born. Most of the Bristol-born people of South Asian origin have had a different experience of life from their parents, and while this can cause real tensions it has not necessarily meant the wholesale rejection of their Asian identity or particular faith community. Arranged marriages are still widespread and accepted, and anecdotal evidence suggests there are more opportunities to negotiate their terms and timing, especially amongst the more educated girls. The rise of Bhangra music and Bollywood films attests to the existence of a generation that is neither wholly British nor Asian but, as one set of scholars have put it, 'BrAsian'. Their varied and often imaginative refashionings of ethnic identity have been influenced by their encounters with western individualism, racism, and newly constituted peer groups, which may replicate or challenge traditional ethnic, gender and class divisions. In addition, the increasing importance of religious, over ethnic, identification has been influenced by generational conflict and by political events in the wider world.[376]

Chapter 14

Displaced People: Poles, Somalis and Others

Bristol has been home to survivors from some of the 20th-century's great upheavals. During the First World War these included Belgian refugees. The Second World War brought a considerable number of displaced civilians and soldiers from Central and Eastern Europe, mostly Poles, but also some from Latvia and a few Jewish survivors of the Nazi genocide.

In the second half of the century, Bristol became home to Hungarians who fled the Soviet invasion in 1956, Ugandan Asians expelled by Idi Amin in 1972, Chileans targeted by Pinochet's military regime from 1973, and the so-called 'boat people' who had escaped from Vietnam by that decade's end. More recent refugees have included civilian survivors of the Balkan conflicts and the Rwandan genocide. Iraqi Kurds, Iranians and Somalis are among the latest exiles to seek security in Bristol.

This chapter begins with a short overview of refugees in Bristol between 1914 and the end of the Second World War, and then focuses on two of the largest post-war refugee groups, the Poles and the Somalis. The first Polish arrivals just after the Second World War predate by nearly half a century the most recent Polish immigration, which occurred after Poland joined the European Community in 2004.

By contrast, aside from a small number of economic migrants who arrived in Bristol just after the Second World War, most of the Somalis came to the city after 1989. An estimated 16,000 Somalis now live in Bristol. Concentrated mainly in the Easton, Eastville, Barton Hill and Horfield areas, they have become a focus for public attention and sometimes hostility in the city.

REFUGEES 1914-1950s

Belgians

When Germany invaded Belgium in 1914, over a million of its six million population fled. Some 250,000 were allowed to enter Britain where their plight generated popular sympathy exceeded only by hatred towards anyone thought to be German. Over 2,500 refugee committees were established in England and Wales and by 1916 Birmingham alone had accommodated nearly 4,000 Belgian refugees.[377]

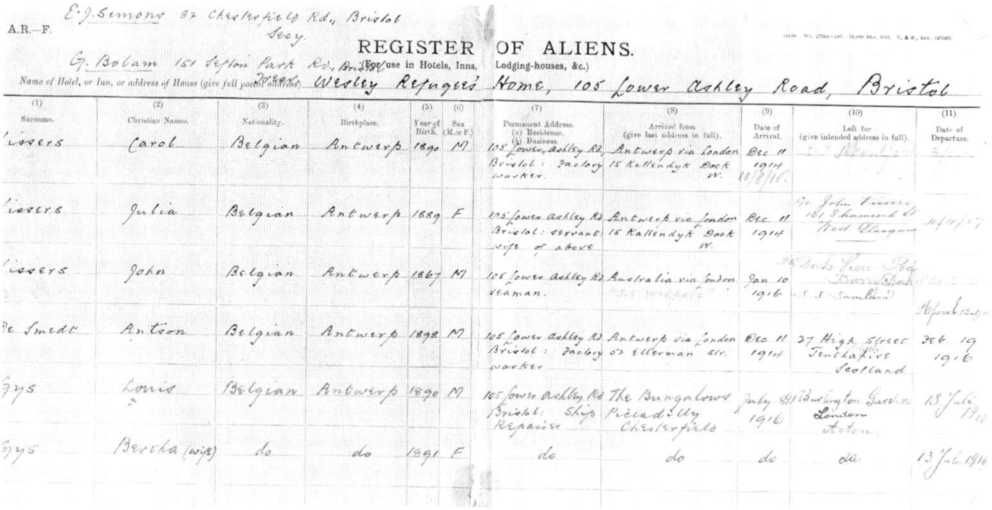

A.R.—F. E. J. Simons 82 Chesterfield Rd., Bristol Secy.

G. Bolam 151 Sefton Park Rd., Bristol

REGISTER OF ALIENS.
(For use in Hotels, Inns, Lodging-houses, &c.)

Name of Hotel, or Inn, or address of House (give full postal address) Wesley Refugees' Home, 105 Lower Ashley Road, Bristol

(1) Surname.	(2) Christian Names.	(3) Nationality.	(4) Birthplace.	(5) Year of Birth.	(6) Sex (M. or F.)	(7) Permanent Address. (a) Residence. (b) Business.	(8) Arrived from (give last address in full).	(9) Date of Arrival.	(10) Left for (give intended address in full).	(11) Date of Departure.
[illegible]ssers	Carol	Belgian	Antwerp	1890	M	105 Lower Ashley Rd, Bristol: Factory worker.	Antwerp via London 15 Kallendyk Dock W.	Dec 11 1914 10/8/16	[illegible]	[illegible]
[illegible]ssers	Julia	Belgian	Antwerp	1889	F	105 Lower Ashley Rd Bristol: servant. wife of above	Antwerp via London 15 Kallendyk Dock W.	Dec 11 1914	To John [illegible] 161 Shamrock St West Glasgow	[illegible]
[illegible]ssers	John	Belgian	Antwerp	1867	M	105 Lower Ashley Rd seaman.	Australia via London	Jan 10 1916	[illegible] S.S. [illegible]	[illegible]
De Smedt	Antson	Belgian	Antwerp	1898	M	105 Lower Ashley Rd Bristol: Factory worker	Antwerp via London 52 Ellerman Str.	Dec 11 1914	27 High Street [illegible] Scotland	Feb 19 1916
[illegible]ys	Louis	Belgian	Antwerp	1890	M	105 Lower Ashley Rd Bristol: Ships Repairer	The Bungalows Piccadilly Chesterfield	July [illegible] 1916	[illegible] Burlington Gardens London Acton	13 July 1916
[illegible]ys	Bertha (wife)	do	do	1891	F	do	do	do	do	13 July 1916

Figure 127 Belgian refugees listed in Bristol's register of aliens during the First World War.

The history of Bristol's Belgian refugees has not been systematically investigated. Some were housed in buildings belonging to the Packer's Chocolate Company in Greenbank (later to become Elizabeth Shaw Chocolates). Churches and chapels also afforded them some support. The Horfield Baptists, for example, housed 10 refugees throughout the war and a member of the Wesley Chapel in St Paul's offered a house rent free in Lower Ashley Road for the use of a refugee family. Just over a dozen people seem to have been accommodated in the nearby parish of Alveston under the direction of the local vicar and assisted in part by voluntary contributions.

But there were growing anxieties about the incomers, too. By 1915, the Alveston and the Bristol Refugee Committees, anxious that refugees should not become dependent on them, scrutinised the economic circumstances of the families under their care, and their willingness to work. The refugees were more welcome as sojourners than permanent settlers and there was national relief when the Belgians were finally able to return home at the end of the war.[378]

Jewish Refugees

New restrictions on 'alien immigration' passed in 1919 and 1920 made it very difficult for people to get into Britain without either a work permit or proof that they would not be dependent on state benefits. Restrictions on those fleeing Nazi persecution were particularly tight in the first part of the 1930s when the policy of appeasement made British politicians wary of alienating Hitler. As the policy became discredited, restrictions were partially lifted, but potential refugees still had to find a sponsor who would guarantee to support them in Britain. Relatively few of the 70,000-80,000 Jewish refugees who came to Britain in 1939 from Germany, Austria and Czechoslovakia found their way to Bristol.

Most of those who were able to gain admittance to the country were from middle-class backgrounds yet, unable to take anything with them, they arrived virtually destitute. A local Refugee Committee was set up in Bristol and Gazina Sacof of the Bristol Hebrew congregation worked closely with others arranging job placements.[379]

One of the 10,000 child refugees rescued by the famous *Kindertransport* operation (a largely Quaker initiative) remembered attending an outing to Bristol in the 1930s funded by the local Jewish community, and an unknown number of other children were hosted by Quakers in Bristol before being sent on to the USA.[380]

Another 'Eva' came at 13 and lived with 16 other girls in a boarding house:

> Each girl was given a room, and food to eat. The English brought us over, and the rest was up to us. We had to work to support ourselves. I wanted to work at the Bristol Aircraft Factory because they were making arms to fight Germany. I kept going back to the foreman of the company until he gave me the job. All the other girls with me in the rooming house worked and grew up to be productive.[381]

William Dieneman, who later became a university librarian in Wales, was evacuated on a *Kindertransport* from Berlin to Bristol in 1939. His parents escaped soon after: 'We were lucky to get to England'. Most were not so lucky.[382]

Figure 128 Mary Moar and Mrs Baker, two Bristol Quakers with the Jewish refugee children Peter, Eva and Stephen Kollisch, whom they fostered after they escaped from Vienna on the *Kindertransport* scheme in 1939, and before the children went on to America.

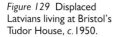

Figure 129 Displaced Latvians living at Bristol's Tudor House, *c.*1950.

The Second World War created refugees all over Europe. In 1951 the government allowed approximately 2,000 displaced people to come to Britain on condition that they would be sponsored for seven years by individuals or groups. That year a public meeting was called by the Bristol Council of Social Services and a small Refugee Aid group was established, comprising about 15 people, some of whom, like Sacof, had been active in refugee work during the war. They had few resources, and assisted only some 20 refugees over the next decade, including 10 Latvians who were accommodated in Tudor House in Ashley Down Road.[383]

A number of Jewish survivors of the Nazis came to Bristol in the first decade after the Second World War. After liberation from a forced labour camp in Kraków and weighing only 4½ stone, 15-year-old Bill Schlesinger came to live with a Jewish family in Bristol. Other arrivals, traumatised by their experiences, were anxious to hide their ethnic identity and so are harder to trace. Shortly after the war, for example, the Stoppard family from India settled in Bristol. Andrew Stoppard was an English Army Major, but his wife Martha and her two sons by her first husband (who had been killed in a Japanese air raid) were Czech Jews who had fled to the Far East. Martha Straüssler's parents and in-laws died in the Holocaust, but she never told her sons of their Jewish parentage. One of them was Tom Stoppard (born Tomáš Straüssler), who worked as a news reporter in Bristol in the mid-1950s before becoming one of Britain's leading playwrights.[384]

THE POLES

The Poles were the largest group of displaced Europeans in immediate post-war Bristol. Many Polish forces had fled the Germans
early in the war and come to Scotland. After fighting for Britain
they were unwilling at the war's end to return to Poland, now
under Soviet domination. The British government's 1945 accommodation with Stalin over Poland, and its subsequent disavowal
of the Polish government in exile, was seen as a betrayal by many
Poles. However, some 114,000 Polish troops and 30,000 of their
dependents were allowed to stay and work in Britain as part of a
formal resettlement scheme. In 1947 another group of Poles, displaced in West Germany, were also permitted to enter as 'European
Voluntary Workers' and were directed into industries experiencing
labour shortages.[385]

Most of Bristol's Poles were from Eastern Poland and had been
deported to Siberia after the Soviet occupation. After a negotiated
amnesty in 1941 to allow the men to fight the Nazis, the Poles were
freed from the labour camps but left without adequate resources

Figure 130 The late
Stanislav Cesarz's war-
time experiences were
published with the help
of Anton Bantock, MBE,
who also illustrated her
work.

to return home. Many joined the Polish Free Forces under General Anders, but other family members were shunted around for years in a chaotic, difficult and often dangerous journey southwards out of the USSR, first to Iran and Pakistan, and from there to the Polish camps scattered throughout Africa, including some in what is now Zambia and Zimbabwe. Many died, weakened by malnutrition and vulnerable to typhoid and typhus. Only in Africa, where some remained for over five years, were the children able to resume some semblance of education and begin to recover their health. Survivors interviewed for this book still remember with emotion the nightmare of that period.[386]

Once in Britain, these families were again shunted around a succession of relocation camps while their papers were processed. Some remained in such camps for years. Re-uniting families was not always easy. Franczek Peszyński and Stanisław Kucharczyk, who had both served in the British forces, went back to Germany to arrange for their families to be smuggled out of Communist Poland. This was done at considerable risk as by then emigration to the West was strictly forbidden. Once reunited in Britain, they had to re-adjust to family life after such a profound rupture in their lives. It took some time before Peszyński's sons would agree to call this strange man 'Papa.'[387]

Many families who ultimately settled in Bristol had lived for years not knowing if husbands, wives or children were still alive. Mirroring the fate of Poland itself, Adolf Jankowski, a railwayman, was sent to Siberia in 1940 while his wife Anna and their three children were later forced to go to a German labour camp. They eventually discovered each other's whereabouts, but when Anna was finally able to get to Britain in 1948, both husband and wife had so aged that they hardly recognised each other.[388]

Around 2,000 men and their dependents had come to Bristol by the early 1950s. Some worked as miners at Radstock or Pensford in nearby Somerset, or as factory workers at the Avonmouth Docks. Franczek Peszyński, a miller by trade, was directed to work at Spillers, the flour manufacturer. Richard Domagala was one of a large group of Poles in Newton Abbot, Devon, who having heard about work in Bristol moved there *en masse* and found factory jobs. Many Polish men, the majority of whom came from rural peasant backgrounds, were absorbed by the local construction industry, like the Irish before them.[389]

If low paid jobs were relatively plentiful, low rent housing was not. While Adolf Jankowski lived in Pensford, where he worked as a miner, his wife and children had to live in Fairford, 25 miles away. One correspondent's father was a carpenter on a Bristol building site but could not find accommodation for his family in the city. He eventually brought them to 'a little hut' near Kingsweston, with no water or electricity, where they spent the winter of 1948, drinking water from a cow trough in a nearby field, before relocating to an ex-army camp in Lockleaze, where there was water and 'a little heating from a cooking stove.'[390]

Bristol's Poles may have been favoured over their West Indian counterparts for being White, but they could not speak English and their fervent anti-Communism and intense Catholicism would not have gone down well in some trade union and Protestant circles. Stanisław Kucharczyk was delighted to find a big house in Zion Hill, Clifton, despite its high rent, because it was near his new factory job. So in 1948 he brought his family to the property, sub-letting rooms to fellow Poles from the army and Bristol University to defray the expense. His two children had just secured free places at two local Catholic schools, La Retraite and St Brendan's College, so everything seemed in place for a bright new beginning. But he was soon in for a shock:

> On my arrival on the first day at my new job, I found that all the workers of that factory went out on strike. The manager told me that I could not start my job because I was Polish and the workers resented this. The manager said that it was out of his hands and he could do nothing to help me.[391]

The family rallied around him. His wife Irena found employment as a tailoress to make ends meet and Stanisław eventually found another job. But a year later they were homeless again. According to Stanisław, 'The reason was we were foreigners and the neighbours had objected. At the time this was quite a common occurrence.'[392]

Adjusting to Bristol Life

Bristol's tight-knit Polish community was quick to develop communal institutions to support its members. Worship was based first at the Pro-Cathedral in Clifton and the nearby Polish Ex-Servicemen's Club provided a friendly social centre. Educated members of the community worked hard to help their fellow Poles find work, learn English and secure benefits. Many soldiers had received professional or technical training but some found themselves reduced to less skilled employment in Britain. Channelling their energies back into their own community was one way of their retaining self-respect and social status. By 1950 a Polish Saturday School had been established to ensure that English-born Polish children knew the Polish language and valued their culture. Some who had come

Figure 131 Anton Bantock depicts Stanislav Cesarz's account of how she and her fellow Poles were left waiting on the bank of the Caspian Sea for transport to Iran after their release from forced labour camps in Siberia in 1941.

to Britain as young children took advantage of the educational opportunities available, although daughters were probably less likely to have been given the chance to study than sons. Franczek Peszynski's son, Ireneusz, studied engineering part-time at Brunel College as an apprentice at the Portishead Power Station.[393]

As the economy grew many Poles enjoyed more comfortable lives. Many stayed in manual jobs but some moved on. Adolf Jankowski escaped the mines of Pensford for a job with Rolls Royce in Bristol, and together with his wife, who worked as a tailoress, purchased a house in Horfield. Franczek Peszynski left his factory job to run a lodgings house, grocery and travel business with his wife, specifically geared to serving Polish workers in Avonmouth. They soon prospered enough to move to a shop in Clifton, just behind the Pro-Cathedral. Sophia Szczech, who had endured many privations in Siberia, Iran, Rhodesia and the potato fields of Staffordshire, took particular pleasure in her parents' new Bristol home in Redland: 'The first bath I had was when I came to Bristol! Because [before then] there was nowhere to wash. I used to stay [in the bath] for so long that my mother used to come and ask me if I were alright! [laughs]'. After working as a tailoress in Bristol, Sophia Szczech secured a relatively well-paid job at Rolls Royce, where she enjoyed the camaraderie of her English workmates and the conditions secured as a trade union member.[394]

The Poles seem to have been scattered around Bristol, with no discernible Polish quarter. There are references to Polish landlords in St Paul's during the 1960s. By the end of that decade, an increasing number had branched out as small shopkeepers, running grocery stores, garages or working as suppliers to the construction industry. Many, like Mr Ludowsky's famous delicatessen in Clifton village, had a distinctively Polish ambience, but others decided it was best to anglicise their image. Franczek Peszynski's son Ireneusz left engineering to retrain as an estate agent, eventually running his own agency with his wife Krystyna under the name of George Press and Co. Stanisław Kucharczyk's garage business in St Andrew's was known simply as 'S.K. Motors'. While there were trends towards integration, with a number of Poles contributing to Bristol public life, counter trends also operated, favouring the retention of a more insular Polish identity.

The Catholic Church was a bulwark against assimilation. By 1968 the Polish community was able to purchase Arley Chapel in Cheltenham Road, Stokes Croft, from the Congregationalists to found the Polish church of our Lady of Ostrabrama, whose liturgy and decorations continue to be distinctively and traditionally Polish. A succession of priests acted as spiritual and cultural leaders, inviting dignitaries from the Polish Diaspora to visit the congregation. Bristol's Poles organised a Polish Scout troop and a Polish dance team, and raised money for relatives and causes 'back home'.[395]

The first generation in particular tended to stay largely within their own community. During the 1960s a secondary wave of Polish immigration strengthened this trend. Economic conditions in Poland were particularly difficult and after Stalin's death pressure had been successfully applied to allow more to leave to be reunited with family members in Britain. Consequently, a number of Polish women applied for entry and married Poles resident in Bristol. The arrival of these new migrants helped to conserve Polish cultural identity and networks.[396]

As the Cold War waned, more Poles took the opportunity to visit relatives back home. They did not always find these visits easy. Richard Domagala, a much decorated veteran of the battles of Monte Cassino and Ancona, returned briefly to Poland in 1973 when it was still under communist rule. He was relieved to get back to Bristol. It was not only the changes wrought by Communism which made him feel this way. Despite the visceral attachment many of the people interviewed expressed to their Polish identity, it was often qualified by recognition that their brand of 'Polishness' was forged within a particular historical and political crucible and differed from that of succeeding generations in Poland.[397]

As the first generation of Polish refugees aged, their social isolation increased, facility with their adopted language declined and long-suppressed memories of war and loss resurfaced. 'I thought if I survived it would be behind me', one respondent said ruefully. The physical and psychological trauma which so many Poles had suffered had resulted in a higher incidence of depression and

Figure 132 Ireneusz Peszynski, Honorary Polish Consul, at home with his wife Krystyna in Bristol (2007).

mental illness in that generation of refugees throughout the UK. As with other minority groups, the elderly felt especially dislocated in their adopted country.[398]

On the other hand, since the fall of Communism in 1989, links between Bristol and Poland have proliferated. These have been aided by the efforts of the Honorary Polish Consul, Ireneusz Peszynski, now a Bristol magistrate who was awarded an MBE in 1993. A regular coach service to Poland, the establishment of a Bristol branch of the Anglo-Polish Society and most recently the establishment of regular flights between Bristol Airport and Kraków have led to many new commercial and cultural contacts.

An unprecedented influx of workers into the city since 2003 has marked a new chapter in the history of Bristol's Polish presence. The existing Polish community has done much to help the newcomers adjust, and the newcomers in turn have swelled the numbers of its once dwindling Catholic congregation. But they have also exposed new fractures within the community itself, whose sense of communal identity has been challenged by these 'New Poles'.

SOMALIS

Somalis have come to British ports as seamen since at least the 19th century, but their presence in Bristol cannot be documented before 1950. Perhaps only around 10 Somali men were working as general labourers in the city in 1960, when the British and Italian colonies on the Horn of Africa merged into an independent Republic of Somalia. Small numbers of marriage partners and other workers joined them, so that a community of around 100 people had been established by 1989.

Yet two years later this number is estimated to have jumped to 2,000. This sudden increase was caused by the collapse of Somalia into civil war in 1991. The Soviet-style regime of Dictator Siyad Barre, who had seized power in the military coup of 1969, was finally toppled after over a decade of clan-based infighting. In the murderous chaos that ensued, some clans in the north-west of the country (formerly under British rule) grouped together to declare the secession of an independent Republic of Somaliland, based on traditional clan structures. Although unrecognised by the international community, Somaliland has enjoyed relative peace and stability since 1997. By contrast, the rest of the country and the surrounding border areas in Kenya and Ethiopia, where ethnic Somalis reside, have descended into barbarous war-lordism. Even in the cities, basic services have been destroyed and rape

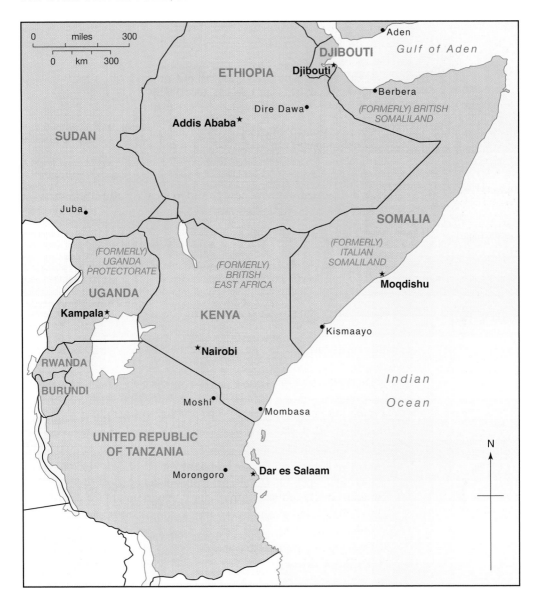

Figure 133 East Africa, showing current boundaries. Present day Somaliland (much of which was previously under British rule) is not formally recognised as an independent nation by international law. Somalia as indicated here was formerly divided between Britain, France and Italy. In the 1960s this region was the site of Cold War contests for power. A significant number of Somali reside as displaced people in Kenya.

Figure 134 Somali
Police visit Bristol Police
Headquarters, 1960.

and murder are routinely perpetrated by 'khat-chewing young
gangsters' in a spiral of factionalism.[399]

The 1990s saw up to one third of Somalis facing starvation and
the displacement of a million of the six million population. Some
of them managed to escape to Europe, despite ever-tightening
restrictions on immigrants and refugees. By 2001 as many as
10,000 Somalis had come to Bristol. Six years later the estimated
number of Somalis in Bristol had doubled. Although 'push' factors
clearly outweigh 'pull' factors in such extreme circumstances, some
respondents expressed a preference for Britain over other European
countries because of the historical links and the status of English
as an international language. The existence of family networks was
another draw, with Bristol preferred to Bath, for example, because
of its ethnic diversity.

The Economic Migrants 1950–c.1989

Mohammed Issa Ahmed and Hashi Jama, who both arrived by
1950, were among the first Somalis to settle in Bristol. Like most
Somalis, they had been rural nomads. Both grew up in northern
Somalia, spending their youth guarding their families' herds of
camels and flocks of sheep and goats from hyenas and lions. Their
formal schooling was confined to studying the Koran at the local
madrassa, where the Arabic text was learned by rote.

They recount with vigour some of the rich oral tradition of
poetry, stories and clan genealogies, often communally recited,

which characterised their culture (before 1972 the Somali language remained unwritten), and are proud of their skills as herdsmen.[400]

Both decided to leave Somalia as teenagers for personal reasons. Issa was outraged at being whipped by the Imam at his *madrassa*, and ran away to live with his aunt for two years before, in 1944, hitching a lift on a *dhow* to the port of Aden, where he joined the Royal Navy. When, as a teenager, Hashi found to his horror that hyenas had attacked his family's herd, he was so worried about the consequences that he, too, left home, stowing away to Aden. From there he eventually found his way to Britain with the help of a network of Somali seamen. Issa arrived in Cardiff in 1949 to stay with a relative before moving to Bristol the following year. Hashi came to the city in 1956.

Both quickly found work. Their lack of formal education may have stymied promotion prospects but did not prevent them from being long-term employees and saving from their earnings. After a stint with Frissell Ltd, Issa worked for Darlington Installation until his retirement 35 years later, by which time he had an English wife, children and his own home.

Hashi, whose wife Ebado is Somali, worked as a machine operator at Cadbury Schweppes in Keynsham, and bought a house in the St Andrew's area where, at the time of writing, he still lives with his family. One of his workmates was another Somali, Ismail Ali who, although from a different clan, shared a similar childhood looking after a sizeable herd of sheep and camels in the northern region of Hergaisse. Ali came to Bristol via Cardiff in 1961 after nine years as a general labourer in Saudi Arabia. He too was 'looking for a different life'. Unlike Issa, he had no family here but he too relied on the friendship and support of Somali seamen. At first he lived with some Somali students who were studying at Bristol University. Within 10 years he had saved enough to own his own home. Two years later he returned to Somalia to marry Saina, who was from his own clan. She had joined him in Bristol by 1975. All three men expressed their appreciation of the opportunity which Britain affords those willing to work hard, a sentiment echoed by others encountered in this investigation. However, as they have aged, two expressed feelings of increasing isolation.[401]

Somalis Seeking Asylum

When Ahmed Duale first arrived in Britain in 1991, he thought the war at home would be over in a few days, but, as he observed, 'everyone I knew was coming out'. He was luckier than most – he was well connected. His father was a chief, his uncle a head teacher and Abdi had recently graduated with a good degree in English

Figures 135 Hodan Ali, Mukhtar Abdi and Suleem Hassan (sitting left to right) gained refugee status in Bristol before 2001 and are now learning English at one of the few available courses in Bristol, 2007.

literature from Somalia National University. His promising career as a junior diplomat in the foreign office enabled him to leave war-torn Mogadishu for Abu Dhabi with a visa. He also had family in both Cardiff and Bristol; he was related to Ahmed Issa. Like many well-educated refugees before him, his qualifications did not cut much ice in Britain. After eight months selling encyclo-paedias in London, he came to Bristol, staying in a refugee hostel in Trelawney Road, Cotham. His paper qualifications were not recognised, and while the Home Office considered his application for 'leave to remain' he stacked shelves at a Safeway depot for two years, and attended Brunel College to become an electrical installa-tion engineer. Two years later, the Home Office offered him excep-tional leave to remain; luck was with him again when two Somali academics came to England in time to provide the references he needed to enrol for an M.Phil. in International Development at Bristol University. His fiancée eventually arrived from Djibouti in 1995, and Ahmed Duale was able to find more congenial work.

But for refugees, even the well-educated, anxiety is a constant companion. Ahmed Duale's elder brother was killed in Somalia; the family, with roots in two warring clans, was reluctant to take sides with either, and is now scattered around the world. For Somalis who were not already English-speakers, life was much tougher. One economics graduate fled first to Italy, and learnt Italian as an adult. Now middle-aged with five children to support, he is finding English much harder to master. Like an estimated 70 per cent of Somali men he remains unemployed, his traditional status within the family undermined and the fate of him and his family agonisingly uncertain.[402]

The 1976 Race Relations Act, which banned racial discrimina-tion in public bodies such as the police, specifically exempted the Immigration Service, an anomaly not rectified by the Race Relations Act of 2000. Although many immigration officials may be fair-minded, vulnerable asylum-seekers have no legal protection against any who abuse their position and act in a discriminatory way. Since the introduction of the Asylum and Immigration Act in 1999, and press campaigns demonising asylum seekers as 'bogus', the Somalis and other asylum seekers, refugees and those with indefinite leave to remain in the city face fresh fears and anxieties. Under the terms of the 1999 Act a dispersal policy has forced asylum-seekers to go where directed rather than to natural support networks of family or friends. Bristol is a dispersal area and it has been argued that those dispersed are more isolated and vulnerable to racial attack. Certainly, racial harassment has been a frequent and widespread experience in Bristol, and this might be exacerbated by grouping Somalis together in highly concentrated and visible groups, without apparent regard for clan divisions. Somalis were settled in scarce social and council housing in the traditionally White estate of Barton Hill and in the backstreets of the tight-knit African-Caribbean area of St Paul's, with a smaller number on the Lockleaze Estate to the north.

Cultural Differences

The average size of a Somali family, larger than that of their English and African-Caribbean counterparts, means that they tend to score more points on the social housing register and so are popularly perceived as getting favourable treatment. Distinctively different in their dress and physical appearance, Somali women – the majority of whom were reportedly 'illiterate' and few of whom can speak English – have been the target of cruel harassment. In Barton Hill's high-rise flats there have been reports of youths setting Somali women's clothes alight as the doors to the lift they have entered are closing.[403]

From the Somali's point of view, urban life in Britain proved a perplexing minefield. Oblivious of the English rituals of waiting in a queue or observing set times for washing in the communal laundry rooms of Barton Hill's tower blocks, Somali women, who often had more children than their neighbours, reportedly occasioned deep resentment for using the washing facilities out of turn. Gardens are another point of tension. When one English neighbour asked why his Somali neighbour did not tend his front garden and keep his lawn properly, he was reportedly told, 'In our culture, once the camel eats the grass, we move on.'[404]

Even many urbanised Somalis are but one generation away from a nomadic or pastoral lifestyle, where time was regulated more loosely and paperwork a mystery. Gaining the skills to navigate the demands of a bureaucratic and technological society, challenging enough for those born here, becomes much more difficult for those with little or no education, poor English and a completely different experience of life. 'My worst fear', related one woman who came in the 1990s and has since become a community worker, 'was that I didn't know how to use the cooker and didn't have the confidence to talk to local people as I could not speak English'.[405]

The local authority was slow to rise to this challenge. In 1991 a Council for Racial Equality report condemned Avon County Council for its failure to help Somalis: 'Many of these families have recently arrived in Bristol and are left to find their own way around the complicated education system.' All this put pressure on the traditional regulatory mechanisms within Somali culture. The strict hierarchies underpinning respect for elders have come under strain. Children face new pressures and situations about which their parents cannot advise them, leaving the way open for a 'gang culture' to take root. The reported involvement of younger children as mules and sellers in the illegal drugs trade is also a growing concern both within and without the Somali community.[406]

Family separation through war and marital breakdown has meant that many, perhaps the majority, of Somali families are headed by single women. A proportion of these women would have been abused during the upheavals at home, where the rape of their womenfolk was used as a means of humiliating men of rival clans. Yet a number of respondents attested to the particular resilience of Somali women and their enthusiasm for taking advantage of the educational and other opportunities afforded them in Bristol. It is also said that many men found it harder to cope with the stresses of dislocation and that an increasing number took solace in the naturally-occurring narcotic root, Khat. Although still legal, its growing use is widely seen as an evil by many community members, who call for Khat to be banned.[407]

Educated Somalis, themselves often un- or under-employed, form a backbone of support for distressed and often traumatised asylum-seekers, providing food and shelter, sometimes in their own homes. More organised institutions such as the Somali mosque in Wade Street, the Elders' Clubs and the Saturday Supplementary School mainly post-date 2001. Ensuring that new Somali arrivals are fully informed about services to which they are entitled is one problem faced by the city authorities and voluntary agencies; another is how to discourage the replication of clan divisions within Britain. Members of the more powerful northern clans tend to be the better educated, so it has been all too easy for vulnerable minorities to be made dependent for service

Figure 136 The Al
Baseera mosque (Somali),
Wade Street, St Jude's,
Bristol (2007). It was
established in 2003 in the
premises of a former pub.

Figure 136 The Al Baseera mosque (Somali), Wade Street, St Jude's, Bristol (2007). It was established in 2003 in the premises of a former pub.

allocation on members of more powerful or even hostile clans. Left unmonitored this could lead to abuse and other, possibly unforeseen, consequences.[408]

Despite the problems they face, a growing number of Somali-owned shops and internet cafes attest to a flair for entrepreneurial enterprise. Whilst this bodes well for the future, it also causes tensions among some of the longer-established African-Caribbean residents, who, like their White counterparts, resent these new incomers.

CONCLUSION

This chapter has focused on the experiences of two very different groups. At first sight they seem, in terms of race, appearance, religious allegiance and historical and cultural backgrounds, to be utterly dissimilar. Yet on closer inspection, both share some things in common. First and foremost, although both groups contain

economic migrants, many have been displaced from their home-
lands under the most traumatic circumstances. The rank and file
of both groups come from rural backgrounds, and if the nomadic
existence of the Somalis seems further removed from modernity
than that of the Polish peasant, both (albeit in different ways)
have found the imperatives of British city life initially alien. Both
groups contain educated elites whose considerable talents have
gone largely unrecognised in the UK job market. Both groups are
religiously homogenous, and tend to favour their own nationally
distinctive religious institutions within the city. Both have a fierce
pride in their national identity, and although the Poles do not have
the complicated clan/family structure which divides the Somali
community, both have a reputation for internal political factionalism. Both Polish and Somali women have had to negotiate their
access to education, employment and individual autonomy within
cultures which are structured on strongly patriarchal lines.

As from 2001, real attempts have been made by voluntary
agencies and some sections of local government in Bristol to help
asylum seekers and refugees to cope in difficult circumstances.
There has been some sympathy among the public at large for what
these incomers have endured, both in their homeland and at the
hands of British officialdom. But these often prove ineffectual in
the face of punitive national policies which continue, at the time of
writing, to cause much suffering. Proponents of 'social cohesion'
should know that a sense of belonging can only flourish where one
feels truly welcome.

Conclusion

Apart from being ethnic minorities in an English city, what links the experiences of Bristol's 21st-century Somalis with those of its 12th-century Jews? If nothing, then what justifies putting them together within the pages of this book? In other words, what if any continuities or indeed instructive contrasts, are to be found across this long period and range of different ethnic groups?

To start with an obvious observation: there is clearly a relationship between ethnicity and urban topography; that is, new immigrants, throughout the centuries, tend to settle first in the poorer areas of the city and then, over time, spread into more economically diverse neighbourhoods. However, this phenomenon should not be overstated. Bristol has never seen ghettoes in the sense of physical spaces into which one ethnic group was exclusively confined. Even in the medieval Jewries there were still Christians and Jews living side by side, and in modern times areas of relatively high ethnic minority population, such as St Paul's, embrace an ethnically diverse population, including a substantial White British element.

Proximity does not necessarily breed tolerance, and contemporary conflicts across the world show that the bitterest antagonisms can be generated between neighbouring ethnic groups. Bristol has had its share of ethnic clashes, from the attack on the Jewry in 1275, to the 19th-century anti-Catholic demonstrations and the post-war riots in St Paul's, but caution is required in interpreting them. The St Paul's riots, for example, were certainly not simply White versus Black affairs. They, like many other eruptions in the city's past, were compounded of a mix of tensions, grievances and misapprehensions that involved class as well as ethnic difference.

This study has shown how the reception of a particular ethnic group largely depends on what skills and capital it brings to the receiving economy and how intolerance can increase against minorities who are perceived to have outlived their economic usefulness. Huguenots were welcomed in part because their elite had the resources and contacts to plug into Bristol's expanding Atlantic economy. Victorian Jewish peddlers and Ugandan Asian refugees were able to find a niche in the expanding retail sector. In this respect it is equally instructive to remember that the rhetoric of outsiders stealing 'our' jobs can be traced back to at least the 15th century, when at a time of economic recession guild masters sought to restrict the employment of aliens. Such defensive strategies were advocated by Sir John Knight, Bristol MP in the 1690s and echoed in the resistance to Black bus drivers in Bristol in the 1960s. The exploitation of foreign workers, probably with little or no command of English, can be documented from the late medieval period, to judge by the evidence for 15th-century Icelandic servants, a phenomenon echoed by the treatment of South Asian homeworkers in 2001.

Another theme which has emerged from this study is the continuing importance of the diaspora network. Like migrants from Bristol's neighbouring counties, those from further afield did not easily forget their family attachments, or cease to seek the regard of friends and compatriots 'back home'. Irish navvies, Jewish peddlers, Italian musicians, Jamaican nurses and Punjabi traders resident in Bristol made considerable sacrifices in order to support relatives and friends outside England. Money was sent to those remaining, jobs and accommodation offered to those arriving. Gossip and gifts were exchanged and marriage partners sought, sometimes with little reference to the host community. The status of minority group members in Bristol was often affected by what property they owned in their country of origin, the regard in which their wider family was held and the generosity, erudition or piety they exhibited within their own communal institutions. The status these institutions afforded could shield recent immigrants and refugees from the worst effects of rejection by the host society. Although these links do tend to weaken over time, and are often difficult to document, they are probably central to understanding how ethnic minority groups both perceive themselves and how they relate to the majority population.

Just as the character of each ethnic group is complex (and to some degree necessarily an artificial construct produced by the – often outside – observer), so are the relationships between those groups. The outside observer is often prone to ignore the manifold differences within broadly-drawn ethnic boundaries or to fix them as unchanging and somehow inscribed in nature. To such an observer, the differences between, say, the Bangladeshi, Indian and Pakistani communities might easily be lost within a crude categorisation of South Asian. The subtleties of other relevant and sometimes overlapping distinctions – ethnic, cultural, religious and political – are even harder to grasp, especially as they change over time. Christian Bristolians in the 19th century were probably largely unaware of the separate characteristics of the more established Jews and the newly arrived East Europeans. The Poles who settled in post-war Bristol find relations with the post-accession Poles problematic. Generational conflict can also reshape identity

Figure 137 Exterior detail of painted house, Shaftesbury Road, Stokes Croft, Bristol.

as children strive to cope in a world very different from that in which their parents grew up. Attitudes within and towards communities can also be influenced by a wide range of gender-related issues. We pose the argument that police relations with the first and second generation African-Caribbeans in the city need to be understood in the context of conflicting perceptions of Black masculinity and its proper relationship to established authority. We note testimony from oral sources attesting to the impact that female participation in the workforce and access to welfare services had on the internal sexual politics within some South Asian and Somali households.

Racial difference has long been a major determinant of one's status and identity in Britain. This has been particularly true for Bristol, where the city's long association with slavery fostered a peculiarly uneasy attitude towards people of African origin. The fear of insurgent African slaves during the era of the slave trade nourished the racialist ideology popularised during the Victorian and Edwardian eras, an ideology which lived on to inform some of the attitudes post-war Caribbean migrants encountered in the city.

By the same token, this study does show the long-term influence that other types of xenophobic ideas can exert in their own right. The 'blood libel' (see panel 5), witnessed locally through the 'Adam of Bristol' story, helped to justify what might be termed the first instance of ethnic cleansing in England, the expulsion of the Jews in 1290. The conviction that Jews posed a threat to the Christian body politic was, as the local press attests, revived in different circumstances in the mid-18th century, to serve other political interests, and was at the root of the resistance to Jewish emancipation in the 19th century.

From the 17th to the 19th centuries, Bristol's majority ethnic population defined itself emphatically as Protestant, of whatever denomination (and the distinction between Anglican and Non-conformist was particularly important in this city). That self-definition, tied up as it was with a sense of Imperial mission, was strongly expressed in the majority population's relations with ethnic and religious minorities. By the 20th century, however, the importance of religion as a marker of the majority group's identity had sharply diminished, as it had in the White Anglican community generally. Today's overwhelmingly secular Britain (Northern Ireland is of course a different matter) is an oddity – a bubble of secularism – when seen in the context of history and of the rest of the contemporary world. Until recently, religion has been a constant identity marker for both minority and majority ethnic groups; today, while the majority has largely lost that marker, it appears by contrast to be even more central to the identity of ethnic minorities, whether it be African-Caribbean Pentecostalism or Polish Catholicism, South Asian Sikhism, or Islam. Since 2001 we have seen religious difference reassert itself even more strongly as a crucial factor in inter-ethnic tensions.

This book has side-stepped current debates about the respective merits of assimilation, integration or ethnic diversity; but we have observed that, since medieval times, the existence of an educated or skilled elite within its ranks could be an important advantage for a minority group, providing its poorer members with patronage and even protection and acting as an advocate for minority interests in the wider community.

Figure 138 Detail of painted mural, showing the parish of St Paul's, Brook Road, St Paul's, Bristol.

The response of the indigenous elite has also been a factor in how well a minority group was incorporated into Bristol life. The fear of disorder, crime and difference discernible in the attitudes of officialdom is often better documented than the sense of hurt, injustice and exclusion experienced by those outside it, as in the case of the Victorian Irish and the post-war African-Caribbean migrants to Bristol. The case of these same two groups also illustrates instances where national government was more willing to exploit a group's economic usefulness than were some local workers and officials, a number of whom saw themselves more directly threatened by economic competition, by a demand for local services or by cultural difference.

It is difficult, in a local study, to do justice to the national and international forces that have both encouraged the inflow of ethnic minorities to Bristol and affected their reception. We have tried to indicate, for example, the historic links between English colonialism and the arrival of the Irish (from the Middle Ages onwards), Africans (from as early as the 16th century), African-Caribbeans and South Asian migrants in the city, as well as those between the policies of foreign powers such as Spain, Portugal and France and the arrival of Jews and Huguenots in the 16th and 17th centuries. While it may be commonplace to link ethnic diversity with post-colonial globalisation, we still think it has been worthwhile to illustrate the process with such specific examples as the case of the Mangla Dam and Bristol's Mirpuri population. Where the evidence

Figure 139 Detail of painted mural, showing market scene with Church of St Paul, St Paul's, Bristol.

has allowed, we have also tried to show how structural inequalities variously affect the life chances of particular ethnic minority groups.

As important as these structural forces are for understanding ethnic relations, so, too, is individual agency. Without sanitising the problems that do exist, we think it distorting to focus on ethnic conflict to the exclusion of instances of cooperation, friendship and negotiated compromise. The positive deserves to be documented. In this regard, we have been particularly struck by the example of Bristol Quakers, who have consistently championed the cause of minorities and asylum seekers for over 300 years.

Ethnic minorities in British cities have variously been ignored, vilified or, more rarely, romanticised. Our findings suggest that a more complex reaction is appropriate. Alongside the undoubted realities of urban stress, deprivation, crime and ethnic tension, we have uncovered many stories of communal self-help and individual resourcefulness and creativity. Those immigrants who have come to Bristol voluntarily have tended to be more dynamic, entrepreneurial and resourceful than average; those who have found refuge in the city, or have been brought here against their will, have often survived horrendous ordeals and have had to find unusual reserves of tenacity and determination to do so. In both cases, such people are likely to have had much to offer in their new home. We are not equipped to enter the debate about the net contribution immigration makes or has made to the host economy, but it is clear that in every period we have studied ethnic minorities have made positive contributions across many areas of the city's life.

To judge from history, people only fully flourish when afforded access to the necessary opportunities and some measure of social acceptance from both the authorities and the general populace. This is not about assimilating to the host community, if by this one means subjugating one culture to another, nor is it about an uncritical multi-culturalism that can inadvertently foster isolationism and a wholesale rejection of British society. It is rather about finding common ground where diversity can be valued and shared goals pursued. A sense of belonging and a sense of history are the necessary first steps.

Endnotes

The following abbreviations are used throughout the endnotes.

ABMS	Archives of the Bristol Malago Society
Ann.	Annual
APC	*Acts of the Privy Council of England*, ed. J. R. Dasent (32 vols, HMSO, 1890-1907)
Arch.	Archaeological
BaJ	*Bath Journal*
BBAP	Black Archives Project, Bristol Record Office
BBHAP	Bristol Branch of the Historical Association Pamphlet
BC	*Bath Chronicle*
BCC	Bristol City Council
BCLL	Bristol Central Lending Library
BCRC	Bristol Community Relations Council
BCRL	Bristol Central Reference Library
BEP	*Bristol Evening Post*
BJ	*Bristol Journal*
BL	The British Library
BM	*Bristol Mirror*
BMer	*Bristol Mercury*
BMGA	*Bristol Mirror and General Advertiser*
BO	*Bristol Oracle*
BREC	Bristol Council for Racial Equality
BRECN	*Bristol Racial Equality Council Newsletter*
BRO	Bristol Record Office
BRS	Bristol Record Society
BTBA	*Bristol Times and Bath Advocate*
BULSC	Bristol University Library Special Collection
CBB	Caroline Barker Bennett
CChR	*Calendar of Charter Rolls ... 1226-[1516]* (6 vols, Public Record Office, 1903-27)
CCR	*Calendar of Close Rolls ... 1271-[1509]* (47 vols, Public Record Office, 1892-1963)
CPR	*Calendar of Patent Rolls ... 1232-1509* (52 vols, Public Record Office, 1891-1916)
CRC	Community Relations Council
CSPDREJ	*Calendar of State Papers, Domestic Series. Edward VI, Mary, Elizabeth I and James I* (12 vols, Public Record Office, 1856-1872)
CUP	Cambridge University Press
Diplomatarium	*Diplomatarium Islandicum* (16 vols, Copenhagen & Reykjavik, 1857-1959)
(E)	Electronic Source (Website): see separate list
FBA	*Farley's Bristol Advertiser*
FDB	Fenton Database
ff.	following
FFBJ	*Felix Farley's Bristol Journal*
Fol(s)	folio(s)
GRBB	*The Great Red Book of Bristol*, ed. E. W. W. (5 vols, BRS, 2, 4, 8, 16, 18, 1931-53)
HBA	Hoare's Bank Archives
Hist.	History/Historical
HMSO	Her/His Majesty's Stationery Office, London
I	Interview, conducted by author, unless otherwise stated

ILN	*Illustrated London News*
JC	*Jewish Chronicle*
JHS	*The Jewish Historical Society of England: Transactions/Jewish Historical Studies*
Jnl.	*Journal*
Letters of Denization	Huguenot Soc, *Letters of Denization* William A. Shaw, 'Lettters of Denization and Acts of Naturalisation for Aliens in England and Ireland 1603-1700', *Proceedings of the Huguenot Society*, vol. 18 quarto series
LPFD	*Letters and Papers, Foreign and Domestic*, Henry VIII, ed. J. S. Brewer, J. Gairdner, R. H. Brodie (21 + 2 vols, HMSO, 1862-1932)
LRBB	*The Little Red Book of Bristol*, ed. F. B. Bickley (2 vols, Bristol: Arrowsmith, 1900)
MHSA	Malago History Society Archives
M LFHS	*The Manchester & Lancashire Family History Society*
Ms	manuscript
n.	note
n.d.	no date
no(s)	number(s)
n.p.	no pagination
N.Y.	New York
OCA	*Oracle Country Advertiser*
OUP	Oxford University Press
Oxford DNB	*Oxford Dictionary of National Biography: From the Earliest Times to the Year 2000*, ed. H. C. G. Matthew, B. H. Harrison (61 vols, Oxford: OUP, 2004) [http://www.oxforddnb.com]
P	Press
PCC	Proceedings of the Common Council (BRO)
PCP	Peter Courtier Papers
Pers. Com.	Personal communication
PND	Peter Newley Database
PP	*Parliamentary Papers*
Proj.	project
Pt.	part
Rec.	Record(s)
Rep.	report
rev.	revised
RO	Record Office
R.S.	Record Society
SCG	*Somerset County Gazette*
SFBJ	*Sarah Farley's Bristol Journal*
SFBN	*Sam Farley's Bristol Newspaper*
Soc.	Society
Studs	Studies
TBGAS	Transactions of the Bristol and Gloucestershire Archaeological Society
TBGPA	*The Bristol Gazette and Public Advertiser*
TBMWCA	*The Bristol Mercury and Western Counties Advertiser*
TBO	*The Bristol Observer*
TBOCA	*The Bristol Oracle and Country Advertiser*
TBW	Transcriptions of Bristol Wills
TNA	The National Archives
Trans.	transactions
TRHS	*Transactions of the Royal Historical Society*
UP	University Press
VLC	Voluntary Liaison Committee
Vol.	volume
WAM	Westminster Abbey Muniments
WDP	*Western Daily Press*

Introduction, pp. 1-8

1 Hutchison & Smith, 4-7.
2 Kidd, pp. 9–72; Fenton (2003), p. 165; S. Hall, 'New Ethnicities', cited in Hutchison & Smith, 161-3.
3 Eriksen, 158–9; Berthoud, Madood & Smith, 9; Commission on the Future of Multi-Ethnic Britain, 27.
4 Mayo (1985); Samuel; Jones & Youseph; Barot (1988), (1992); Jeffrey; Edwards; Campbell; Hussain, M; Dresser (1983), (1996), (2001a); Irwin-Zarecka, 17-19; Burrell & Panayi (2005); Myers (2006).

CHAPTER 1 The Bristol Jewry to 1290, pp. 9-18

5 Roth; Skinner; Chazan, 154-67; Samuel, 20-40.
6 TNA E101/249/2; Hillaby (2003), 21, 33; Stacey (1985), 175-249. Hillaby (2001), 77-81.
7 Howlett, vol. 1, 294; Richardson, H. G., 166-73; Roth, 35.
8 Tovey, 77; *CPR, 1216-25*, 157; Hardy, vol. 1, 378, 359; Stacey (2003), 41-54; Hillaby (1984), 368; *CCR, 1250-53*, 312-13.
9 CPR, 1216-25, 157; Powicke & Cheney, vol. 2, 55, 177-8, 318; Grayzel, Pt 1, Introduction & Pt 2, 314-15, 330-1.
10 Treharne & Sanders, 87; Stacey (1991), 137-50; Roth, 59-62.
11 Rigg (1902), li-liv, lv, lxi; Mundill, 55-70.
12 Bund, vol. 2, 71; Rigg, Jenkinson & Richardson, vol. 1, 266-7, vol. 2, 297, 301, vol. 3, 51, 123, 202, 221; *CCR, 1272-9*, 166, 170, 172; *CPR, 1281-92*, 107; Adler, 225-9; Roth, 77, 82.
13 Rokéah (1988), 96 (1992), 159-218.
14 Rigg (1902), 121, 127.
15 *CPR, 1281-92*, 378, 381-2; *GRBB*, vol. 1, 74 (25), 75 (22-3); Stacey (1997), 77-101; Roth, 85-90; Samuel, 37-9; Adler, 245-7; TNA E101, 249/27/12.
16 Neale (2000), nos 46, 200, 270, 320, 353, 369; Leech, R. (1997), 118-19; Howlett, vol. 1, 294.
17 Benedict of Winchester: Brown & McCartney, 19-23; Adler, 245-7.
18 Boore (1982), 7-11; Boore (2001), 179-82; Emanuel, 308-15.
19 Honeybourne, 145-59.
20 Holmes, M., 184; *GRBB*, vol. 1, 74 (34-5); Hillaby & Sermon, 127-36, 139-41.
21 Hillaby & Sermon, 127-51.
22 Hillaby (1993), 182-98; Livock, 94; Neale (2000), nos 46, 200; Smith, L. T., 87-8.
23 *CCR, 1251-53*, 312-13; *1268-72*, 522; *C ChR, 1257-1300*, 245-53; *GRBB*, vol. 1, 75 (6, 17), 76 (31), 100 (17); TNA E101/249 ff 27, 30; Leech (1989), 241-3.
24 Jacobs, 95, 97, 142, 253.
25 WAM, 3507-8, 6899, 6933, 6937, 9005.
26 Samuel, 31-2.

CHAPTER 2 Ethnic Minorities in the Middle Ages, pp. 19-32

27 Darlington, 43, 91; Grinsell, 25, 57-8, 47; Walker, 4-8.
28 Duffy, 57-80; Bowly, 15-17. Irish Mead: BRO, 5139/451; Neale, nos 61, 167.
29 Davies, 24-55; Penn, 33-4, 42-4.
30 Crawford, 1-2.
31 *CCR, 1402-05*, 267; *CPR, 1452-61*, 440; Prestwich, 501-2; Kowaleski, 482-3.
32 Down, 449; Cosgrove (1987a), 553; TNA SC8/118/589; Bolton (2000); Childs.
33 *CPR, 1391-96*, 451, 454-6, 461.
34 *CPR, 1413-16*, 122, 124-5; Vanes, 190-1, 198; Childs, 35; BRO 40365/D/2/11, 17-8, 21, P.AS/D/LM/D/1, P.AS/D/NA/7; Wiltshire & Swindon RO, 1728/40-1; GRBB, I, 136.
35 Childs, 34-5; Roskell, Clark & Rawcliffe, vol. 2, 113-5.
36 Orme, 38-40.
37 Carus-Wilson (1933), 195-6; TNA E179/113/103.
38 Jurkowski, Smith & Crook, xxxix-xli, 94-5; Cosgrove (1987b), 530, Bolton (2000), 3-4.
39 TNA E179/113/03, 104. Thrupp (1957), 270; Thrupp (1969), 251-72; Bolton

(2000), 5; Bolton (1998), Introduction; Childs, 36 & n. 43; Dyer & Slater, 626, 636; Fleming, P.

40 Cosgrove (1987b), 530; Griffiths (1981), 167-71, 551-61; Bolton (2000), 3-4; *LRBB*, vol. 1, 86-8; *GRBB*, vol. 1, 151.

41 *GRBB*, vol. 2, 49-50; Childs, 37-42; TNA C1/1489/77, C4/6/7, 32, C4/48/47, C44/31/4.

42 Davies, ch. 17; *CPR, 1399-1401*, 359, 555; Dimmock (2004); Dimmock (2005); Griffiths (1978); Griffiths (1994b); Griffiths (2000a); Griffiths (2002).

43 TNA JUST 3/20/9; BRO JTol/J/1/2, ff. 2-45; *CPR, 1413-16*, 122, 124-5; Roskell, Clark & Rawcliffe, vol. 2, 806, vol. 4, 939-40.

44 Griffiths (1994b), 17-18; *CPR, 1494-1509*, 43, 171.

45   Wadley, 126-7, 147-8; Griffiths (2000b), 231; Griffiths (1978), 153, 156-7. TNA PROB 11/6, quire 47; Pugh, 83. Vaghan: TNA PROB 11/15, quire 28.

46 Griffiths (1981), 171; *CPR, 1429-36*, 545, 549-50, 553, 559-60, 565, 567, 576-7, 582-3, 587.

47 TNA E179/113/137, 157.

48 Bolton (1998), 8; Bolton (1998), 28-33.

49 *CPR, 1441-46*, 79, *1461-67*, 41; Carus-Wilson (1933), 211; Carus-Wilson (1937), 111; TNA E179/113/103; *GRBB*, vol. 1, 238-9.

50 Roskell, Clark & Rawcliffe, vol. 4, 869-71.

51 *LRBB*, vol. 1, 246; *GRBB*, vol. 1, 151, 159.

52 TNA E179/270/54; Quinn, 47-51.

53 *Diplomatarium Islandicum*, vol. 4, nos 381, 558, 715, vol. 5, 72-4, vol. 6, 62-5; Carus-Wilson (1967); Þorsteinsson, 102, 159, 177-8, 207, 269; Seaver, 178-93, 198-207.

54 *LRBB*, vol. 2, 128.

55 BRO FC/BB/1 (a-f); Latimer (1903), 134-7.

CHAPTER 3 Ethnic Minorities, 1500–1685, pp. 33-48

56 TNA C1/831/60; Williams (1908), 26; Nott & Ralph, 48-9; Owen (1962), 106, 126-9, 131-2, 159-60.

57 BRO BK/101/GMF 1-4, BRO FCP/St W/R/1 (a) 3, FCW/1662/1/Fram; Sabin, 117-8, 122, 125, 128.

58 TNA PROB 11/23, quire 10, 30, quire 44; Lang & McGregor, 117.

59 McGrath, 275-6.

60 McGurk, 165-74.

61 *APC, 1587-1588*, 109; *1601-1604*, 502; *1628-1629*, 297; *CSPDREJ, Addenda, 1580-1625*, 468; Sabine, 17-21, 23-5, 27, 29, 57-8; Latimer (1900), 13, 102; McGurk, 165-74.

62 Barnard, 34-46, 54.

63 *APC, 1618-19*, 322; *1619-21*, 99; Latimer (1900), 155, 176; Nott, 21, Nott & Ralph, 138-9; BRO Great Audit Book, 04026 (21), first quarter, 1643. Church wardens' accounts: BRO P/St P and J/ChW/3a (SS Philip and James), P.StMR/ChW/1/d (St Mary Redcliffe), P/Xch/ChW/1c (Christchurch), P/StW/ChW/3b (St Werburgh), P/AS/ChW/3(a) (All Saints); Sabine, 80-1, 87, 91; Lynch, 15, 18; Bagnall, 152. Transportation: Smith, A. E., 165, 167.

64 Jurkowski, 132-70; TNA E179/113/192, 205, 114/229, 253, 115/308, 317, 330, 386, 394, 247/6, C1/667/32-3, 983/13, 1427/68.

65 Burgess (2004), 335, 337-8, 341-2, 345-6, 350, 393, 445, 461; TNA E179/113/205; *Letters of Denization*, VIII, 43, 72; Hollis, 92, 123.

66 BRO FC/BB/1 (c) 4 f. 88; *Letters of Denization*, VIII, 76; TNA E179/115/394, 247/6, REQ 2/182/29, 234/33, PROB 11/88 quire 19.

67 TNA E179/115/330, 386, 394; PROB11/60 quire 36, 61 quire 3, 75 quire 3; Ralph (1992), nos 884, 955, 1280, 1324, 1541.

68 BRO P/St J/F/28, FC/BB/1 (c) 4, f. 87, (d) 1, ff. 5, 17, 22, 49, 102.

69 *LPFD*, vols. 4, pt. 3, no. 6654 (i), vol. 7, no. 1430, vol. 8, nos. 1457, 1575; *Letters of Denization*, VIII, xlvii, 7, 51, 62, 109, 127, 156-7, 162, 195-6, 209, 211, 215, 221, 249-50; TNA PROB11/56 quire 25; Connell-Smith, 363-70; Ellis (2006), 142-5; Gough, 64-6.

70 Wolf (1934), 84-90; Katz, 10-13.

71 American Jewish Historical Society (E).

72 TNA STAC 5/514/26; Latimer (1900), 344; Dresser (2001), 8-15; Lindegaard (n.d.a), 25, 28, 33, 40, 42, 44-6; Jones & Youseph, 2.

CHAPTER 4 Religion and Refugees, 1685–1835, pp. 49-58

73 Colley; Wilson.
74 Defoe, vol. 2, 270; BRO, PrCC, c 1695-1701, 133,156, M/BCC/CCP/1/8, 1687-1702, 1750-1753, 153, 159; Barry, 37-38.
75 Latimer (1893), 78; Lindegaard (n.d. b), no. 3, 40, 52, no. 4, 10; Goldwin; Latimer (1893), 78; *SFBJ*, 27/11/73.
76 Gunnis, 33-38; Latimer 178-179; Goldwin.
77 Latimer (1893), 451; BRO, JQS/p/1642.
78 TNA, HO43/25, cited in Poole (1996), 81.
79 *FBA*, 30/06/44.
80 *OCA*, 01/02/46,15/02/46, 01/03/46.
81 Vlaeminke, 4, 113-114. *BC*, 18/10/92; BRO, JQS P/151.
82 Gwynn, 35, 39.
83 Mayo (1985), 9; Kershaw & Pearsall, 8-9, 84-87; *Lettters of Denization,* vi-xiii, 1; Firth, 2424-2426.
84 Mayo (1985), 6.
85 BRO, AF/F/1 ufp; Mayo (1985), 2-11.
86 Beckerdite (E).
87 Knight; Latimer (1900), 476; Taylor.
88 Bosher, 80; Mayo (1996), 188, 194; Beckerdite (E).
89 Pellew, 1-2; Mayo (1996), 188, 194; Morgan (1993), 143.
90 Cruger; Gilder (E); Agnew, 42; 'Cruger, Henry (1739–1827)', *Oxford DNB*; Richardson (198-), 13, 27, 105, 124; House of Commons Journal (E); TNA, PROB 11/536, 538, 639, 712, E190/1195/3; Huddleston, 30299/9; BRO, AC/JS/49ab, 08840/18a.
91 HBA, Ledger 2,434, 3/434, 14/228/17/264, 22/75, 24/129, 26/121-122 & pp. 313-14, Ledger for Plate: 1697 (pp. 244, 255, 1260).
92 Mayo (1996), 131, 205; TNA, PROB 11/508, 460.
93 TNA, PROB 11/460, 508, 639; Mayo (1996), 185.
94 'Cruger, Henry (1739–1827)', *Oxford DNB*; Bill Thomas, 'America's Mr. Bristol, (undated newspaper cutting, probably from *BEP, c.*1995); BRO, 30299/9.
95 Adherents: Lart, 16. Raoul: TNA, PROB/11/715.

CHAPTER 5 The Welsh in the 18th Century, pp. 59-72

96 Powell, 33; London: Whyte, 100; Jenkins, P. (2000), 133-7; 1825 Matthews (1825), 179.
97 Denning, 16-17.
98 Defoe (E); Skeel, 142; Williams, G., 355. Cattle market: Latimer (1887), 123.
99 Powell, 23; Williams, M. I., 334-53.
100 Goldwin.
101 BRO, F/M/We1, Bk, 1776-1807; Anon. (*c.*1970); John, 98.
102 *FFBJ*, 25/02/75; Stoddard, 45, 74-5; Sketchley; BCRL (E).
103 *BJ*, 14/05/65, 18/05/65, 14/12/65, 28/12/65; *FFBJ*, 02/03/54.
104 Powell, 55; BRO, 04356/10-14.
105 Pike (1996), 274.
106 TNA, C107/6; BRO, 04356/13, 15, 00228/25a.
107 Hobhouse.
108 TNA, PROB 11/467, 527, 726, 767.
109 Pike (n.d.); TNA PROB11/527.
110 BRO , TBW, 1745, Mary Lewis, Dorothy White, 1749, George Jones, 1750, Thomas Pritchard, Thomas Williams; TNA, PROB 11/1181.
111 Jenkins & Ramage; Jones, T.; N.A, 12.
112 *BJ*, 02/03/65; *FFBJ*, 10/02/72; *FFBJ*, 17/02/70, 04/03/75, 01/03/80.
113 Denning; BRO, TBW, 1745, William Howell; Powell, 35.
114 Bristol and Avon Family Hist. Soc.; Jenkins, P. (1992), 146.
115 Jenkins, G. H.; Swaish, 16; Moon, 4-5. 10-26; Foyle; membership registers

of Welsh congregational chapels in England in National Library of Wales,
Aberystwyth.

116　Powell, 36-9; Bristol Baptists (E); Morgan (1994), 65-70; Day, 35. Lloyds: Bosher,
83n.

117　Powell, 36; Moon, 4-5. 10-26; Churchcrawler (E); Hutton.

118　Dresser (2001b), 138.

119　*BJ*, 03/08/65.

120　Hippisley.

121　Lindegaard (n.d. b), nos 2, 64.

122　Hippisley; E. Collins, *The Saints Backsiding* (*c*.1756) cited in Poole (2007), 115-17.

123　*FFBJ*, 01/01/80, 22/04/80, 29/04/80, 16/09/80, 31/03/81, 17/04/81.

CHAPTER 6 The Irish, 1685–1835, pp. 73-84

124　BRO, 8930/9a-b, 40297/Per/1; TNA, PROB20/2238; 'Burke, Edmund (1729/30–
1797)', *Oxford DNB*.

125　Ralph (1985), 47; Little, 46; BRO, TBW, 1741, Anne Maddox, 1743, James Moore,
1746, Thomas Kelly, 1746, David Regan, 1747, James Kennady, 1748, Michael
Casey.

126　Papists: BRO, List of Papists, P.Tem/E/5. Ralph , 47; Little (1987), 46; BRO,
37553/R/1/1, FCNC/RCB/2/1/4, pp.39-45.

127　*BO*, 24/08/45; *FFBJ*, 21/09/54, 09-10/03/65, 30/03/65, 11/05/65, 23/04/1803; *BaJ*,
28/08/49; Latimer (1893), 171-2; TNA, SP 36/21 Fols 140-5.

128　Anstey, 33-4.

129　*The Times*, 28/03/99.

130　*SFBN*, 07/08/36; Latimer (1893), 227.

131　BRO, 04343(5).

132　TNA, C107/2; Richardson, D. (1996).

133　*The Times*, 19/09/1806; BCRL, undated cutting, Braikenridge Collection, Temple
Vol. 22, 291.

134　Irish names: Hansom, 181-329. Casual workers: Worrall, 168-9. Malone &
Kennady: Sketchley, 55, 63.

135　Stoddard, plates 53, 55; Anon. (1973).

136　Redford, 138-9. Militia man: *The Times*, 27/08/1812.

137　*BM*, 20/05/1820; *The Times*, 04/04/1820, 15/04/1820, 28/04/1820.

138　Johnson, 24n ; *The Times*, 18/06/1824.

139　*The Times*, 09/05/1828, 07/01/1829, 17/02/1829, 25/02/1829; *BM*, 18/02/1828;
Latimer (1887), 128-9; Whidder, 207-28.

140　BRO, 8Feb/JQS/p/1642; Latimer (1887), 129; Dresser (1996), 113; Poole (1996),
81.

141　Redford; Irish Vagrants (E).

CHAPTER 7 The Black Presence, 1688-1835, pp. 85-92

142　Werner, 73.

143　Bristol Africans: tabulated at www.englandspastforeveryone.org. Bristol & Avon
Family Hist. Soc. (2005 & 2006); Lindegaard (n.d.a); Jones & Youseph; Eickelmann
& Small; Karen Garvey (pers. comm.).

144　Eickelmann & Small, 35-52.

145　Linebaugh & Rediker, 76-80; BRO 'Minutes of Church Meetings 1779-1817'
(Broadmead), 30251/Bd/M1/3; Dresser (2003), xx-xxi, 51, 56.

146　Dresser (2001a), 8-11, 72-85.

147　1759: BULSC, Moravian Collection, Bristol Minister's Diary, 04/04/59. Kinsmen:
Dresser (2001a), 64, 82-5; Sparks (2002), (2004). Franks: Crossley Evans, 203.

148　TNA, 'Prisoners of War at Stapleton 18051811', ADM104/416; Hathaway.

149　Poole (1996), 81; *FFBJ*, 07/05/20.

150　*TBGPA*, 07/06/21.

151　*FFBJ*, 02/09/80, 07/09/11; *FFBJ*, 16/02/88.

152　Ibid., 169, 178-9.

153　Report on the Bristol Missionary Society, *The Times*, 05/10/22.

CHAPTER 8 Jews in Georgian Bristol, pp. 93-102

154 *Cesarani*, 141-56.
155 Poliakov, 3; Bartal, 20-37; Pollins, 73-85.
156 Dresser (1996), 98-101; BCRL, B10942.
157 BCRL, B10942; Evans, 1.
158 Evans, 2.
159 Dresser (1998); Dresser (1996), 98-101, 118.
160 Wolf, 137; Latimer (1893), 327; BRO, 00401(5)a, Town Clerk's Correspondence, 1763-5, bundle 2 & 27 Sept. 1765, bundle 9.
161 BRO, Town Clerk's Correspondence 1763-5, bundle 9, 3 August 1765; 'Isaac Jacobs', *Oxford DNB*; Samuel, 82-3.
162 BCRL, Braikenridge Collection, St James and St Paul's part 1, 81; *FFBJ*, 13/01/70, 24/02/70.
163 *TBOCA*, 29/12/44; Old Bailey (E); BCRL, newspaper notice (*c*.1745), Jefferies Collection, vol. 12, 29; BRO, JQS/0/11 (1748-53), 27; *FFBJ*, 06/02/90, 15/03/55.
164 *FFBJ*, 11/03/91.
165 Samuel, 66-7.
166 BRO, 39490/ Jtol/J/5/1.
167 Susser (E); Samuel, 46-7.
168 'Isaac Jacobs', *Oxford DNB*.
169 Pigot's Directory (E); TNA, HO45/8948.
170 Dresser (1996), 115-16.

CHAPTER 9 Protestant Culture, pp. 103-16

171 Brace, 123-8; Latimer (1887), 424-5.
172 PND; www.englandspastforeveryone.org.uk/Bristol for further details.
173 Meller, 78-80; Latimer (1887), 514.
174 Sassen, 36-7; Latimer (1887), 292, *Oxford DNB*.
175 Pryce, G., 607-12; Sugar refiners (E).
176 Brown, H. G., 160.
177 TNA, RG11/2475, fol. 9, 5; Holmes (1991), 132.
178 'George Frederick Müller', *Oxford DNB*; Latimer (1887), 224-6; Pierson; *ILN*, 29/11/73, 515.
179 BRO, 1336/78; Robe Family (E); Richardson (1996), passim; Torrens; Mcarthurs (E); 'John Loudon Macadam', *Oxford DNB*; Latimer (1887), 63-5.
180 A. Jones, private research on 1851 Census.
181 A. H. Dinwoodies, I. Thomas, 'Letters to the Editor', *Dumfries and Galloway Family History Society Newsletter* (July 2001); Brace, 132; A. Jones, letter to I. Thomas (11/08/2001); Latimer (1887), 370.
182 Penny, 22; Latimer (1887), 357; *WDP*, 26/01/05; BRO, 41876.
183 BCRL, 'Lavars's new Map of Bristol', 1849; *WDP*, 27/01/05, 03/02/05.
184 BRO, 40499.
185 Hannam, 186, 192.
186 Latimer (1887), 414-15.

CHAPTER 10 Catholics and Jews, 1837-1910, pp. 117-34

187 *WDP*, 02/03/03.
188 Strachan (E); Information (E). Shoemakers: PND.
189 PND; *PP*, House of Commons, 1861, vol. 7, 128; Large (1985), 42-7.
190 PND; Large (2006); Gilbert, 76; TNA, HO45/248; Atkinson, 6.
191 Large (1985), 42-6; Large (2006); Davis, 26; Letford & Pooley, 100-4.
192 Large (1985), 55; *WDP*, 14/04/62; Clifton Diocese Archives, box of correspondence for St Nicholas de Tolentino.
193 *BTBA* 15/03/51; Gilbert, 303.
194 *PP*, House of Commons, 1861, vol. 7, 124.
195 De la Beche, vol. 1, 258 & 262.
196 Large (1985), 51.
197 *TBO*, 06/08/87; Gilbert, 89, 104.
198 Ibid.

199 Hankins, 60.
200 TBMWA, 09/11/50; FFBJ, 26/10/50.
201 Dye, 357-9; Hankin, 34; MacRaild, 75-99; BCRL, B2463; Hankins, 17; Harding, 64; Gilbert, 104; BRO, 375534.
202 BM, 20/4/1830; 27/3/1841.
203 *BMGA*, 25/10/45, 8/11/45.
204 Samuel, 62, 72,139-42; BRO, 33290 (7); *SCG*, 15/06/50; TNA, PROB11/2087; Crossley-Evans, 205.
205 TNA, PROB 11/2063.
206 *JC*, 14/02/72.
207 Samuel, 71-3, 113-15, *JC*, 22/01/04, 113-15.
208 Brothers: *BMGA*, 15/11/45, 22/11/45. Reid; Samuel, 120-1.
209 Leech (1884), 51-4.
210 Leech (1888). 25-31.
211 Feldman, 121-4; Endelman, 153, Samuel, 131.
212 TNA, HO144/899/17-725, /32/138533; Samuel, 195.
213 Census Enumerators' Reports, 1901, RG/13/2374.
214 *JC*, 15/05/03; Samuel, 151; *JC*, 17/02/05;http://www.familyrecords.gov.uk/focuson/ rosenberg/early-life.htm consulted 17 August 2007.
215 *JC*, 06/11/03, Samuel, 147.
216 *JC*, 25/11/81; Feldman, 121-4; Endelman, 156 ff.
217 *JC*, 18/02/81.
218 Thomas (c1985), 129-30; *JC*, 03/06/81, 21/06/81.
219 *JC*, 12/05/05; Holmes (1988), 71-2; *JC*, 23/06/05, 15/12/05.
220 Feldman, 166-84.

CHAPTER 11 Ethnic Diversity in the 20th Century, pp. 135-56

221 Few Bristolians: Jenkinson; TNA, a list of Bristol residents naturalized (Gary Evans on-line catalogue search);Mosley: Webber, 582; *The Times*, 11/04/34, 23/04/34, 16; BEP 11/04/34, 17; WDP 29/03/34, 1; 23/04/27, 1; JC, 20/04/34, 12.
222 2001 Census. Standard Tables. Table 13 Theme Table on Ethnicity-Bristol; 2001 Census Key Statistics Table KS06, Standard Table S201.in http://www.london.gov. uk/gla/publications/factsandfigures/dmag-briefing-2003-23.pdf, accessed 24/8/07.
223 BRO, 40499/1.
224 St Patricks (E); *WDP*, 8 July 1930, 6.
225 Samuel, 170.
226 Wright & Blease; BRO Exhibition: Bristol's Italian Community, 8/01/07; E: 'The Verrecchia Ice-Cream Company', http://weldgen.tripod.com/id64.html, accessed 1 August 2007.
227 Raymond and Betty St Clair (son and daughter in law of Joseph St Clair) (I: 17/01/06): family papers of Dr Lindsay St Clair (Joseph St Clair's granddaughter).
228 Holmes, 153; Phelps (E); Thomas Brookman (I: Sian White, 9/12/05); anon., Parkway Methodist Fellowship Centre Reminiscence Session, 20/02/06 (pers. comm. CBC); Mark Steed (2/11/06) & Dixie Brown's granddaughter Kathleen Charles (pers. comm.).
229 Hussain, M., 61-4.
230 Hussain, M., 114; Visram, 282-3.
231 Fletcher (E); BRO, Po/M/3/3, 34908.
232 BRO, Pol/CD/5/2; Smith, 205; Wynn; Pers. Com.; brown babies: *Rose, 1175*.
233 Richmond (1973), 43; Peach, 372.
234 TNA, HO344/122; BRO, Pol.LG/1/1; *BEP*, 31/10/61; Richmond (1973), 43; Jones (1978), 518.
235 TNA, CO1028/25; Banton (1953), 2-13; *BEP*, 2/11/61.
236 BRO, 'Liaison with coloured immigrants', 4 December 1960, Pol/LG/1/1.
237 Hughes, *Ladies Mile*.
238 Morant Bay: 'The Black Race', BTM, 13/11/1865; Co-habitation: H. Goulbourne and M. Chamberlain, ed, *Caribbean families in Britain and the Trans-Atlantic World* (London: Macmillan, 2001), 48-62.
239 Police: BRO, 34908, Pol/LG/1/1-2. Black masculinity: Collins. 'Hustler' minority: Pryce, 185, 267; *BEP*, 29/08/58; Laurence Hoo (I, Nov. 2006); Steve Wilkes (I, June 2005).

240 BRO, Pol/LG/1/1.

241 BRO, 34908, Pol/LG/1/1-2.

242 BRO, Pol/LG/1/1.

243 Derek Lane, Community Relations Officer, Bristol and Avon Constabulary, 1980s (I: 23/02/06).

244 BCRC Ann. Rep. 1972, 1819. Liaison officer: BRO, Pol/LG/1/1. Metropolitan Police: Whitfield (E).

245 'Sister Jaycock', 4; Mary Perkins (I).

246 Rt. Rev. Oliver Tomkins (Bishop of Bristol), 'Race problem success', detached cutting, probably from the *New Statesman*, *c*.1967.

247 VLC, CRC, minutes & reps, 1967-9.

248 VLC, CRC, minutes & reps, 1968; Rt. Rev. Oliver Tomkins (Bishop of Bristol), 'Race problem success', detached cutting, probably from the *New Statesman*, *c*.1967; Colin Holmes, *John Bull's Island: Immigration and British Society 1871-1971* (London: Macmillan, 1988), 264-7; Phillips and Phillips, *Windrush,* 226-9.

249 Goulbourne, 53; Thatcher (E).

250 PCP, CRC Ann. Rep. 1974, 24.

251 *BEP*, 18/02/67; *WDP*, 1/08/72, 5/12/72; BRO, Pol/LG/1/1; Dresser (1986); Muktyar Singh (I: 14/11/06).

252 Brown, C.

253 *BEP*, 2/05/77, 3; 3/05/77, 3.

254 PCP, CRC Ann. Rep. 1976, 21; BCRE Ann. Rep. 1978, 13; 'E', former Bristol headteacher (I: CBC, 2006).

255 PCP, BCRE Ann. Rep. 1978, 20.

256 PCP, BCRE Ann. Rep. 1980, 9-11, 12-19; *BRECN* (May 2004); Peter Courtier (I, 29/8/06, 13/11/06); Serpico (E); *The Times*, 3/04/80, 1, 4; Joshua & Wallace, 57-119.

257 PCP, BCRE Ann. Reps 1983, 23; 1985, 23; Rex & Cross, 12-13; Mohammed Sadiq (I, 6/12/06).

258 PCP, BCRE Ann. Rep. 1980, 9-11, 12-19, 39; *BRECN* (May 2004); Peter Courtier (I, 29/08/06, 13/11/06); impending raid, Harris and Wallace, 75.

259 PCP, BCRE Ann. Reps 1978, 1980, 13, 35-37, 1983, 28; community liaison not informed of impending raid: Harris and Wallace, 75 and *The Times, 5/02/1981,4.*

260 PCP, BCRE Ann. Reps, 1983, 28, 1984, esp. 15, 21, 1985, 1-8, 1986, 1-8.

261 *The Times*, 21/03/1981, 02/04/1981, 4 07/04/1981, 4.

262 Gilroy, 238-9; PCP, BCRE Ann. Rep. 1987, 5-7; Peter Courtier former Chair of BREC ((I, 13/11/06I); *WDP*, 15/9/1986, 17/9/1986, 18/9/1986; EP, 17/9/1986; *Guardian*, 13/9/1986; 200 estimated *The Guardian*.

263 *The Times*, 15/05/1981, 2; PCP, BCRE Ann. Rep. 1988, 5, 1989, 15; Gilroy, 137; Austin.

264 PCP, BCRE Ann. Reps, 1990, 1, 1991, 10.

265 national problem: Bowling, 231-2, 'not exist': PCP, BCRE Ann. Rep., 1990, 2; national problem: Bowling, 231-2.

266 Fascist link, *The Times*, Thursday, 02/05/1981, 1; Bristol attacks: 'BREC's Evidence to part II of the Inquiry into the Matters Arising from the Death of Stephen Lawrence' (Bristol, 3 November 1998), 2-4, 5-6; PCP, BCRE Ann. Rep., 1994, 12-13, 1995, 11-13, 1996, 10-11; *BRECN (*May 2004); Batook Pandya (I, April 2007); *The Independent*, 11/05/1995; PCP, BREC Ann. Rep., 1999, 9-10, 2000, 8.

267 Street robberies, *The Guardian*, 27/12/1986; drugs, *The Independent*, 26/06/04; Laurence Hoo (I, Nov. 2006); Steve Wilkes (I, June 2005); Derek Lane, Community Relations Officer, Bristol and Avon Constabulary, 1980s (I, Feb. 2006).

268 Peter Courtier, Malcolm X Centre staff (I, Feb. 2007).

269 PCP, BREC Ann. Rep., 1996, 9; *BEP* 17/04/96, 1; Hoo.

270 Travellers: *EP,* editorial, 16/07/1997; PCP, BREC Ann Rep, 1998, 16; Colston controversy: *EP,* 29/1/1998, unpublished letters and calls made to *Evening Post*.

CHAPTER 12 African-Caribbeans, 1948–1990, pp. 157-76

271 Brathwaite, 51.

272 Tidrick; Rose et al, 67; Goulbourne & Chamberlain; Derek Sealy (I: Raj Lalal, BCRL, Oral Hist. Proj., 1997).

273 Pryce, K., 20-1.

274　BRO, Pol/LG/1/1; Peter Courtier former Chair of BREC (I, 1997). Chain migration: Castles & Kosack; FDB.

275　FDB; Fenton (1987), 6.

276　parishes, FDB; Fenton (1987), 6; 1957 TNA, HO344/122; anticipation' G', Retired elderly white professional (I, 18/10/06); FDB; BRO, Pol/LG/1/1.

277　Not allocated.

278　Richmond (1973), 54; Rex, 19; Fleming, T., 110.

279　Avon County Council (1994), 4-5.

280　BRO, CRC Ann. Rep. 1971, 18.

281　BRO, Pol/LG.1/1/.

282　'C', elderly male Jamaican, retired skilled worker St Paul's (I, 27/06/06); Campbell; Downer.

283　Richmond (1961), 54; Fleming, T., 97, 28n.

284　Malpass & Walmsley, 7-8; McNeil.

285　BCC.

286　Peter Courtier (1 March 1997); FDB.

287　 Richmond (1961), 25; Banton, 56; Patterson, 80; Glass, 72.

288　Derek Sealey (I).

289　Testimony Films; Banton; Pers. Com.

290　Ramdeen, 28-9.

291　Campbell.

292　Dresser (1986), 40; Richmond (1961), 85; Foot; Layton-Henry.

293　BRO, Pol/LG/1/1; Dresser (1986); BRO, Pol/LG/1/1.

294　Paul Stephenson (I: Raj Lalal, BRL, Oral Hist. Proj.); PCP, VLC rec., 1967–9, Liaison officer report no 7, 8th October 1968; 'D', Dominican-born woman professional, Montpelier (I, July 2006).

295　Mr & Mrs Hibbert, Jamaican shopkeepers, St Marks Road (I, August 2006).

296　Assaulted: 'C' Elderly Jamaican male St Paul's (I, 30/06/06); Dresser (1986), 10. Arrested: Paul Stephenson (I: Raj Lalal, BRL, Oral Hist. Proj.); Johnson, H.

297　Thomas.

298　Mr & Mrs Hibbert (I)

299　British Empire and Commonwealth Museum; Guy Bailey (I: Raj Lalal, BCRL); BBC 2.

300　Burton.

301　Roy Hackett (I, 23/07/06); BRO, Pol/LG/1/1.

302　James & Harris.

303　Pryce, xii, 184; BCRL, Inkworks Newsletter nos 25-8, 1986, St Paul's Festival Programme, vol. 42, 1987.

304　Bristol Black Writers Group, 37-8.

305　'After the Fire', Equal Opportunities Sub-Committee, Bristol Teachers Association (NUT), (report of Avon Division of NUT, Sept. 1980); 'G', elderly Englishwoman, Henbury (I, 18/10/06); Coard.

306　'G' (I).

307　PCP, CRC rep., 17.

308　'H' mixed race Bristolian male professional mid-40s (I).

309　'F' Black Bristolian woman professional Stapleton (I, July 2006).

310　BRO, 'Rep. of the Employment Working Party', CRC, 1978, 20; PCP, CRC Ann. Rep., 1975, 6, 1977, 14-16.

311　Roy Hackett (I: Raj Lalal, BCRL, Oral Hist. Proj., 1997).

312　Nicholls, 87.

313　' D', Dominican woman professional, Montpelier (I, 21/07/06).

314　'E', Jamaican born Bristolian, Lockleaze (I); Asher Craig (I: Raj Lalal, BCRL, Oral Hist. Proj., 1997).

315　'E' (I); Shawn Napthali Sobers (I, 18/05/07); Pryce, 167-87.

316　'E' (I) .

317　'E' (I); Inkworks: 'E' (I). Ekome: Higgins, 4; Martin, 3; Richard Davis, a founder member of Ekome (I, 28/07/06).

318　'H', mixed race male professional (I, 26/07/06); Massive Attack (E).

319　Johnson, L. K., 29.

320　OPCS 1991 Bristol Census (HMSO 1993); Avon County Council (1994); Barry Gosworth, formerly Director of Bristol Task Force (I).

321 PCP, Carmen Beckford CRC 1975 Rep., 6; Roberts; Reiner; Hall et al.
322 *WDP*, 28/07/87; Russell, Fenton et al., 32.
323 Waithe: Cathy Waithe, MBE (I, 21/07/06). Osbourne: M. Dresser (1993), 'Draft Oration for Olive Osbourne's Honourary Degree in Humanities, UWE'; *WDP*, 28/07/87.
324 HTV.
325 *BEP*, 24/11/84.
326 BCC, 'The Final Report of the Black and Other Minority Ethnic Pupil Exclusion Working Group' Feb. 2002, 'Poverty in Bristol' (1994); Morgans, 5. *WDP*, 28/07/87.
327 *WDP*, 24/02/90; *BEP*, 29/04/91; Sherrie Eugene (I, 10/07/06); BCLL, G. Clarke, 'Star's Sunday Faith Ban', cutting in General Sports file.

CHAPTER 13 South Asians, 1947–2001, pp. 177-200

328 Werbner, 11; Charsley, 85-6.
329 Brah, 71.
330 Gardner & Shukur, 143; Pandey, 4, 28-9.
331 Hussain, M., 152.
332 Rais Hyder (I, Feb. 2007).
333 Table T13, 'Theme Table on Ethnicity, Bristol', 2001 census Standard Tables; *The Guardian*, 8/09/05, 13.
334 Charsley, 87; 2001 census.
335 Table T13, 'Theme Table on Ethnicity, Bristol', 2001 census Standard Tables.
336 Barot (1988), 25-6; 2001 census, Table KS06, cited in *BRECN*, 288 (Sept. 2003).
337 Ballard, 93, 5n.; Bhatlines (E); Barifi (E); Nesbitt (E).
338 Singh; FDB, 102, 15; Maan, 106-44.
339 Singh; Hussain, M.; Sikh Temple (E).
340 Ballard, 95; 'B', Bhat Sikh (I, March 2007).
341 FDB, 71, 79, 91; Hussain, M., 152, 179; Mukhtyar Singh (I, 14/11/06).
342 *BEP*, 18/12/87; *WDP*, 9/02/88.
343 Jeffery, 60; FDB, nos. 7, 8, 9, 10, 13, 14, 15, 19, 21.
344 'Fatima' (I, 05/03/07); 'Rani' (I, 28/02/07).
345 I (Katherine Charsley, n.d. (*c*.2000-2002)), Dhek Bhal women's group, Barton Hill; Jeffery, 66.
346 Mirpuris in Bristol: Hussain, 94-6; Mangla Dam & British Immigration: Kulra, 66-73; Himal Southasian (E); World Commission (E); Jeffery, 16; Rais Hyder (I, Jan. & Feb. 2007); Hussain, K., 38-9.
347 Hussain, M., 109; 'Ms S' (I, March 2007).
348 M. Yunis (I, 31/1/04).
349 I (Katherine Charsley, n.d. (*c*.2000-2002)), Dhek Bhal women's group; (I, 19/02/07).
350 Dahya, 90-8.
351 FDB, 34; Shaw (1994), 45-6.
352 'E' (I: CBB, 21/09/06).
353 FDB, 39.
354 Edwards, 46.
355 FDB, 85.
356 Barot (1992), 54; Barot (1994-5); FDB, 83, 100; Hussain, M., 9, 20; Zy Siddiqi (I, 6/12/06).
357 Thajdin, 135.
358 Zy Siddiqi (I, 6/12/06); Bhachu, 10-22.
359 Amlani, 133.
360 BCRC Ann. Rep., 1978, 26; Britain Today (E); Ideas Festival (E).
361 BCR Ann. Rep., 1972, 29; *BEP*, 05/12/72.
362 Zehra Haq (I, 16/02/07).
363 Shaw (1988), 147-9; Foyle.
364 BCRC, Ann. Rep., 1977, 28.
365 Sikh Temple (E); BCRC Ann. Rep., 1979, 12ff.; Foyle.
366 Barot (1999), 58.
367 Wailing tower: *BEP*, 14/06/68; BCC Planning Envelope 62806, Street File: G66 (Green Street).
368 BCRC, 1985, 13; Boreham (E); Ballard, 100-2.

369   FDB, 18, 19, 29, 45, 61, 73.
370   FDB, 26, 61.
371   FDB, 12, 14, 22, 62, 73, 74, 76, 77, 103; Muhktyar Singh (I, 14/11/07, 30/11/07); Singh; BCRC, 1977, 46.
372   Zehra Haq (I, 19/2/07); 'BB' & 'RF' (I, 5/3/07); FDB, 96.
373   Sunamganj (E); Malek, 13-15.
374   Moklis Miah (I).
375   Gujeratis: Barot (1999), 62-3. Debate: Modood & Berthoud, 140-9, 341-5. Newport: 'Ms U' (I). Education: Malek, 51.
376   Sayyid, 5.

CHAPTER 14 Displaced People: Poles, Somalis and Others, pp. 201-18

377   Kushner & Knox, 47-54; *The Times*, 22/09/14, 12.
378   Greenbank (E); Companies (E); BRO, P/ALV/M/2(a-b), 35123 W/M/3; Horfield (E).
379   Ritchie, 63-4; Samuel, 177-8; Edwards, 10, 32.
380   Kershen, 146-7; Samuel, 177-8.
381   Greene (E).
382   Stephen Bates, 'Survivors with a message: lest we forget Nazi genocide', *The Guardian*, 27/01/06.
383   BRO, 27155(2) a-n.
384   See n. 2; Edwards, 10, 32; Kelly, 1-14.
385   Kushner & Knox, 220-1; Miles, 432.
386   Stachura (2004a & b); Lane, 43-50; Kushner & Knox, 217-28; Sword & Ciechanowski ; Burrell, 71; Cesarz, 12-16; Domagala, 127-9.
387   Kucharczyk, 3-8; Ireneusz G. Peszynski (I, 26/04/07).
388   *BEP*, 24/11/95, 28; Janina Wozniak (I, 25/02/07).
389   Ireneusz G Peszynski (I, 26/04/07); Celina, Alla & Richard Domagala (I: Sian White, 23/08/06).
390   'Jan' (I: Pam Sheppard, 25/02/07).
391   Kucharczyk, 9.
392   Kucharczyk, 9.
393   Ireneusz G. Peszynski (I, 26/04/07); Janina Wozniak (I, 25/02/07).
394   Sophia Szczech (I, 25/02/07).
395   Celina, Alla & Richard Domagala (I: Sian White, 23/08/06); Anon. (1993); Ireneusz G. Peszynski (I, 26/04/07); Souvenir of 150th Anniversary of Arley Chapel (2006).
396   Ireneusz G Peszynski (I, 26/04/07).
397   Celina, Alla & Richard Domagala (I: Sian White, 23/08/06); Burrell, 77-8; Krystyna Studzinska (I, 30/08/06 & 2/09/06).
398   Bülbring, 108, 112; Winslow, 85-93; Krystyna Studzinska (I, 30/08/06 & 2/09/06).
399   Al Haj Jama, 14-19, 61-91; Gardner & El Bushra, 1-5; 228-36; Lewis (1993), 1-3; Lewis (1988);
400   Mr Mumin (I, 11/02/04); Ahmed Duale (I, 19/04/07).
401   Mohammed Issa Ahmed & Hashi Jama (I, 24/04/07); Ms 'S', Somali refugee (25/04/07); Ms 'Z', refugee adviser (19/04/07); Ahmed Duale (I, 19/04/07).
402   Ahmed Duale (I, 19/04/07); Boch, 118-19.
403   Cole (E); Sue Njie, refugee support worker (I: Dresser & P. Sheppard, 5/03/07); S. Clark, 'Mobility and Unsettlement in Contemporary Britain', Project transcripts.
404   Batook Pandya, director of Support Against Racist Incidents (I, April 2007); Parkway Methodist Reminiscence Group (I: CBB, February 2006).
405   Skills: Sue Njie (I, March 2007). Could not speak English: Layla Ismail (talk, 26/04/07).
406   BCRE Ann. Rep. (1991), 9-13; Peevers (E).
407   Immigration lawyer & refugee advisors (I, 05/06/07); Ms 'Z' (refugee) (I, June 2007); Affi, 107-8, 110-13; Peevers (E).
408   Mahamad Mohamud (I: Pam Sheppard, 23/02/07); Somali Saturday School organisers (I, 10/12/05); Hussein (E); Boch, 123; Duale & Luling.

Bibliography and Sources

Adler, J. with Schlesinger, A. and Emanuel, R. (n.d.) *The Bristol Hebrew Congregation: A Guide to the Park Row Synagogue* (Bristol)

Adler, M. (1939) *Jews of Medieval England*, Jewish Hist. Soc. of England

Affi, L. (2004) 'Domestic Conflict in the Diaspora: Somali Women Asylum Seekers and Refugees in Canada', in J. Gardner and J. El Bushra (eds), *Somalia – The Untold Story: The War Through the Eyes of Somali Women* (London: Pluto)

Agnew, D. C. A. (1866) *Protestant Exiles from France in the Reign of Louis XIV or the Huguenot Refugees and their Descendants in Great Britain and Ireland* (London)

Al Haj Jama, I. (2007) *Somalia: A Forgotten Issue*

Amlani, Y. (1998) 'What is to be, is to be! My destiny …' in G. Edwards (ed.), *Origins: Personal Stories of Crossing the Seas to Settle in Britain* (New Words: Bristol)

Anon. (1753) *The Case and Appeal of James Ashley of Bread Street London … in Relation to I. The Apprehension of Henry Simons, the Polish Jew, on a Warrant Issued Out Against Him for Perjury*

Anon. (1883) *Work in Bristol: a Series of Sketches of the Chief Manufactures in the City of Bristol* (Bristol: reprinted for the *Bristol Times and Mirror*)

Anon. (*c.*1970) 'Welsh Back – an Account of its History' (unpublished ms, n.d., BCRL)

Anon. (1973) *Zion Street Chapel, The Church of the Vow Bedminster Bridge-Bristol Bicentenary of 'The Vow' 1773-1973 – Souvenir Programme*

Anon. (1993) *Ksiega Pamiatkowa Polskief Paraffii Matki Boskiefj Ostrobramskiej 1948-1993* (London)

Anstey, C. (1756) *Memoirs of the Noted Buckhorse. In Which, Besides a Minute Account of his Past Memorable Exploits …*, vol. 2. (London: S. Crowder and H. Woodgate)

Atkinson, B. (1982) *Trade Unions in Bristol* (BBHAP)

Austin, R. (1988) 'Racial Violence and Harassment in Local Authority Housing: Case Study [of] Bristol City Council', Working Party of the Centre for the Study of Community and Race Relations, Brunel University

Avon County Council (1981) 'Report of the Employment Working Group: Planning Dept., Census: Birthplace Statistics for Bristol and Avon.'

Avon County Council (1988) 'The Ethnic Minority Population and Workforce Bristol and Avon' (Planning Dept.)

Avon County Council (1994) 'Selected Statistics' (Dept. of Public Relations and Publicity)

Bagnall, R. (1909) *Ireland under the Stuarts and during the Interregnum, Volume I, 1603-1642* (London: Longmans)

Ballard, R. (c1994) 'Differentiation and Disjunction among the Sikhs', in R. Ballard (ed.), *Desh Pardesh:The South Asian Presence in Britain* (London: Hurst), pp. 88-116

Banton, M. (1953) 'Recent Migration from West Africa and the West Indies to the United Kingdom', *Population Studs.*, 7, pp. 2-13

Banton, M. (1959) *White and Coloured: The Behaviour of British People towards Coloured Immigrants* (London: Jonathan Cape)

Barnard, T. C. (1975) *Cromwellian Ireland: English Government and Reform in Ireland, 1649-1660* (London: OUP)

Barot, R. (1988) *Bristol and the Indian Independence Movement* (BBHAP)

Barot, R. (1999) 'Ethnicity and Religion Among Bristol Hindus', *Scottish Jnl of Religious Studs.*, 20/1

Barot, R. (1994/5) 'South Asians in Britain: a Historical Profile', published in French as 'Une Perspective Historique sur l'immigration et le peuplement de provenance d'Asie du sud en Grand-Bretange', *Migrance*, 6/7, Personal translation from Rohit Barot.

Barot, R. (1999) 'Ethnicity and Religion: The Formation and Adaptation of a Hindu Community in Bristol', *Scottish Jnl of Religious Studs.*, 20, pp. 51-72

Barry, J. (1996) 'Bristol Pride: Civic identity in Bristol, *c.*1640-1775' in M. Dresser and P. Ollerenshaw (eds), *The Making of Modern Bristol* (Tiverton: Redcliffe), pp. 25-47

Bartal, I. (2002) *The Jews of Eastern Europe, 1772-1881* (Pennsylvania UP)

BBC2 (1980) 'The Western Star Domino Club' (documentary)

BCC (1994) 'A survey into the Housing Needs of Black Elders in Bristol' (Policy and Information Unit, Housing Services)

Berthoud, R., Madood, T. and Smith, P. (1997) 'Introduction', in T. Modood and R. Berthoud (eds), *Ethnic Minorities in Britain: Diversity and Disadvantage: the Fourth National Survey of Ethnic Minorities*

Bhachu, P.K. (1985) *Twice Migrants: East African Sikh Settlers in Britain* (London: Tavistock)

Blackman, M. (2007) (ed.) *Unheard Voices* (London: Corgi)

Boch, A. (1999) 'As If Being a Refugee Isn't Hard Enough: The Policy of Exclusion', in P. Cohn (ed.), *New Ethnicities, Old Racisms* (NY, London: Zed Books)

Bolton, J. L. (1998) (ed.) *The Alien Communities of London in the Fifteenth Century: The Subsidy Rolls of 1440 and 1483-4* (Stamford: Richard III & Yorkist Hist. Trust/Paul Watkins)

Bolton, J. L. (2000) 'Irish Migration to England in the Late Middle Ages: the Evidence of 1394 and 1440', *Irish Hist. Studs.*, 32, pp. 1-21

Boore, E. J. (1982) 'Excavations at Peter Street, Bristol, 1975-1976', *Bristol & Avon Arch.,* 1, pp. 7-11

Boore, E. J. (2001) 'A Medieval Lamp from Peter Street, Bristol', *TBGAS,* 119, pp. 179-82

Bosher, J.F. (1995) 'Huguenot Merchants and the Protestant International in the Seventeenth Century', *The William and Mary Quarterly*, 3rd Series, 52, pp. 77-102

Bottignolo, B. (1985) *Without a Bell Tower: a Study of the Italian Immigrants in South West England* (Rome: Centro Studi Emigrazione)

Bowling, B. (1993) 'Racial Harassment and the Process of Victimization: conceptual and methodological implications for the local crime survey', *British Jrnl. of Criminology*, 33, pp. 231-50

Bowly, T. (2005) 'Bristol's trading network with Ireland in the later Middle Ages' (Univ. of the West of England, Bristol, MA thesis)

Brace, K. (1971) *Portrait of Bristol* (London: Robert Hale)

Brah, A. (2006) 'The "Asian" in Britain', in N. Ali, V.S. Kalra, and S. Sayyid (eds), *A Postcolonial People: South Asians in Britain* (London: Hurst)

Brathwaite, E. (1973) *The Arrivants: New World Trilogy* (London: OUP)

Bristol & Avon Family Hist. Soc. (2005) *Bristol Diocese Baptismal Registers1812-1837 Index and Transcripts* (Bristol: BAFHS, CDRom)

Bristol & Avon Family Hist. Soc. (2006) *Bristol Diocese Baptismal Registers 1754-1812, Index and Transcripts* (Bristol: BAFHS, CDRom)

Bristol Black Writers Group (1999) *The Reality is …The Bristol Black Writers Anthology* (Bristol)

British Empire & Commonwealth Museum (2004) 'Sheet 2: Who's Who?', Crossing Continents Education Pack Information

Brown, C. (2002) *Bovver* (London: John Blake)

Brown, H.G. (*c.*1935) *Our Bristol: The Story of the City of Bristol* (Bristol)

Brown, R. B. and McCartney, S. (2004) 'David of Oxford and Licoricia of Winchester: Glimpses of a Jewish Family in Thirteenth-Century England', *Jewish Hist. Studs,* 39, pp. 19-23

Bülbring, M. (1954) 'Post-War Refugees in Great Britain', *Population Studs.*, 8, pp. 99-112

Burgess, C. (2004) (ed.) *The Pre-Reformation Records of All Saints' Church, Bristol. Part III: Wills, the Halleway Chantry Records and Deeds,* BRS, 56

Burrell, K. (2004) 'Homeland Memories and the Polish Community in Leicester', in P. D. Stachura (ed.), *The Poles in Britain 1940-2000: From Betrayal to Assimilation* (London: Cass), pp. 69-84

Burell, K. and Panayi, P. (2006a) (eds) *Histories and Memories* (London: Tauris)

Burell, K. and Panayi, P. (2006b) 'Immigration, History and Memory in Britain', in Burrell and Panayi (2006a), pp. 3-25

Burton, E. (1997) 'A Profile of Bristol's Black Community and Black Worship in Bristol'

Campbell, P. (2003) (ed.) *'Many Rivers to Cross': Our History* (Bristol: Malcolm X Elders Forum)

Carus-Wilson, E. M. (1933) 'The Overseas Trade of Bristol', in E. Power and M. M. Postan (eds), *Studs. in English Trade in the Fifteenth Century* (London: Routledge), pp. 20-64

Carus-Wilson, E. M. (1937) (ed.) *The Overseas Trade of Bristol in the Later Middle Ages,* BRS, 7

Carus-Wilson, E. M. (1967) 'The Iceland Venture', in E. M. Carus-Wilson, *Medieval Merchant Venturers* (CUP), pp. 98-142

Castles, S. and Kosack, G. (1973) *Immigrant Workers and Class Structure in Western Europe* (OUP)

Cesarani, D. (2006) 'The Jews of Bristol and Liverpool, 1750–1850: Port Jewish Communities in the Shadow of Slavery', *Jewish Culture & Hist.*, 7.2

Cesarz, S. (1998) 'Has This Suffering any Meaning?', in G. Edwards (ed.), *Origins, Personal Stories of Crossing the Seas to Settle in Britain* (Bristol: New Words), pp. 12-16

Charsley, K. (2005) 'Unhappy Husbands: Masculinity and Migration in Transnational Pakistani Marriages', *Jnl of the Royal Anthropological Institute,* 11, pp. 85-105

Chazan, R. (2006) *The Jews of Medieval Western Christendom, 1000-1500* (CUP)

Childs, W. (2000) 'Irish Merchants and Seamen in Late Medieval England', *Irish Hist. Studs.*, 32, pp. 22-43

Coard, B. (1971) *How the West Indian Child is Made Educationally Sub-Normal in the British School System*

Colley, L. (1992) *Britons: Forging the Nation 1707-1837* (London: Pimlico)

Collins, M. (2001) 'Pride and Prejudice: West Indian Men in Mid-20th Century Britain', *Jnl of British Studs.*, 40, pp. 391-418

Commission on the Future of Multi-Ethnic Britain (2000) *The Future of Multi-Ethnic Britain* (HMSO)

Connell-Smith, G. (1951) 'The ledger of Thomas Howell', *EcHR*, new ser. 3, pp. 363-70

Cooper, W. (1798) (ed.) *The Messiah Revealed to a Jewess; Or, The Merciful Dealings of God with Hannah Nonmus, Born at Frankfort, in Germany, of Jewish Parents, and Brought Up In Jewish Prejudices; But Divine Providence Brought Her to England, and Divine Grace Drew Her to Christ*

Cosgrove, A. (1987a) 'The Emergence of the Pale, 1399-1447', in A. Cosgrove (ed.), *A New History of Ireland: Volume II, 1169-1534* (Oxford: Clarendon P), pp. 533-56

Cosgrove, A. (1987b) 'England and Ireland, 1399-1447', in A. Cosgrove (ed.), *A New History of Ireland: Volume II, 1169-1534* (Oxford: Clarendon), pp. 525-32

Crawford, A. (1984) *Bristol and the Wine Trade* (BBHAP)

Crossley-Evans, M. (2004-2005) 'The Origins and Values of Bristol Masonry', *Corona Gladiorum: Trans of the Bristol Masonic Soc.*

Cruger, D. W. (*c.*2002) 'The Family of John Cruger: Colonial Mayor of New York City' (unpublished ms n.d.)

Dahya, B. (1974) 'The Nature of Pakistani Ethnicity in Industrial Cities in Britain' in A. Cohen (ed.), *Urban Ethnicity* (London: Tavistock), pp. 77-118

Darlington, R. R. (1928) (ed.) *Vita Wulfstani of William of Malmesbury*, Camden Soc., 3rd ser., 40

Davies, R. R. (2000) *The Age of Conquest: Wales, 1063-1415* (2nd edn, OUP)

Davis, G. (1991) *The Irish in Britain 1815-1914* (Dublin: Gill and Macmillan)

Davis, G. (2000) 'The Irish in Britain, 1815-1939' in A. Bielenberg (ed.), *The Irish Diaspora* (Harlow: Longman), pp. 19-36

Day, J. (1973) *Bristol Brass: A History of the Industry* (Newton Abbot: David & Charles)

De la Beche, T. (1845) *The Second Report of the Commissioners for Inquiring into the State of Large Towns and Populous Districts* (HMSO)

Defoe, D. (1742) *A Tour Thro' the Whole Island of Great Britain. Divided into Circuits or Journeys* (3rd edn, London)

Denning, R.T.W. (1995) (ed.) *The Diary of William Thomas of Michaelstone-super-Ely near St. Fagans, Glamorgan, 1762-1795*, South Wales Record Soc., 11

Dimmock, S. (2004) 'Haverfordwest: An Exemplar for the Study of Southern Welsh Towns in the Later Middle Ages', *Welsh Hist. Review*, 22, pp. 1-28

Dimmock, S. (2005) 'Reassessing the Towns of Southern Wales in the Later Middle Ages', *Urban Hist.*, 32, pp. 33-45

Domagala, W. (1998) 'Life in a Soviet Labour Camp', in G. Edwards (ed.), *Origins, Personal Stories of Crossing the Seas to Settle in Britain* (Bristol: New Words), pp. 127-9

Down, K. (1987) 'Colonial society and economy', in A. Cosgrove (ed.), *A New History of Ireland: Volume II, 1169-1534* (Oxford: Clarendon), pp. 439-91

Dresser, M. (1986) *Black and White on the Buses* (Bristol Broadsides)

Dresser, M. (1996) 'Protestants, Catholics and Jews: Religious Difference and Political Status in Bristol 1750-1850' in M. Dresser and P. Ollerenshaw (eds.), *The Making of Modern Bristol* (Tiverton: Redcliffe), pp. 96-123

Dresser, M. (1998) 'Minority Rites: Jewish Circumcision in British Thought', *Jewish Hist. and Culture*, 1, pp. 72-87

Dresser, M. (2001a) *Slavery Obscured: The Social History of the Slave Trade in an English Provincial Port* (London and New York: Continuum)

Dresser, M. (2001b) '"The Book of Your Own Heart". Some Observations on Women's Spiritual Memoirs of the Eighteenth Century: The case of the Bristol Moravians,' in J. H. Bettey (ed.), *Historic Churches and Church Life In Bristol* (Gloucester: Bristol and Gloucestershire Arch. Soc.), pp. 134-47

Dresser, M. (2003) (ed.) *The Diary of Sarah Fox*, BRS, 55

Dresser, M. (2004) 'Isaac Jacobs', *Oxford Dictionary of National Biography* (OUP)

Duale, A-K and Luling, V. (2005) 'Somali Social and Legal Issues with Reference to UK Asylum Seekers' (Report Commissioned by Advice Centres for Avon)

Duffy, S. (1997) *Ireland in the Middle Ages* (Basingstoke: Macmillan)

Dye, R. (2001) 'Catholic Protectionism or Irish Nationalism? Religion and Politics in Liverpool, 1829-1845', *Jnl of British Studs.*, 40, pp. 357-90

Dyer, A. (2000) 'Ranking lists of English medieval towns', in D. M. Palliser (ed.), *The Cambridge Urban History of Britain, vol. 1: 600-1540* (CUP), pp. 747-70

Dyer C. and Slater, T. R. 'The Midlands', in D. M. Palliser (ed.), *The Cambridge Urban History of Britain, vol. 1: 600-1540* (CUP), pp. 609-38

Edwards, G. (1998) (ed.) *Origins: Personal Stories of Crossing the Seas to Settle in Britain* (Bristol: New Words)

Eickelmann, C. and Small, D. (2003) *Pero: the Life of a Slave in Eighteenth-Century Bristol* (Tiverton: Redcliffe)

Ellis, P. (2006) 'Revenue from rocks', in B. Cunliffe (ed.), *England's Landscape: The West* (London: Collins), pp. 135-52

Elrington, C. R. (2003) (ed.) *Abstract of Feet of Fines Relating to Gloucestershire, 1199-1299*, Gloucester Rec. Ser., 16

Emanuel, R. R. (2000) 'The Society of Antiquaries' Sabbath Lamp', *Antiquaries Jnl.*, 80, pp. 308-15

Endelman, T. M. (2002) *The Jews of Britain, 1656-2000* (Berkeley and London: University of California)

Eriksen, T. H. (2004) *What is Anthropology?* (London: Pluto)

Evans, W. (2003) 'Norborne Berkeley and Jewish Naturalisation' (unpublished paper)

Feldman, D. (1994) *Englishmen and Jews: Social Relations and Political Culture 1840-1914* (New Haven and London: Yale UP)

Fenton, S. (1987) 'Black Elderly People in Bristol' (research pamphlet, Bristol Univ.)

Fenton, S. (2003) *Ethnicity* (CUP)

Firth, G.H. (1914) (ed.) *Macaulay's History of England with Illustrations* (London), vol. V

Flavell, J.M. (2004) 'Cruger, Henry (1739–1827)', *Oxford Dictionary of National Biography* (OUP)

Fleming, P. (2007) 'Identity and belonging: Irish and Welsh in fifteenth-century Bristol', in L. Clark (ed.), *The Fifteenth Century, VII* (Woodbridge: Boydell, forthcoming)

Fleming, T. (1998) 'Rearticulating Tradition Translating Place. Collective Memories of Carnival in Leeds and Bristol' (Sheffield Univ., Ph.D. thesis)

Foot, P. (1969) *The Rise of Enoch Powell* (London: Cornmarket)

Foyle, A. (2007) 'Bristol: Ethnic Minorities 1001-2001: Places of Worship by Denomination' (unpublished report for the Bristol EPE project)

Franklin, P. (1993) (ed.) *The Taxpayers of Medieval Gloucestershire: An Analysis of the 1327 Lay Subsidy Roll with a New Edition of its Text* (Stroud: Sutton)

Fuller, E. A. (1894-5) 'The tallage of 6 Edward II and the Bristol rebellion', *TBGAS*, 19, pp. 171-278

Gardner, J. and l Bushra, J. (2004) (eds) *Somalia-The Untold Story: The War Through the Eyes of Somali Women* (London: Pluto)

Gardner K. and Shukur, A. (1994) '"I'm Bengali, I'm Asian, And I'm Living Here": The Changing Identity of British Bengalis' in R. Ballard (ed.), *Desh Pardesh: The South Asian Presence in Britain* (London: Hurst), pp. 142-64

Gilbert, P.J. (1995) 'In the Midst of a Protestant People: The Development of the Catholic Community in Bristol in the Nineteenth century' (Bristol Univ. Ph.D. thesis)

Gilroy, P. (1987) *There Ain't No Black in the Union Jack* (London: Hutchinson)

Glass, R. (1960) *Newcomers, The West Indians in London* (London: Centre for Urban Studs./George Allen & Unwin)

Goldwin, W. (1712) *A Poetical Description of Bristol* (London and Bristol: Joseph Penn)

Gough, J. W. (1967) *The Mines of Mendip* (rev. edn., OUP)

Goulbourne, H. (1988) *Race Relations in Britain Since 1945* (Basingstoke: Macmillan)

Goulbourne, H. and Chamberlain, M. (2001) *Caribbean Families in Britain and the Caribbean World* (London: Caribbean)

Grayzel, S. (1966) *The Church and the Jews in the Thirteenth Century* (NY: Hermon)

Griffiths, R. A. (1978) (ed.) *Boroughs of Medieval Wales* (Cardiff: Wales UP)

Griffiths, R. A. (1981) *The Reign of King Henry VI* (London: Ernest Benn)

Griffiths, R. A. (1994a) *Conquerors and Conquered in Medieval Wales* (London: St Martin's)

Griffiths, R. A. (1994b) 'Medieval Severnside: the Welsh Connection', in R. A.

Griffiths, *Conquerors and Conquered in Medieval Wales* (Stroud: Sutton), pp. 1-18

Griffiths, R. A. (2000a) 'Wales and the Marches', in D. M. Palliser (ed.), *The Cambridge Urban History of Britain, vol. I : 600-1540* (CUP), pp. 681-714

Griffiths, R. A. (2000b) 'Urban colonization in England and Wales in the Later Middle Ages: Examples and Implications' in M. Boone and P. Stabel (eds), *Shaping Urban Identity in Late Medieval Europe* (Leuven: Garant), pp. 221-35

Griffiths, R. A. (2002) 'After Glyn Dŵr: An Age of Reconciliation?', in *Proceedings of the British Academy*, 117, pp. 139-64

Grinsell, L. V. (1986) *The Bristol Mint* (BBHAP)

Gruenewald, H. (1998) 'Last Train from Hell', in G. Edwards (ed.), *Origins: Personal Stories of Crossing the Seas to Settle in Britain* (Bristol: New Words), pp. 10-11

Gunnis, R. (1953) *Dictionary of British Sculptors 1660-1851* (London: Odhams)

Gwynn, R. D. (1985) *Huguenot Heritage: the History and Contribution of the Huguenots in Britain* (Brighton: Sussex Academic)

Hall, S. et al. (1978) *Policing the Crisis: Mugging, the State, and Law and Order* (London: Macmillan)

Hankins, K. (1993) *In My Father's House: St Mary-on-the-Quay – Bristol's Oldest Catholic Church* (Bristol)

Hannam, J. (1996) '"An Enlarged Sphere of Usefulness": the Bristol Women's Movement, *c*.1860-1914', in M. Dresser and P. Ollerenshaw (eds), T*he Making of Modern Bristol* (Tiverton: Redcliffe), pp. 184-209

Hansom, J. S. (1903) (ed.) 'Catholic Registers of St Joseph's Chapel Trenchard Street, 1787-1808', *Catholic Records*, 3, pp. 181-329

Hardy, T. D. (ed.) (1833/44) *Rotuli Litterarum Clausarum in Turri Londinensi Asservati …, 1204-1227* (2 vols, London: Rec. Commission)

Hathaway, E. (2000) (ed.) *A True Soldier Gentleman, the Memoirs of Lt. John Cooke 1791-1813* (Swanage: Shinglepicker)

Higgins, K. (1990) 'Black Dance Development in Bristol and Avon', *Southwest Arts*

Hillaby, J. (1984) 'The Hereford Jewry, 1179-1290. Part I', *Trans of the Woolhope Club* 44 (iii), pp. 20-33

Hillaby, J. (1993) 'Beth Miqdash Me'at: The Synagogues of Medieval England', *Jnl. Ecclesiastical Hist.*, 44 (ii), pp. 182-98

Hillaby, J. (2001) 'Testimony from the Margin: the Gloucester Jewry and its neighbours c1159-1290', *JHS,* 37, pp. 77-81

Hillaby, J. (2003) 'Jewish Colonisation in the Twelfth Century' in P. Skinner (ed.), *The Jews in Medieval Britain: Historical, Literary and Archaeological Perspectives* (Woodbridge: Boydell & Brewer), pp. 15-40

Hillaby J. and Sermon, R. (2004) 'Jacob's Well, Bristol: *Mikveh* or *Bet Tohorah?*', *TBGAS*, 122, pp. 127-51

Hippisley, J. (*c*.1731) *A Journey to Bristol or the Honest Welch-man. A Farce of Two Acts* (London)

Hobhouse, C. P. (n.d.) *Some Account of the Family of Hobhouse and Reminiscences* (Leceister: Johnson Wykes and Co.)

Hollis, D. (1948) (ed.) *Calendar of the Bristol Apprentice Book, 1532-1565, Part I, 1532-1542*, BRS, 14

Holmes, C. (1988) *John Bull's Island: Immigration and British Society, 1871-1971* (London: Macmillan)

Holmes, C. (1991) 'Historians and Immigration' in C.G. Pooley and I.D.Whyte (eds), *Migrants, Emigrants and Immigrants: A Social History of Migration* (London: Routledge), pp. 191-207

Holmes, M. (1956) 'St Bartholomew's Hospital, Bristol: Some New Material' *TBGAS*, 74, pp. 180-7

Honeybourne, M. B. (1959-61) 'The Pre-Expulsion Cemetery of the Jews in London' *Trans. Jewish Hist. Soc. of England,* 20, pp. 145-59

Hoo, L. (2006) *Bristol: Inner-City Tales*

Hoskins, M. and Fox, D. (2001) *Bristol Football Club (RFU) 1888-1945* (Stroud: Tempus)

Howlett, W. (1884-9) (ed.) *Chronicles of the Reigns of Stephen, Henry II and Richard I* (Rolls Series)

HTV (1994) 'The West Story "Voices Over Bristol"' (documentary)

Huddleston, C.R. (n.d) 'Notes and correspondence on Huguenots' (typescript notes, BRO)

Hughes, V. (1977) *Ladies Mile* (London: Absom Press)

Hussain, K. (2006) *Going for a Curry? A Social and Culinary History* (Middlesbrough: Ed Zuban)

Hussain M. (2006) (ed) *A Century of Migration: Bristol's Asian Communities* (Bristol: Bristol Library Service)

Hutchison, J. and Smith, A. D. (1996) (eds.) 'Introduction', *Ethnicity* (OUP)

Hutton, J.H. (1909) *History of the Moravian Church* (London: Moravian Publication Office)

Irwin-Zarecka, I. (1994) *Frames of Remembrance* (New Brunswick [N.J.]: Transaction Publishers)

Jacobs, J. (1893) (ed.) *English History from Contemporary Writers: The Jews of Angevin England* (London: Powell)

James, W. and Harris, C. (1993) *Inside Babylon: The Caribbean Diaspora in Britain* (London: Verso)

Jeffery, P. (1976) *Migrants and Refugees: Muslim and Christian Pakistani Families in Bristol* (CUP)

Jenkins, G. H. (1977-78) 'A Welsh Quaker', *Jnl of the Flintshire Hist. Soc.,* 28

Jenkins, P. (2000) 'Wales' in P. Clark (ed.), *The Cambridge Urban History of Britain, vol. 2: 1540-1840* (CUP), pp. 133-50

Jenkins, P. (1992) *A History of Modern Wales* (London: Longman)

Jenkins, R.T. and Ramage, H. M. (1951) *A History of the Honourable Society of Cymmrodorion and of the Gyneddigion and Cymreigyddion Societies, 1751-1951* (London: the Honourable Soc. of Cymmrodorion)

Jenkinson, J. (1996) 'The 1919 riots,' in P. Panayi (ed.), *Racial Violence in Britain in the Nineteenth and Twentieth Centuries* (rev, edn, London: Leicester UP), pp. 92-103

John, A.H. (1951) 'Iron and Coal in a Glamorgan Estate 1700-1740', *EcHR,* 2, pp. 93-103

Johnson, H. (n.d.) 'Under the Swing' (HTV/Minus 4 documentary)

Johnson, J. (1820) *An Address to the Inhabitants of Bristol on the Subject of the Poor Rates With a View to Their Reduction and the Ameliorating the Present Condition of our Poor* (Bristol)

Johnson, L. K. (1996) *Selected Poems* (London)

Jones, P. and Youseph, R. (1994) *The Black Population of Bristol in the Eighteenth Century* (Bristol)

Jones, P. N. (1978) 'The Distribution and Diffusion of the Coloured Population in England and Wales 1961-1971', *Trans. of the Institute of British Geographers,* n.s., 3, pp. 53-81

Jones, T. (1717) *The Rise and Progress of the Most Honourable and Loyal Society of Antient Britons established in honour to Her Royal Highness's Birthday and the Principality of Wales, in St. David's Day the first of March, 1714-1715* (Kidib: W. Wilks for W. Taylor at the Ship in Pater Noster Row)

Joshua, H. and Wallace, T. (1983) *To Ride the Storm: the 1980 Bristol 'Riot'*

Jurkowski, M., Smith, C. L. and Crook, D. (1998) *Lay Taxes in England and Wales, 1188-1688* (Kew: Public Record Office)

Katz, D. S. (1994) *The Jews in the History of England, 1485-1850* (OUP)

Kelly, K. (2001) (ed.) *The Cambridge Companion to Tom Stoppard* (CUP)

Kershaw, R. and Pearsall, M. (2000) *Immigrants and Aliens: A Guide to Sources on UK Immigration and Citizenship* (Kew: Public Record Office)

Kershen, A. J. (2003) 'Immigrants, Sojourners and Refugees: Minority Groups in Britain, 1900-1939' in C. Wrigley (ed.), *A Companion to Early 20th Century Britain* (Oxford: Blackwell and the Historical Association), pp. 137-51

Kidd, C. (1999) *British Identities Before Nationalism: Ethnicity and Nationhood in the Atlantic World, 1600–1800* (CUP)

Knight, J. (1693) *A Speech in the House of Commons, against the Naturalizing of Foreigners* (London)

Kowaleski, M. 'Port towns: England and Wales, 1300-1540', in D. M. Palliser (ed.), *The Cambridge Urban History of Britain, vol.1 : 600-1540* (CUP), pp. 482-3

Kucharczyk, S. (n.d.) 'Memories: short true story of my life during and after World War II (1939-1997)' (unpublished ms)

Kulra, V. S. (2000) *From Textile Mills to Taxi Ranks: Experiences of Migration, Labour and Social Change* (Aldershot: Ashgate)

Kushner, T. and Knox, K. (2003) *Refugees In An Age of Genocide: Global, National and Local Perspectives during the Twentieth Century* (London: Frank Cass)

Lane, T. (2001) 'Victims of Stalin and Hitler: The Polish Community at Bradford', *Immigrants and Minorities*, 20, pp.43-50

Lang, S. and McGregor, M. (1993) (eds) *Tudor Wills Proved in Bristol, 1546-1603*, BRS, 44

Large, D. (1985) 'The Irish in Bristol in 1851: A Census Enumeration' in R. Swift and S. Gilley (eds), *The Irish in the Victorian City* (Beckenham, Kent: Croom Helm), pp. 37-58

Large, D. (2006) 'The Irish in Bristol in the Nineteenth Century' (unpublished study undertaken for the EPE project)

Lart, C.E. (ed.) *Registers of the French Church of Bristol, Stonehouse and Plymouth*, Huguenot Soc. Quarto Series, CD Rom 5b

Latimer, J. (1887) *The Annals of Bristol in the Nineteenth Century* (Bristol: W. & F. Morgan)

Latimer, J. (1893) *Annals of Bristol in the Eighteenth Century* (Bristol: J. W. Arrowsmith)

Latimer, J. (1900) *The Annals of Bristol in the Seventeenth Century* (Bristol: J. W. Arrowsmith)

Latimer, J. (1903) 'The Maire of Bristowe is Kalendar: its list of civic officers collated with contemporary legal MSS', *TBGAS*, 26, pp. 108-37

Layton-Henry, Z. (1984) *The Politics of Race in Britain* (London: Allen & Unwin)

Leech, J. (1884) 'A Tooth for a Tooth', in J. Leech, *Brief Romances from Bristol History* (Bristol: William George), pp. 51-4

Leech, J. (1888) *Supplemental Papers by the Church Go-er: Making the Fourth Collection from the Same Sources* (Bristol: William George)

Leech, R. H. (1989) 'Aspects of the Medieval Defences of Bristol: the Town Wall, the Castle, the Barbican and the Jewry' in M. Bowden, D. MacKay, P. Topping (eds), *From Cornwall to Caithness: Some Aspects of British Field Archaeology* (BAR, British ser., 209), 241-3

Leech, R. H. (1997) *The Topography of Medieval and Early Modern Bristol, vol. 1*, BRS, 48

Letford, L. and Pooley, C.G. (1995) 'Geographies of Migration and Religion: Irish women in Mid-Nineteenth Century Liverpool', in P. O'Sullivan (ed.), *The Irish World Wide, Vol. 4: Irish Women and Irish Migration* (London & N. Y.: Leicester UP), pp. 89-112

Lewis, I. M. (1988) *A Modern History of Somalia* (Boulder: Westview)

Lewis, I. M. (1993) 'Misunderstanding the Somali Crisis', *Anthropology Today*, 9, pp. 1-3

Liebmann, M. (1998) 'The Long Journey of Beginning', in G. Edwards (ed.), *Origins: Personal Stories of Crossing the Seas to Settle in Britain* (New Words: Bristol), pp. 30-8

Lindegaard, D. P. (n.d.a) *Black Bristolians of the Seventeenth, Eighteenth and Nineteenth Centuries* (Bristol)

Lindegaard, D.P. (n.d. b) *Brislington Bulletins* (Bristol)

Linebaugh, P. and Rediker, M. (2000) *The Many-Headed Hydra: Sailors, Slaves, Commoners, and the Hidden History of the Revolutionary Atlantic* (London and New York: Verso)

Little, B. (1987) 'Catholic Bristol: Some Eighteenth-Century Facts', *South Western Catholic Hist.*, 5, pp. 45-50

Livock, D. M. (1926) (ed.) *City Chamberlain's Accounts in the Sixteenth and Seventeenth Centuries*, BRS, 24

Lynch, J. (1999) *For King and Parliament: Bristol and the Civil War* (Stroud: Sutton)

Maan, B. (1992) *The New Scots: The Story of Asians in Scotland* (John Donald)

MacRaild, D. M. (1995) *Irish Migrants in Modern Britain, 1750-1822* (Basingstoke: Macmillan)

McGrath, P. (1955) (ed.) *Merchants and Merchandise in Seventeenth-Century Bristol*, BRS, 19

McGrath, P. (1985) (ed.) *A Bristol Miscellany*, BRS, 37

McGurk, J. (1997) *The Elizabethan Conquest of Ireland: The 1590s Crisis* (Manchester UP)

McNeil, J. (2001) 'Easton in the 20th Century' (Bristol: Living Easton)

Malek, M. (1986) 'Bengali Migrants in the Indian Restaurant Trade' (MSc. thesis, Bristol Univ.)

Malpass, P. and Walmsley, J. (2006) '100 Years of Council Housing Report' (Bristol City Council & Univ. of the West of England Faculty of the Built Environment)

Martin, B. (1997) 'Black African and Caribbean Arts in Bristol' (unpublished paper)

Mayo, R. (1985) *The Huguenots in Bristol* (BBHAP)

Mayo, S. (1996) 'Les Huguenots à Bristol (1681-1791)' (doctoral thesis, la Faculté des Lettres et Sciences Humaines de Lille, Institute Française du Royaume-Uni)

Medaglia, A. (2001) *Patriarchal Structures and Ethnicity in the Italian Community in Britain* (Aldershot: Ashgate)

Meller, H.E. (1976) *Leisure and the Changing City, 1870-1914* (London: Routledge & Kegan Paul)

Miles, R. (1989) 'Nationality, Citizenship and Migration to Britain, 1945-1951', *Jnl of Law and Society*, 16, pp. 426-42

Moon, N. (1979) *Education for Ministry: Bristol Baptist College, 1679-1979* (Bristol)

Morgan, K. (1993) *Bristol and the Atlantic Trade in the Eighteenth Century* (CUP)

Morgan, K. (1994) (ed.) 'The John Evans List of Dissenting Congregations and Ministers in Bristol, 1715-1729', in J. Barry and K. Morgan (eds), *Reformation and Revival in Eighteenth-Century Bristol*, BRS, 45, pp. 65-70

Morgans, C. (1996) 'Facing the Future A Report of St Pauls Anglican Parish Church' (Bristol)

Mundill, R. R. (2003) 'Edward I and the final phase of Anglo-Jewry', in Skinner, 55-70

Myers, K. (2006) 'Historical Practice in the Age of Pluralism: Educating and Celebrating Identities' in Burell and Panayi (2006a), pp. 35-53

N.A. [Bishop Saunders?] (*c*.1966) *The United Bristol Hospitals* (Bristol: Board of Governors of the United Bristol Hospitals, n.d.)

Neale, F. (2000) *William Worcestre:The Topography of Medieval Bristol*, BRS, 51

Nicholls, G. (1983 rep. 1990) *I Is a Long Memoried Woman* (London: Karnak House)

Nott, H. E (1935) (ed.) *The Deposition Books of Bristol, Vol. I, 1643-1647*, BRS, 6

Nott, H. E and Ralph, E. (1948) (eds) *The Deposition Books of Bristol, Vol. II, 1650-1654*, BRS, 13

OPCS (1993) *1991 Bristol Census* (HMSO)

Orme, N. (1976) *Education in the West of England, 1066-1548* (Exeter UP)

Owen, G. D. (1962) *Elizabethan Wales: The Social Scene* (Cardiff: Wales UP)

Pandey, G. (1997) 'In Defence of the Fragment: Writing about Hindu-Muslim Riots in India Today', in R. Guha (ed.), *A Subaltern Studs. Reader 1986-1995* (Minnesota UP)

Patterson, S. (1963) *Dark Strangers: A Study of West Indians in London* (Harmondsworth: Penguin)

Peach, G. C. K. (1975) 'Immigrants in the Inner City', *Geographical Jrnl.*, 141, pp. 372-9

Pellew, G. (1890) *John Jay* (Boston [Mass.])

Penn, S. A. C. (1989) 'Social and economic aspects of fourteenth-century Bristol' (Birmingham Univ. Ph.D. thesis)

Penny, J. (2001) *All the News That's Fit to Print: A Short History of Bristol's Newspapers since 1702* (BBHAP)

Phillips, M. and Phillips, T. (1998) *Windrush: The Irresistible Rise of Multi-Racial Britain* (London: Harper Collins)

Pierson, A. T. (1902) *George Müller of Bristol* (London)

Pike, J. (1996) 'Dyfed Apprentices in Eighteenth Century Bristol Part 1', Dyfed Family Hist. Jnl, 7, pp. 274ff

Pike, J. (n.d.) 'Dyfed Strays in Bristol' (BRO, microfiche)

Poliakov, L. (1968, rep 2003) *The History of Anti-Semitism*, vol. 3 (Pennsylvania UP)

Pollins, H. (1982) *Economic History of the Jews in England* (London: Associated University)

Poole, S. (1996) 'To Be a Bristolian: Civic Identity and the Social Order, 1750-1850', in M. Dresser and P. Ollerenshaw (eds), T*he Making of Modern Bristol* (Tiverton: Redcliffe), pp. 76-95

Poole, S. (2007) '"Bringing great shame upon this city": sodomy, the courts and the civic idiom in eighteenth-century Bristol', *Urban Hist.*, 34, pp. 115-17

Pooley, C. (1989) 'Segregation or Integration: The Residential experience of the Irish in Mid-Victorian Britain' in R. Swift and S. Gilley (eds), *The Irish in Britain 1815-1939* (London: Pinter), pp. 60-83

Powell, J. H. (2000) 'Bristol and West Wales: Economic and Social Links 1689-1837' (Univ. of Bristol, M.A. dissertation in Local Hist.)

Powicke, F. M. and Cheney, C. R. (1964) (eds) *Councils and Synods with other Documents relating to the English Church 1205-65* (Oxford: Clarendon)

Prestwich, M. (2005) *Plantagenet England, 1225-1360* (OUP)

Pryce, G. (1861) *A Popular History of Bristol …* (Bristol: W. Mack)

Pryce, K. (1979) *Endless Pressure: A Study of West Indian Lifestyles in Bristol* (Middlesex)

Pugh, R. B. (1963) (ed.) *The Marcher Lordships of South Wales, 1415-1536: Select Documents* (Cardiff: Wales UP)

Quinn, D. B. (1974) *England and the Discovery of America* (London & NY)

Ralph, E. (1985) (ed.) 'Bishop Secker's Diocese Book' in J. H. Bettey (ed.), *A Bristol Miscellany*, BRS, 37

Ralph, E. (1992) (ed.) *Calendar of the Bristol Apprentice Book, 1532-1565, Part III, 1552-1565*, BRS, 43

Ralph, E. and Hardwick, N. M. (1980) (eds) *Calendar of the Bristol Apprentice Book, 1532-1565, Part II, 1542-1552*, BRS, 33

Ralph, S. (2007) 'One Evening on the Internet', *Jnl of the Bristol and Avon Family Hist. Soc.*, 128

Ramdeen, H. (1991) ' Mother Country, 1955-75' (Univ. of the West of England, BA dissertation)

Redford, A. (1976) *Labour Migration in England, 1800*-1850, (3rd edn. Manchester UP)

Reicher, S.D. 'The St. Pauls' Riot: An Explanation of the Limits of Crowd Action in terms of a Social Identity Model,' *European Jnl of Social Psychology,* 14, 1-21

Reid, H. (2005) *Life in Victorian Bristol* (Bristol: Redcliffe)

Reiner, R. (1991) 'Crime and Policing' in S. MacGregor and B. Pimlott (eds), *Tackling the Inner Cities: The 1980s Reviewed, Prospects for the 1990s* (Oxford: Clarendon), pp. 44-64

Rex, J. (1968) 'The Social Segregation of the Immigrant in British Cities', *The Political Quarterly,* 39, pp. 15-24

Rex, J. and Cross, M. (1981) 'Unemployment and Racial Conflict in the Inner City', working Papers on Ethnic Relations, 16, S.S.R.C. Research Unit on Ethnic Relations, The University of Aston in Birmingham

Richardson, D. (198) *Bristol, Africa and the Eighteenth-Century Slave Trade to America,* vol. 1, BRS, 38

Richardson, D. (1996) *Bristol, Africa and the Eighteenth-Century Slave Trade to America,* vol. 4, BRS, 47

Richardson, H. G. (1960) *The English Jewry under the Angevin Kings* (London: Methuen)

Richmond, A. (1961) *The Colour Problem* (Harmondsworth: Penguin)

Richmond, A. (1973) *Migration and Race Relations in an English City: A Study in Bristol* (OUP)

Rigg, J. M. (1902) (ed.) *Select Pleas, Starrs, and other Records from the Rolls of the Exchequer of the Jews, 1220-84,* Selden Soc., 15

Rigg, J. M., Jenkinson, C. H., Richardson, H. G. (1905-72) (eds) *Calendar of the Plea Rolls of the Exchequer of the Jews, Preserved in the Public Record Office and British Museum,* 4 vols, Jewish Hist. Soc. of England

Ritchie, J.M. (2002) 'Holocaust Refugees: Great Britain and the Research Centre for German and Austria Exile Studs. in London', *Immigrants and Minorities,* 21, pp. 63-80

Robbins, C. (1962) 'A Note on General Naturalization under the Later Stuarts and a Speech in the House of Commons on the Subject in 1664', *Jnl. of Modern Hist.,* 34, pp. 168-77

Roberts, B. (1982) 'The Debate on "Sus"', in E. Cashmore & B. Troyna (eds) *Black Youth in Crisis* (London: George Allen and Unwin), pp.100-28.

Rokéah, Z. E. (1988/1992) 'Money and the Hangman in late 13th-century England: Jews, Christians and Coinage Offences Alleged and Real', *Trans Jewish Hist. Soc. of England,* 31, pp. 83-109, 32, pp. 159-218

Rose, E. J. B. et al. (1969) *Colour and Citizenship: A Report on British Race Relations*

Roskell, J. S., Clark, L. and Rawcliffe, C. (1993) (eds), *The History of Parliament: The House of Commons, 1386-1421* (Stroud: Sutton/History of Parliament Trust)

Rose, S. (1998) 'Sex, Citizenship, and the Nation in World War II Britain', *American Hist. Rev.,* 103, pp. 1147-76

Roth, C. (1941) *A History of the Jews in England* (Oxford: Clarendon)

Russell, J., Fenton, S. et al. (1987) 'Facts in the City Faith in the People: A Report of St Paul's Anglican Parish Church, Bristol City' (University of Bristol report)

Sabin, A. (1956) (ed.) *The Registers of the Church of St Augustine's the Less, Bristol, 1577-1700* (Bristol and Gloucestershire Arch. Soc. Rec. Section, 3)

Samuel, J. (1997) *Jews in Bristol: A History of the Jewish Community in Bristol from the Middle Ages to the Present Day* (Bristol: Redcliffe)

Sassen, S. (1999) *Guests and Aliens* (English edn, N.Y.: Tauris)

Seaver, K. (1996) *The Frozen Echo: Greenland and the Exploration of North America ca A.D. 1000-1500* (Stanford UP)

Sayyid, S. (2006) 'Introduction', in N. Ali, V.S. Kalra and S. Sayyid (eds), *A Postcolonial People: South Asians in Britain,* (London: Hurst and Company)

Shaw, A. (*c.*1994) 'The Pakistani Community in Oxford' in R. Ballard, *Desh Pardesh: The South Asian Presence in Britain* (London: Hurst), pp. 35-57

Shaw, A. (1988) *A Pakistani Community in Britain* (London: Blackwell)

Singh, H. (1977) 'Bhatra Sikhs in Bristol: Development of an Ethnic Community' (Bristol Univ. undergraduate dissertation)

'Sister Jaycock' (1983) *St Paul's People Talking* (Bristol Broadsides)

Skeel, C. (1926) 'The Cattle Trade Between Wales and England', *TRH S*, 4th series, 9, pp. 135-58

Sketchley, J. (1971) *Sketchley's Bristol Directory, 1775* (1971 edn., Bath: Kingsmead Reprints)

Skinner, P. (2003) (ed.) *Jews in Medieval Britain: Historical, Literary and Archaeological Perspectives* (Woodbridge: Boydell & Brewer)

Smith, G. A. (1987) *When Jim Crow Met John Bull: Black American Soldiers in World War II Britain* (London: Tauric)

Smith, L. T. (1910) (ed.) *The Itinerary of John Leland* (London: Bell)

Sparks, R. J. (2002) 'Two Princes of Calabar: an Atlantic Odyssey from Slavery to Freedom', *William and Mary Quarterly*, 59, pp. 555-84

Sparks, R. J. (2004) *The Two Princes of Calabar: An Eighteenth-Century Atlantic Odyssey* (Harvard UP)

Stacey, R. C. (1985) 'Royal Taxation and the Social Structure of Medieval Anglo-Jewry: the Tallages of 1239-42', *Hebrew Union College Annual* 56, pp. 175-249

Stacey, R. C. (1991) 'Crusades and the Baronial *Gravamina* of 1263-64' in P. Coss and S. D. Lloyd (eds), *Thirteenth-Century England* (Woodbridge: Boydell), vol. 3, pp. 137-50

Stacey, R. C. (1997) 'Parliamentary Negotiation and the Expulsion of the Jews from England', in R. H. Britnell, R. Frame and M. Prestwich (eds), *Thirteenth-Century England* (Woodbridge: Boydell), 77-101

Stacey, R. C. (2003) 'The English Jews under Henry III', in Skinner (2003), 41-54

Stachura, P. D. (2004a) 'Towards and Beyond Yalta', in P. D. Stachura (ed.), *The Poles in Britain 1940-2000: From Betrayal to Assimilation* (London), pp. 6-20

Stachura, P. D. (2004b) 'The Poles in Scotland, 1940-1950', in P. D. Stachura (ed.), *The Poles in Britain 1940-2000: From Betrayal to Assimilation* (London), pp 48-58

Stoddard, S. (2001) *Bristol Before the Camera: The City in 1820-30* (Bristol: Redcliffe and Bristol City Museums and Art Gallery)

Swaish, J. (n.d.) *Chronicles of Broadmead Church, Bristol 1640-1923* (Bristol: Young & Humphries)

Swift, R. (1990) *The Irish in Britain 1815-1914: Perspectives and Sources* (London: The Historical Association)

Sword, K and Ciechanowski, J. (1989) *The Formation of the Polish Community in Great Britain 1939-1950* (London: School of Slavonic & East European Studs)

Taylor, J. (n.d.) 'Notes on Bristol Huguenots, extracted from minutes of the third meeting of the session of the Huguenot Soc., 1889-1890, III, iii, 357-374', reprinted as BRO pamphlet 12

Testimony Films (2002) 'Hope and Glory' Episode 5, 'A Journey Across the Seas' (HTV)

Thajdin, K. (1998) 'A Long Trauma' in G. Edwards (ed.), *Origins: Personal Stories of Crossing the Seas to Settle in Britain* (Bristol: New Worlds)

Thomas, C. (1968) 'Celebrate What?' (BBC Documentary)

Thomas, C. (c.1985) '"With Paste Pot and Brush": Origins of the Bristol Labour Party', in I. Bild (ed.), *Placards and Pin Money: Another Look at Bristol's Other History* (Bristol Broadsides)

Thrupp, S. (1957) 'A Survey of the Alien Population of England in 1440', *Speculum*, 32, pp. 262-73

Thrupp, S. (1969) 'Aliens in and around London in the Fifteenth Century', in A. E. Hollandaer and W. Kellaway (eds), *Studs. in London Hist. Presented to P. E. Jones* (London: Hodder), pp. 251-72

Tidrick, G. (1973) 'Some Aspects of Jamaican Migration to the United Kingdom 1953-1962' Rep. in L. Comitas and D. Lowenthal (eds), *Work and Family Life: West Indian Perspectives.* (NY: Anchor/Doubleday), pp. 189-219

Torrens, H.S. (1984) *Men of Iron: The History of the MacArthur Group* (privately printed)

Tovey, D'B (1738) *Anglia Judaica: Or, the History and Antiquities of the Jews in England* (Oxford: J. Fletcher)

Treharne, R. E. and Sanders, I. J. (1973) (eds) *Documents of the Baronial Movement of Reform and Rebellion, 1258-67* (Oxford: Clarendon)

Vanes, J. (1937) (ed.) *The Overseas Trade of Bristol in the Later Middle Ages*, BRS, 7

Visram, R. (2002) *Asians in Britain: 400 Years of History* (London: Pluto)

Vlaeminke, M. (1981) 'Bristol During the French Revolutionary Wars 1793-1802' (Bristol Univ. M.A. thesis)

Wadley, T. P. (1886) (ed.) *Notes or Abstracts of the Wills contained in the Great Orphan Book of Wills* (Bristol & Gloucester Arch. Soc.)

Walker, D. (1971) *Bristol in the Early Middle Ages* (BBHAP)

Webber, G. C. (1984) 'Reassessments of Fascism', *Jnl of Contemporary History*, 19, pp. 575-606

Werbner, P. (2002) *Imagined Diasporas among Manchester Muslims: The Public Performance of Pakistani Transnational Identity Politics* (Oxford: James Currey)

Werner, A. (1906) 'Language and Folklore in West Africa', *Jnl of the Royal Africa Soc.*, 6, pp. 65-83

Whidder, M. (1985) 'Samuel Colman 1780-1845' (Edinburgh Univ. Ph.D. thesis)

Whyte, I. D. (2000) *Migration and Society in Britain, 1550-1830* (Basingstoke: Palgrave)

Williams, G. (1974) *Glamorgan County History*, vol. 4 (Cardiff: Glamorgan County History Trust Ltd.)

Williams, M. I. (1956) 'Contribution to the Commercial History of Glamorgan, 1666-1735', pt. 2, *National Library of Wales Jnl*, 9, no. 3, pp. 334-53

Williams, T. W. (1908) (ed.) *Bristol Memoranda* (Bristol)

Willis-Bund, J. W. (1898-1902) (ed.) *Register of Bishop Godfrey Giffard, 1268-1301*, 2 vols, Worcester Hist. Soc.

Wilson, K. (2003) *The Island Race: Englishness, Empire and Gender in the Eighteenth Century* (London and New York: Routledge)

Winslow, M. (2004) 'Oral History and Polish Émigrés in Britain' in P. D. Stachura (ed.), *The Poles in Britain 1940-2000: From Betrayal to Assimilation* (London: Cass), pp. 85-93

Wolf, L. (1934) *Essays in Jewish History*, ed. C. Roth (London: Jewish Historical Soc. Of England)

Worrall E.S. (1989) (ed.) *Church of England. Diocese of Chester: Returns of Papists, 1767. Vol.2, Dioceses of England and Wales, except Chester. Diocese of Bristol* (Catholic R.S. Occasional Pubs., no.2), pp. 168-9

Wright, S. and Blease, M. 'Sicilian Rhapsody', *Venue Magazine*, no. 668 (June 2005), 17

Wynn, N. (1976) *The Afro-American and the Second World War* (London: Elek)

Þorsteinsson, B. (1970) *Enska Öldin í Sögu Íslendinga* (Reykjavik: Mál og Menning)

Electronic Sources (Websites)

Date accessed in brackets.

American Jewish Historical Society 'The Jew with Sir Walter Raleigh', http://
    beta.ajhs.org/publications/chapters/chapter.cfm?documentID=249
    (20/03/07)Apna
Jhelum http://www.apnajhelum.net/ (04/03/07)
Barifi 'Sikh Surnames And The Castes To Which They Belong' http://www.
    barficulture.com/community/main/topic.php/47999/index.html; (15/02/07)
Beckerdite Luke Beckerdite, 'Religion, Artisanry and Cultural Identity: The
    Huguenot Experience in South Carolina, 1680-1725', American Furniture
    1997, www.chipstone.org (December 2006)
Bhatlines 'Who Are The Bhat Sikhs?', http://www.freewebs.com/bhatline/
    whoarethebhatsikhs.htm (15/02/07)
Boreham P. Boreham, 'Trade Unions, Industrial Relations and Economic Policy
    Instituitons: the Implications for Unemployment in OECD Countries,' (Dept.
    of Human Resources, University of Strathclyde, Occasional paper no. 12,
    2001), 13, http://www.hrm.strath.ac.uk/research/publications/occ-12.pdf.
    (04/03/07)
Bristol Baptistshttp://www.broadmeadbaptist.org.uk/historypage.
    php?content=history/ewins.htm (03/04/06)
BCRL [Brian Little?],'Welsh Back: an Account of its History', http://www.mid-
    landspubs.co.uk/pubsigns/l.htm (30/03/06)
Bristol Rugby http://www.bristolrugby.co.uk/31_86.php (12/04/07)
Britain Today 'Britain Today', UK India website (May 2004) http://www.ukinin-
    dia.com/magazines/britaintoday/BTInnerpage.asp?IssueId=71&magzineId=3
    &SectionId=462&ArticleId=1228; (May 2007)
ChurchCrawler http://www.churchcrawler.co.uk;
Cole Ian Cole & David Robinson, 'Somali Housing Experiences in England'
    (Centre for Regional & Economic Research, Sheffield Hallam University)
    (2003) http://www.shu.ac.uk/cresr/downloads/publications/10-SOMALI per
    cent20Housing.pdf (01/05/07)
Companies 'History of Bristol Companies: Packer Chocolates-Elizabeth Shaw'
    at http://weldgen.tripod.com/id57.html (29/04/07)
Defoe D. Defoe. Curious and diverting journies, thro' the whole island of
    Great-Britain. Containing, I. A particular description of the principal cities
    and towns, ... II. The customs, manners, speech, as also ... employment of the
    people. III. The produce and improvement of the lands, ... IV. The sea ports
    and fortifications, ... V. The publick edifices, ... With useful observations on
    the whole. ... By A. B. gent.. London, 1734. 18th Century Collections Online.
    Gale Group. http://galenet.galegroup.com/servlet/ECCO (29/04/07)
Dixie Brown: www.englandspastforeveryone.org.uk/Bristol; (11/06/07)
Downer Sandola Downer's story, www.bristolstories.org (11/06/07)
Eleanor Nesbitt, 'Faith Guides for Higher Education: A Guide to Sikhims',
    http:www.prs.heacademy.ac.uk/publication/sikhism.pdf. (15/02/07)
Fletcher Tom Fletcher, 'Civvy Street in World War Two' http://www.macksites.
    com/ (02/11/06)
Gilder www.gilderlehrman.org.http://www.gilderlehrman.org. (25/05/07)
'Going for a Curry' The Works of Khadim Hussain, http://www.neukol.org.uk/
    teesblog/index.php/gfac?cat=257; (15/02/07)
Greenbank 'The History of Greenbank Bowling Club', http://www.bristolgreen-
    bank.org.uk/History.html (29/04/07)
Greene Roberta R. Greene, 'Holocaust Survivors: a Study in Resilience', If Not
    Now [Journal of the Baycrest Organisation], vol. 3, (spring 2002) http://
    www.baycrest.org/If_Not_Now/Volume_3_Spring_2002/7121_7309.asp#
    (15/02/07)

Himal Southasian Himal Southasian, The Southasia Trust, Lalitpur, Nepal
    http://www.himalmag.com/2003/november/commentary_2.htm (29/04/07)
Horfield 'The History of Horfield Baptist Church' http://www.digitalbristol.org/
    members/hbchurch/history.htm (29/04/07)
House of Commons Journal http://www.british-history.ac.uk/report.
    asp?compid=39623 (December 2006)
Hussein Ayan Hussein 'Case Study: St Paul's Learning and Family Centre' http://
    www.bristol-city.gov.uk/ccm/cms-service/stream/asset/?asset_id=5161006
    (20/03/07)
Ideas Festival http://www.ideasfestival.co.uk/multicultural.html (07/03/07)
Information 'Bristol Information', http://www.bristolinformation.co.uk/srch/
    srchit.asp?list=list&gdoc=bs&howmany=200 (20/07/06)
Irish Vagrants Select Committee on Irish Vagrants: with minutes of evidence
    and appendix summarised in 'Enhanced British Parliamentary Papers on
    Ireland 1801-1922', http:>>www.bopcris.ac.uk/eppi/ref296.html (28/05/07)
Jimmy Peters "Jimmy Peters Exhibition", Museum of Rugby, http://www.rfu.
    com/index.cfm/fuseaction/RFUHome.Touchline_Detail/storyId/3957/
    sectionId/85 (12/04/07)
Massive Attack http://www.bbc.co.uk.music.profiles/massiveattack (03/03/07)
Mcarthurs 'The Mcarthurs group', http://www.mcarthur-group.com (27/07/06)
Old Bailey 'Proceedings of the Old Bailey" available at http://www.hrionline.
    ac.uk/luceneweb/hri3/display_20050804.jsp?mode=bailey&file=html_
    units%2F1740s%2Ft17450116-16.html&hil=content:(castai**)%20AND%20
    decade:bhea#firsthil (04/11/05)
Peevers Simon Peevers, 'Drugs Threat to Somali Youths' The Somaliland Times,
    21 September 2006, http:..www.somalilandtimes.net sl/2005/245.028.shtml
    (01/05/07)
Phelps 'Jack Phelps-the voice of Bristol boxing;' http://weldgen.tripod.com/
    fighters-of-the-est-country/id22.html (22/10/06)
Pigot's Directory Pigot's Directory for Bristol (Bristol, 1830) http://www.genuki.
    org.uk/big/eng/GLS/Bristol/Pigot1830.html (12/07/05)
Robe Family http://www.electricscotland.com/webclans/minibios/r/robe_fam-
    ily.html (27/07/06)
St Patricks http://www.saint-patricks-church.com/history.html (24/11/06)
Serpico John Serpico, 'Southmead Riots' http://www.brh.org.uk/articles/south.
    htm (06/11/06)
Sikh Temple http://www.bristolsikhtemple.co.uk (25/02/07)
Strachan Strachan & Henshaw, 'Histories of Bristol Companies' weldgen.tripod.
    com/id48.htm (15/02/07)
Sugar Refiners "Sugar refiners and Sugarboilers Database" http://home.clara.net/
    mawer/sugarff.html (25/11/06)
Sunamganj 'About Sunamganj', CyberSylhet http://www.cybersylhet.com/mod-
    ules.php?name=Sylhet&file=sunamgonj (10/03/07)
Susser B. Susser, 'Jewish inventors, writers and artist in the South-west of
    England', Susser Archives, http://www.jewishgen.org/jcr-uk/susser/thesis/
    thesischapternine.html (15/05/06)
Thatcher http://www.margaretthatcher.org/document/93030FB632E147999
    D4BEB655587A134.pdf (06/11/06)
Tony McClean Sports Network http://www.blackathlete.com/Othersports/index.
    shtml (12/04/07)
Whitfield James Whitfield, 'Policing the Windrush Generation', History and
    Policy papers, http://www.historyandpolicy.org/archive/pol-paper-print-45.
    htm (30/10/06)
World Commission World Commission on Dams, Case Study. Pakistan: The
    Tarbela Dam and Indus River Basin' http://www.dams.org/kbase/studies/pk/
    pk_exec.htm (03/04/07)

Index

Picture Credits

The author and publisher would like to thank the following for permission to reproduce their material. Any infringement of copyright is entirely inadvertent and accidental. Every care has been taken to contact or trace all copyright owners. We would be pleased to correct in future editions any errors or omissions brought to our attention.

Guy Bailey, 167
BBC Museum, 92
Berlin Kupferstichkabinett BPK/SMB (Jörg P. Anders), 37
Bristol and Gloucestershire Archaeological Society, 24
Bristol Central Reference Library, x, 6, 15 (Fig. 7), 59, 99, 122 (accordion player), 131 (Fig. 80), 133; Braikenridge Collection, 63 (Fig. 38), 132
Stanisława Cesarz and family, 205, 208
Bristol Evening Post, 139 (Fig. 90), 142, 161
Bristol Hebrew Congregation, 101, 127
Bristol Library Service, 139 (Fig. 89)
Bristol Municipal Charities (Lee Davis), 58 (all Figs)
Bristol Museums, Galleries and Archives, 15 (Fig. 8), 29, 56, 57, 60, 37, 63 (Fig. 39), 77, 78 (Fig. 49), 81, 87 (Figs 55a and b), 96, 97, 122 (detail of organ grinder)
Bristol Record Office, 61 (Figs 35 and 36), 64, 69, 74, 87 (Fig. 54), 88, 91, 100, 112, 120, 136, 137 (Fig. 84), 168 (Fig. 107), 202, 204; with Bristol Black Archives Partnership, 150, 151, 164, 170, 173, 169; (David Emeney), xii, 23, 26, 36
British Council, 178, 212
British Library, 12, 34, 55, 71
Kathleen Charles, 138 (Fig. 88)
Lee Davis, 48, 54, 112 (Fig. 69)
Dhek Bhal Association, 189, 197
Edinburgh University Library, 38
English Heritage (James Davies), 126, 137 (Fig. 85), 155, 162, 176, 177, 184, 193, 195, 196, 199, 210, 217, 221, 223
English Heritage. NMR, 73, 83, 117, 124, 128
Family History Centre, 131 (Fig. 79)
The George Muller Foundation, 106, 107, 110
Elaine Hicks, 145 (Fig. 94), 146
Rais Hyder, 154
Images of England (Mr Cyril N. Chapman LRPS), 87 (Fig. 55c)
Llyfrgell Genedlaethol Cymru/The National Library of Wales, 20
Lord Mayor's Office, Bristol, 165
Zahir Malik, 139 (Fig. 89), 145 (Fig. 93), 184 (Fig. 120), 195 (Fig. 123), 214 (Fig. 135)
Mitchell Library Collection, 112 (Fig. 70)
Museum of London Archaeology Service, 9
The National Archives, 25 (Figs 15a and b), 40, 86 (Figs 53a and b), 102, 123 (census report), 27
National Portrait Gallery, 78
Mary Perkins, 144
Reece Winstone Archive, 123 (Italian women), 158
Mark Simmons, 168 (Fig. 106)
Mark Steed, 138 (Fig. 86)
United States Holocaust Memorial Museum, 203
University of London, 16, 104, 105, (Matthew Bristow) cover image
Waterford Museum of Treasures, 21
Westminster Abbey Dean and Chapter, 11
Worcester Cathedral (David Nash Ford), 19
www.bristolinformation.co.uk, 115

Maps were drawn by Cath d'Alton (Figs 3, 10, 19, 41, 46, 52, 59, 71, 99, 114, 119, 133 and both maps in Panel 4). Fig. 3 was based on M.D. Lobel and E.M. Carus-Wilson, Atlas of Historic Towns and Fig. 71 was based on material supplied courtesy of Bristol Reference Library. Other UK maps were drawn using Ordnance Survey 1st edition maps © University of London.